BEST OF
SPORTS ILLUSTRATED
2001—2002

BEST OF
SPORTS ILLUSTRATED
2001—2002

ISBN: 1-929049-71-4
Manufactured in the United States of America
First printing 2002

THE BEST OF SPORTS ILLUSTRATED 2002

Editorial Director: Morin Bishop
    Project Editor: John Bolster
    Managing Editor: Theresa M. Deal
    Researchers: Andrew Blais, Ward Calhoun, Jeff Labrecque
    Copy Editor: Lee Fjordbotten
    Photography Editors: John S. Blackmar, Alan Gottlieb
Designers: Barbara Chilenskas, Jia Baek

THE BEST OF SPORTS ILLUSTRATED 2002 was prepared by
Bishop Books, Inc.
611 Broadway
New York, New York 10012

TIME INC. HOME ENTERTAINMENT
President: Rob Gursha
Vice President, Branded Businesses: David Arfine
Executive Director, Marketing Services: Carol Pittard
Director, Retail & Special Sales: Tom Mifsud
Director of Finance: Tricia Griffin
Marketing Director: Kenneth Maehlum
Product Manager: Dana Pecoraro
Prepress Operations Manager: Emily Rabin
Associate Product Manager: Victoria Alfonso
Assistant Product Manager: Ann Gillespie
Special thanks to: Suzanne DeBenedetto, Robert Dente, Gina Di Meglio, Peter Harper, Natalie McCrea,
Jessica McGrath, Jonathan Polsky, Mary Jane Rigoroso, Steven Sandonato, Meredith Shelley, Bozena
Szwagulinski, Marina Weinstein, Niki Whelan.

We welcome your comments and suggestions about SPORTS ILLUSTRATED Books.
Please write to us at:
SPORTS ILLUSTRATED Books
Attention: Book Editors
PO Box 11016
Des Moines, IA 50336-1016

If you would like to order any of our
hardcover Collector's Edition books,
please call us at 1-800-327-6388.
(Monday through Friday, 7:00 a.m.— 8:00 p.m., or Saturday, 7:00 a.m.— 6:00 p.m.,
Central Time).
Please visit our Web site at **www.TimeBookstore.com**

10   9   8   7   6   5   4   3   2   1

Contents

Time Out

After pausing to honor the victims of the Sept. 11 terrorist attacks, the sports world resumed play in the spirit of healing

MERRELL NODEN

01.08.01

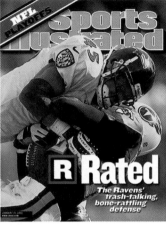

01.15.01

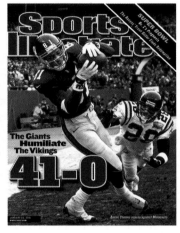

01.22.01

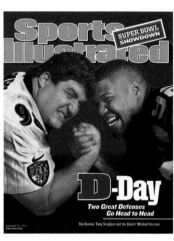

01.29.01

This was the year we were all reminded, suddenly, terribly, and perhaps irrevocably, of exactly where sports stand in the grand scheme of things. The Sept. 11 terrorist attacks on the World Trade Center and the Pentagon—and the crash of a fourth hijacked plane in rural Pennsylvania—left the entire nation and much of the world in a stupor of disbelief and horror, bringing the world of games to a stunned halt. For blinkered sports nuts, this was a strong dose of perspective.

Whereas only days earlier, on Sept. 8, 9 or 10, we had spent our time wondering whether or not Barry Bonds would break Mark McGwire's single-season home run record, or if Michael Jordan would come out of retirement to play for the Washington Wizards, by mid-morning on Sept. 11, nobody cared. In the anxious, eerie aftermath of the attacks, sports were the last thing on anyone's mind. Sports rivalries were instantly replaced by a somber awareness of the many more things we shared: We were all Americans, and we were all pretty shaken up.

Here and there, you heard talk of playing on as an act of defiance and community. "In times of sorrow and fear," argued SPORTS ILLUSTRATED's Frank Deford, "the chance for Americans to gather in any huge stadium, to stand together, bound together, provides a powerful—even patriotic—nectar."

And perhaps sports would have supplied that nectar—had anyone been able to muster the will to play. At only one major U.S. professional event did officials follow Deford's advice. The Big Island Championships, a Women's Tennis Association event in Hawaii, suspended play on Sept. 11 but resumed it the following day. Everyone else followed the example of NFL Commissioner Paul Tagliabue, who, mindful of what former NFL commissioner Pete Rozelle called the biggest mistake of his career—allowing play to go forward the weekend after the Kennedy assassination—canceled that week's games, saying, "At a certain point, playing our games can contribute to the healing process. Just not at this time." Major league baseball did not resume its schedule until the following Monday, Sept. 17, creating the longest suspension of play since World War I. The Ryder Cup, scheduled for Sept. 28–30, at the Belfry in England, was postponed until next year.

And when sports did resume—a week or so later, in most cases—it was with a pronounced deference to the nation's somber mood and an awareness that, starting on Oct. 7, the U.S. was bombing Afghanistan, the nation har-

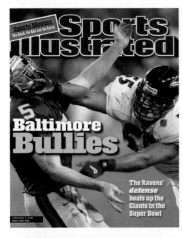

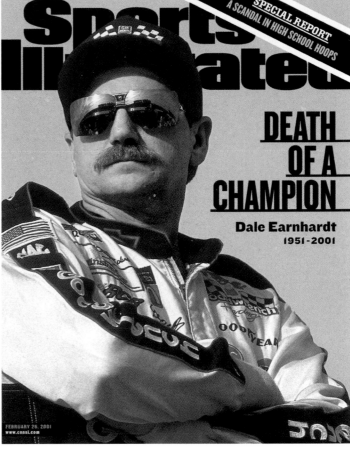

DEATH OF A CHAMPION

Dale Earnhardt
1951-2001

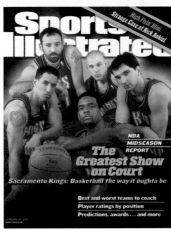

boring the prime suspect in the attacks, Saudi militant Osama bin Laden. At a preseason NHL game between the Flyers and the New York Rangers in Philadelphia's First Union Center, fans booed until arena officials stopped the game so that the crowd could watch and listen to President Bush's address to Congress on the scoreboard screen. The game was not resumed.

The communal "nectar" that Deford longed for was much in evidence, as flags were unfurled across end zones, in outfields and on the back of every major league baseball uniform. New York City firefighters and police officers found themselves guests of honor at sports events everywhere, and the New York Mets were given special dispensation by the league to abandon their usual caps in favor of dark blue ones bearing the initials NYPD and FDNY. The Mets wore the new caps as they made a late-September charge that brought them to the brink of the playoffs and salvaged an otherwise dismal season.

Of course, there was more to 2001 than that one horrific day. The surprise attacks of Sept. 11 ripped the year into two very different parts. From our vantage point now, on the far side of that date, the first eight months of 2001 look blessedly carefree. Those months bear witness to the sports world's usual smorgasbord of miracles and chokes, of dynasties in the making and brilliant newcomers. At a time when we need to believe that comebacks are possible, we can look back on more than a few inspiring comebacks. There were painful reminders of mortality, too, in the form of several untimely deaths, which, unhappy though they were, forced us to re-examine the practices that may have caused them. So let's go back, with a sense of something like nostalgia, to the start of 2001, when we could afford to place undue importance upon such matters as the fate of a splashy, trashy new football league.

That outfit, dubbed the XFL and launched by World Wrestling Federation owner Vince McMahon in cahoots with NBC, made its televised debut on Feb. 3 in, appropriately enough, Las Vegas. The XFL banned fair catches, put helmeted cameramen on the field, and R- if not X-rated cheerleaders on the sidelines. Instead of a coin toss, games began with a 20-yard race between two players for a loose football at midfield. The winner's team would receive the kickoff. The fanfare was clamorous, the curiosity factor high, the quality of play dismal. After a successful debut, TV ratings for the league fell by 50%, and on May 10, less than a month after the end of its inaugural season, the XFL folded.

03.05.01

03.12.01

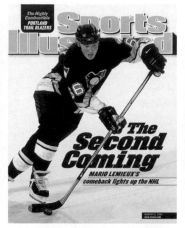

03.19.01

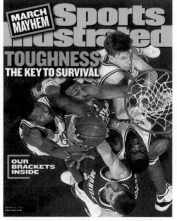

03.26.01

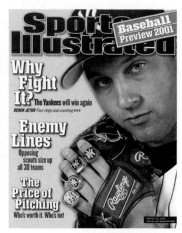

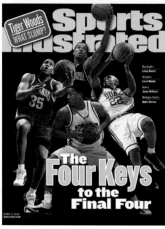

04.02.01

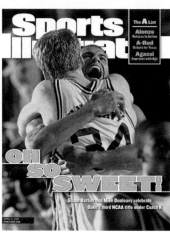

04.09.01

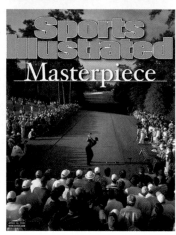

04.16.01

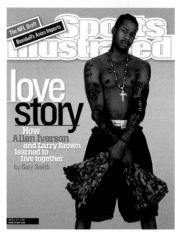

04.23.01

Fate foreshadowed the defining events of 2001 when it whipped sports fans' attention from the folly of the XFL to a tragedy in NASCAR's premier event, the Daytona 500. On Feb. 18, as he entered Turn 4 of the race's final lap, Dale Earnhardt, arguably the sport's brightest star, died instantly when his Chevy Monte Carlo crashed head-on into the wall. "Dale was the Michael Jordan of our sport," said Humpy Wheeler, president of Lowe's Motor Speedway near Charlotte. "To think he is not around anymore is incomprehensible. This is a terrible, terrible loss."

It was ruled that Earnhardt died as a result of a severe injury at the base of his skull. Dr. Steve Bohannon, Daytona's EMS director, said that he did not think that either a HANS (head-and-neck support) device or a full-face helmet would have saved Earnhardt, but his death did have the positive effect of training a spotlight on NASCAR's safety precautions, spurring several changes.

One reassuring antidote to life's nasty jolts is continuity, and for that, one turns to the Blue Devils hoopsters of Duke who, under coach Mike Krzyzewski, have made the NCAA title game six times in 12 years, and won three times. This year's team was led by senior Shane Battier, an academic-minded forward. After coming back from a 39–17 deficit to

beat Maryland in the national semis, the Blue Devils shook off pesky Arizona in the title game to win 82–72. At 54, Krzyzewski has coached Duke to three NCAA titles, putting him in the exclusive company of Bob Knight, Adolph Rupp and John Wooden as the only men with three or more national championships.

In the women's championship game, Notre Dame held off cross-state rival Purdue, 68–66. Ruth Riley, Notre Dame's 6'5" center, dominated in the paint, grabbing 13 rebounds, scoring 28 points and blocking seven shots. As impressive as Riley was, she had to share the spotlight with Southwest Missouri State's tireless sharpshooter, Jackie Stiles, who, after setting an NCAA career scoring record during the regular season, carried her upstart team to the Final Four, where she scored 22 points in a semifinal loss to Purdue.

Six days after Duke's impressive victory, Tiger Woods won the Masters by two strokes over David Duval. Not only did that put an end to all the early-season talk of a slump, it made Woods the first person to hold all four of golf's major championships simultaneously. But with the Holy Grail of a single-year Slam on the horizon, Woods seemed to falter. His best finish at a major after the Masters was 12th, in the U.S. Open.

04.30.01

05.07.01

05.14.01

05.21.01

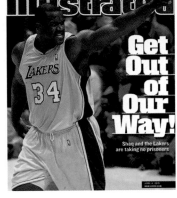

05.28.01

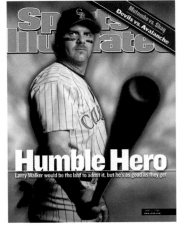

06.04.01

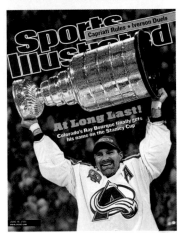

06.11.01

06.18.01

No one could have guessed that with Woods seven strokes adrift, the three men in contention at the U.S. Open at Southern Hills would be Stewart Cink, Mark Brooks and South Africa's Retief Goosen. Or that all three would three-putt the final green, Goosen from only 15 feet. And he turned out to be the winner, edging Brooks by two strokes in an 18-hole playoff. In July, Duval won his first Grand Slam event, taking the British Open at Royal Lytham and removing the cumbersome label of "best player never to have won a major." And at the PGA Championship, in Atlanta, David Toms got up and down from 88 yards on the monstrous par-4 490-yard 18th to finish one stroke ahead of Phil Mickelson.

If the respected Duval's triumph was heartening, the comeback of superstar hockey player Mario Lemieux was downright inspiring. The National Hockey League got a huge midseason boost when the 35-year-old cancer survivor announced that he would come out of retirement to play for the team he partially owns, the Pittsburgh Penguins. On Dec. 27, 2000, just 33 seconds into his first game, Lemieux set up a goal by Jaromir Jagr, then added an assist and a goal of his own in Pittsburgh's 5–0 win over Toronto. Lemieux's return proved to be a boon to Jagr, who won his

fourth straight NHL scoring title with 121 points on 52 goals and 69 assists. With their superstar back in the fold, the Penguins made it all the way to the Eastern Conference finals, where they fell in five games to the defending champion New Jersey Devils.

In the Stanley Cup finals, the Devils ran into the Colorado Avalanche and goaltender Patrick Roy, who won in seven games. Though Roy was magnificent, stopping 49 of 50 shots in Games 6 and 7 to win a record third playoff MVP trophy, it was his graybeard teammate, Ray Bourque, who was the sentimental hero. In his 22nd season and fourth decade of play, Bourque finally won the hallowed Cup. He announced his retirement several weeks later.

Another stirring argument for hanging in there was made by Jennifer Capriati, who overcame the scars of child stardom to win the Australian and French Opens and seize the No. 1 ranking in October. Capriati reached the Wimbledon semis, but lost to Justine Henin, who was herself beaten by Venus Williams in the final. In the U.S. Open, Williams and her sister, Serena, made history by meeting in the final, the first sibling matchup in a Grand Slam final since 1884. Venus won in straight sets, and, having won four of the last six Grand Slam events, she is

06.25.01

07.02.01

07.16.01

07.23.01

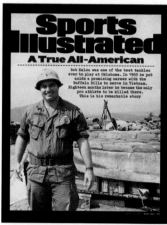

07.30.01

08.06.01

08.13.01

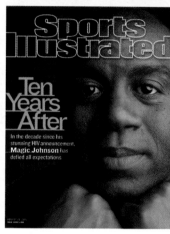

08.20.01

arguably the most talented player on the tour. There were no double winners among the men in Grand Slam play, as Andre Agassi won his seventh major at the Australian Open, clay-court specialist Gustavo Kuerten won the French, Goran Ivanisevic beat Patrick Rafter in a Wimbledon final for the ages, and Lleyton Hewitt downed Pete Sampras for the U.S. Open title.

While parity reigned in men's tennis, a dynasty grew in men's basketball as Shaquille O'Neal, Kobe Bryant and the Lakers defended their NBA title. But the championship was by no means a foregone conclusion, as the Lakers' two stars, O'Neal and Bryant, feuded all season over who was the team's true go-to guy, causing the team to sputter and clearing the way for several other contenders. Among them were the steady San Antonio Spurs, led by David Robinson and Tim Duncan; the flashy Sacramento Kings, led by Chris Webber; and the Philadelphia 76ers, an anonymous cast content to support the league's leading scorer and regular-season MVP, Allen Iverson.

Surely it took all of Phil Jackson's skill as a zen psychologist and motivator to do so, but he managed to restore balance and harmony to his team. The Lakers swept all pretenders from their path, beating the Blazers, the Kings and the Spurs without a loss to set up a finals showdown with the 76ers. After losing Game 1, the Lakers won four straight to seize the title.

Like the Lakers in the NBA—but for reasons of strategy rather than ego—Lance Armstrong started slowly in the Tour de France before turning it on in the mountains to win the 21-stage race for the third straight year. He beat Jan Ullrich of Germany by six minutes and 44 seconds. Like Lemieux, Armstrong is a cancer survivor and, seemingly, a flesh-and-blood advertisement for courage in hard times. But some of the delight was sucked out of Armstrong's win because of reports that he'd made several visits to Italian doctor Michele Ferrari, who is awaiting trial on charges of providing riders with the dangerous blood-boosting drug EPO.

In track and field, fans and athletes said goodbye to Michael Johnson, the sport's biggest star in the '90s, who retired. Olympic 100 champ Maurice Greene made another claim to the title of greatest 100 man in history by winning his third straight world title, clocking 9.82 on an injured leg. Marion Jones didn't fare so well. At the world championships, she lost her first 100 after 42 straight wins, to Zhanna Pintusevich-Block of the Ukraine, though Jones did

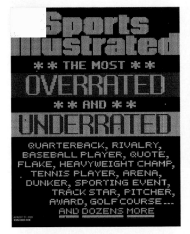

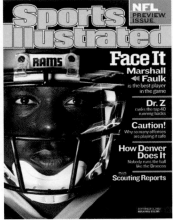

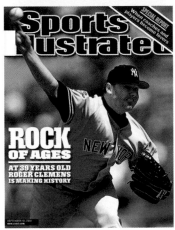

08.27.01

09.03.01

09.10.01

09.17.01

09.24.01

come back to win the 200 and anchor the U.S.'s triumphant 400-meter relay team.

While Jones appeared unfocused or tired after her heroics in Sydney, Stacy Dragila took over as the top woman in track and field, setting eight world records in the pole vault. Other barriers fell in the decathlon, where Roman Sebrle of the Czech Republic became the first person to top 9,000 points, and in the women's marathon, in which Japan's Naoko Takahashi became the first woman to break 2:20, clocking 2:19:46 in Berlin—only to see her record broken seven days later by Catherine Ndereba of Kenya, who ran 2:18:47 in Chicago.

Still, there was no doubt who the most exciting star in U.S. track and field was this year. It was Alan Webb, an 18-year-old from Reston, Va., who ran a staggering 3:53.43 mile to break Jim Ryun's 36-year-old national high-school record by 1.87 seconds. That was the fastest mile run by an American of any age since 1998.

A teenager stole the spotlight in swimming, too, though that was hardly a surprise since the youngster in question was Ian Thorpe, who has starred for three years now. The sensational Australian looks to be on his way to becoming the greatest swimmer in history. At the world champi-

onships in Fukuoka, Japan, Thorpe won a meet-record six gold medals and set world records in the 200, 400 and 800 freestyles, plus the 4x200 freestyle relay. The U.S. star in Fukuoka was Michael Phelps, a 16-year-old junior at Towson (Md.) High School, who won the 200 butterfly in a world-record 1:54.58.

Pro football absorbed a tragic hit on August 1, when Korey Stringer, the Minnesota Vikings' popular All-Pro tackle, died from heat exhaustion after a preseason workout. Stringer's death was bookended by the heat-related deaths of University of Florida fullback Eraste Autin and Northwestern safety Rashidi Wheeler, an asthma sufferer, during preseason practices. The Vikings never recovered from Stringer's death, enduring a dismal 5–11 season that ended with the departure of coach Dennis Green and a 19–3 loss to the defending champion Baltimore Ravens.

The Ravens, who lost running back Jamal Lewis to injury in the preseason, needed to win that game to qualify for the playoffs, and their opponents in the previous season's Super Bowl, the New York Giants, missed the playoffs altogether, finishing 7–9. Once again, the NFL boasted lots of pretty good teams, few great ones. The St. Louis Rams, champions of the 1999 season, found their form again with

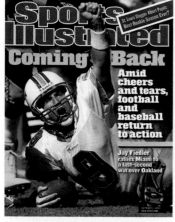

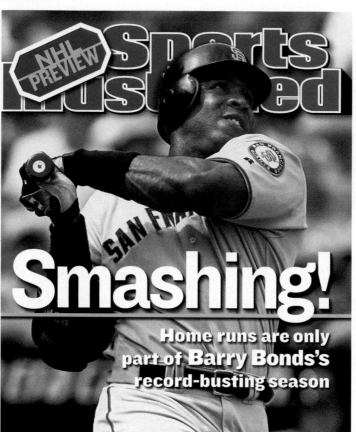

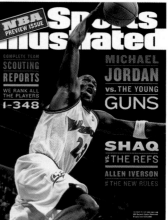

a healthy Kurt Warner at quarterback and cruised to a 14–2 record, the league's best. In the AFC, the Pittsburgh Steelers rumbled to their best record since 1978, going 13–3 behind bruising fullback Jerome Bettis (1,072 yards rushing in 11 games) and the versatility of quarterback Kordell Stewart (3,109 yards passing, 536 rushing).

On the eve of the playoffs, St. Louis looked like the favorite in the NFC, followed by the surprising Chicago Bears (13–3) and the rejuvenated Green Bay Packers (12–4). In the AFC, the Steelers would play all of their playoff games at their home Heinz Field, and—watch out, bad pun ahead—it was surely without relish that visitors anticipated playing in frigid Pittsburgh in January. Of those potential visitors, New England (11–5) appeared to be the most formidable. After losing their first two games of the year (and quarterback Drew Bledsoe to injury), the Patriots went 11–3 to win the AFC East. The Pats finished the season with six straight wins.

College football's much maligned BCS system once again produced an undisputed national champion—something it has done in each of its four years of existence, over the increasingly loud gripes of coaches, players, fans and commentators. In 2001 it was Oregon which appeared to have

the biggest beef with the BCS. Heading into the Fiesta Bowl, the 10–1 Ducks voiced their displeasure at not being picked to play in the Rose Bowl for the national championship against Miami (11–0). That honor went to 11–1 Nebraska, whose only loss was a doozy: a 62–36 trouncing by none other than Colorado, Oregon's opponent in the Fiesta Bowl. Imagine the muddle if Nebraska had beaten Miami in the Rose Bowl. At 12–1, the Cornhuskers would have been crowned national champions by the BCS. But whichever team won the Fiesta Bowl would have made a legitimate claim to the title as well: Oregon because of its won-loss record and its having defeated the one team that beat Nebraska; Colorado on the strength of its thoroughly convincing win over the Cornhuskers. Luckily for the BCS, and college football fans, Miami stilled the rising tide of complaint by routing Nebraska 37–14 in Pasadena to finish 12–0 and remove any doubt. It was the Hurricanes' fifth national title.

Baseball's long season was the last one for three classy future Hall of Famers. Bowing out with their customary good grace were Cardinals slugger Mark McGwire, eight-time batting champ Tony Gwynn of the San Diego Padres, and Cal Ripken Jr. who set the record for consecutive games played (2,632) during his 21-year career with Baltimore.

11.05.01

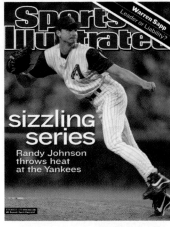

11.12.01

11.19.01

11.26.01

12.03.01

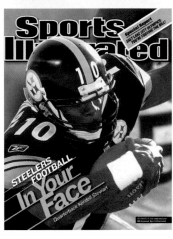

12.10.01

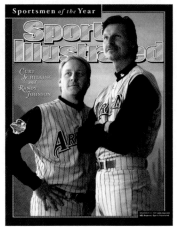

12.17.01

12.24.01

The Seattle Mariners, who lost All-Stars Randy Johnson, Ken Griffey Jr. and Alex Rodriguez in the previous three years, won 116 games, tying the 1906 Chicago Cubs. Leading the way for Seattle was rightfielder Ichiro Suzuki, who won seven straight batting titles in Japan before signing with the Mariners and threatening George Sisler's single-season hits record of 257. He settled for 242 (and an AL-leading .350 average), tops in the majors since 1930. The Mariners rallied to beat the Cleveland Indians in the first round of the American League playoffs but then fell to the New York Yankees in the ALCS. The Yankees themselves had to come back from 2–0 down to shock the young Oakland A's in the Division Series.

Joining oldtimers Gwynn and Ripken in the late-season spotlight was 42-year-old Rickey Henderson of the Padres, who scored career run No. 2,246 to break Ty Cobb's record. But home run hitters, as they had in 1998, once again raised the bar. Arizona leftfielder Luis Gonzalez hit 57 homers—and finished third in the National League home run race. Sammy Sosa hit 64 to become the first player to top 60 in three seasons. But the undisputed star of this power-mad year was Barry Bonds, who walked a record 177 times yet still cracked 73 homers to break McGwire's record

of 70. His slugging percentage of .863 was another record, topping Babe Ruth's 81-year-old record.

Yet for a number of reasons Bonds's heroics failed to ignite the excitement McGwire's and Sosa's had in 1998. And in the end, his chase was overshadowed by the attacks of Sept. 11. So too was Michael Jordan's tease of a return, at 38, to play for the Washington Wizards, a team of which he was part owner. On Oct. 30, having divested his stake in the team, Jordan played in the Wizards' season opener, scoring 19 points in a sloppy 93–91 loss to the Knicks in New York. But Air Jordan would fly again, producing 45- and 51-point games in late December as Washington went on a nine-game winning streak. As 2002 dawned the once-lowly Wizards looked like a playoff team.

But even glimpses of vintage Jordan only served to distract us temporarily from the many ways in which the world of sports was changed by the Sept. 11 calamities. For further evidence, we need only wait for the Super Bowl, which is scheduled for Feb. 3 in New Orleans; and for the 2002 Winter Olympics, which will begin on Feb. 8 in Salt Lake City.

Security will be tighter than ever before, but that nectar will still draw us, irresistibly, even if we look both ways before leaning in for a taste.

Double Feature

Capping a season of infighting with a dominating title run, the team from Hollywood gave fans two dramas to savor in 2000—01

MARK BEECH

In hindsight it seems almost impossible that anyone could have foreseen a different ending to the 2000–01 season. The Los Angeles Lakers steamed to their second straight NBA championship, and after their title-clinching victory over the Philadelphia 76ers, the words dynasty and greatness started popping in the air like the champagne corks the players released in celebration.

Could there really have been doubts about this team? With the 7' 1", 315-pound Shaquille O'Neal in the pivot—an irresistible force on offense and an immovable object on defense—and the silky Kobe Bryant slashing from the perimeter, the Lakers went 67–15 en route to the 1999–2000 NBA title. There was no reason they couldn't repeat the feat in 2000–01. Yet there were doubts, and they surfaced early in the season.

Both Bryant and O'Neal came into the season with their eyes fixed firmly on the game's most coveted prize. Bryant claimed to have spent his summer in the gym, not leaving each day until he'd sunk 2,000 jumpers from 15 feet and beyond; O'Neal re-upped with the purple and gold for three more years and $88.4 million. "Winning one championship trophy is like having one car," he said after signing the deal, with his Rolls-Royce waiting in the parking lot. "It's not enough for me."

Unfortunately for L.A., Shaq and Kobe didn't agree as to how that second championship should be won. O'Neal wanted his teammates to climb aboard his broad shoulders, as they had during his MVP season the previous year, and let him return them to the promised land. Bryant, for his part, seemed to want a more prominent role on the team. He was sure he was capable of leading the Lakers, and he refused to defer to Shaq on offense. Befitting a team from Tinseltown, a jealous squabble ensued. The feud enthralled and exasperated Angelenos for most of the season. The defending champs were plagued by inconsistency for much of the year before the two stars worked out a tentative time-share agreement for the Hollywood spotlight. Reeling off eight wins to end the regular season, L.A. lifted its record to a respectable 56–26, tied for second best in the league.

But on the eve of the playoffs, Los Angeles was considered vulnerable. Many of the courtside cognoscenti predicted that the Lakers wouldn't make it beyond the Western Conference finals, a notion that vaporized faster than *Pearl Harbor*'s Oscar prospects. The Lakers rolled through the postseason, dispatching opponents with arrogance and gusto, trampling them with O'Neal one night and dazzling them with Bryant the next. They swept Portland in the first round, Sacramento in the second, and then, in the hotly anticipated conference finals against San Antonio, the 1999 NBA champion and the team with the league's best regular-season record (58–24), the Lakers removed all doubts about their dominance.

The Spurs had suggested that the 1999–2000 season might have been different had their star big man, Tim Duncan, not gone down with an injury. They were eager to match their inside tandem of Duncan and David Robinson against Shaq and the Lakers, and many observers expected an epic series. Instead, San Antonio was blown right out of the water. The Lakers won the first two games at the Alamodome and then routed the Spurs twice in L.A. to complete the sweep and return to the NBA Finals, carrying an 11–0 postseason record. They hadn't lost a game in two months, and they had a chance to run the table in the playoffs, something no NBA team—not Jordan's Bulls, Chamberlain's Lakers or Russell's Celtics—had done. Just like that, they'd gone from vulnerable to invincible. "There's no way any Eastern team can beat them," said Robinson.

But in Game 1 of the championship series, this Hollywood sequel had a most unexpected twist:

Led by the irresistible Bryant (opposite, 8) and the immovable O'Neal, the Lakers repeated as NBA champions, ousting the feisty 76ers 4–1 in the Finals. An overtime loss to Philadelphia in Game 1 would be Los Angeles's only defeat in 16 playoff games.

the second half) and induced O'Neal to foul out with more than two minutes left, only to be undone by a three-pointer from reserve forward Robert Horry. Games 4 and 5 were a Shaq-alanche, as O'Neal scored a combined 63 points and grabbed 27 rebounds. "The guy is the best," said Philadelphia coach Larry Brown. "He's unstoppable."

O'Neal, though, knew better than to claim he'd done it all by himself. "Kobe and I got on the same page," he said. "Once that happened, it was pretty much all over for the rest of the league."

While that turned out to be true, the rest of the league provided enough highlights and exciting players to keep the season interesting and its conclusion in doubt until the turnaround in La-La Land.

Leading the way was Iverson, the Sixers' six-foot shooting guard, who fulfilled the brilliant promise he had flashed since he entered the league in 1996. In his first four NBA seasons, the man known as the Answer had often seemed determined to make a riddle of himself. Undeniably superb on the court, he had a knack for controversy off of it. In 1997 his car was stopped for speeding and police found marijuana and a gun in the vehicle; before the 2000–01 season

The tenacious 76ers toppled the mighty Lakers in overtime 107–101. Foregoing the usual strategy of double-teaming O'Neal, Philadelphia let center Dikembe Mutombo play one-on-one against Shaq and concentrated on shutting down everybody else. O'Neal scored 44 points, but Bryant shot just 7 for 22 from the field and blew a chance to win the game in regulation when he turned the ball over with 18 seconds left and the score tied 94–94. Philadelphia's explosive, scrappy guard, Allen Iverson, the regular-season MVP, poured in 48 points to lead the Sixers.

But the plot reverted to form during the next four games, as the Lakers rolled to the title even as the irrepressible, overmatched Sixers kept finding ways to make the games close. In Game 3, a 96–91 Lakers victory, Philadelphia pressured Bryant into an uneven shooting night (3 for 14 in

he recorded a hardcore gangsta rap album whose lyrics made sure to offend almost every segment of society; and through it all, he feuded with Brown, a conflict that, to say the least, was a distraction to the interests of the team.

The situation deteriorated so much that Philadelphia nearly traded Iverson during the summer. Sixers president Pat Croce had a sit-down with the player in the offseason, and the Answer found himself, producing the best season of his five-year career. He led the NBA in scoring for the second time, averaging 31.1 points a game. More importantly, he began showing a commitment to his team. He arrived on time for practices, participated in team workouts and made an effort to get along with his coaches.

The results were electrifying. Philadelphia started the season with 10 straight victories and

had the NBA's best record for most of the year. They won the Atlantic Division by six games and rolled into the playoffs as the top seed in the Eastern Conference. "You're always trying to learn, but sometimes it doesn't stick with you," Iverson said early in the season. "Because of the s--- I went through, I'm a more mature person and a better basketball player."

In the playoffs Iverson, 25, squared off against two young stars who could eventually challenge his status as the best player in the East: Vince Carter, 24, of the Toronto Raptors, and Ray Allen, 25, of the Milwaukee Bucks. The gravity-defying Carter was already one of the most popular players in the game. The graceful Allen, on the other hand, had a more gradual emergence, honing his deadly jumper in relative obscurity in Milwaukee. Iverson brought out the best in both players. Carter rained 50 points on Philadelphia in Game 3 of the Eastern Conference semifinals, while Allen went for 38 in Game 2 of the conference finals. Alas, both the Raptors and the Bucks fell to Philadelphia in seven games, but the promise of future playoff showdowns between the three young stars bodes well for the future of the league. "A year or two ago," said Toronto coach Lenny Wilkens, "when people were talking about how some of the young players in the league hadn't

won anything yet, I said, 'Give them time. Let them mature, and you'll see them start to accomplish some things.' It doesn't happen overnight, especially with players spending less and less time in college. Now, a few years later, you're seeing the emergence of some mature players, guys who are capable of leading their teams to the postseason." Wilkens might also have pointed out that Michael Jordan, the benchmark for NBA greatness, didn't win his first title until his seventh season.

There were other young players who excelled in the playoffs, including 25-year-old Duncan, who already has one championship, and of course Bryant, who is only 22, with two titles and counting. And then there was 21-year-old Tracy McGrady, of the Orlando Magic. His team fell to the Bucks in four games in the first round, but McGrady's performance was the most memorable part of the series. He scored 33 points and made eight assists in Game 1, followed that up with 20 consecutive points in Game 2, then exploded for 42 in the next game to become the second-youngest player, behind Magic Johnson, to score 40 or more points in a playoff game. McGrady scored his points with style to burn, driving for layups, posting up, burying three-pointers and throwing down poster-perfect dunks. "I should probably tell you he's not all that good and we can

McGrady (above, center) played with poise beyond his years, finishing seventh in the NBA in scoring with a 26.8 average and winning the league's Most Improved Player award. The Magic lost to the Bucks in the first round of the playoffs, but McGrady gave Milwaukee all it could handle by scoring 135 points in four games.

Shaquille O'Neal (above, 34) was his usual dominant self in Game 1 of the NBA Finals, pouring in 44 points and grabbing 20 rebounds, but Philadelphia rode Allen Iverson's 48 points to a 107–101 overtime victory. Despite leading his team in scoring, blocks and field-goal percentage, Portland's Wallace (opposite, with ball) received more attention for incurring 41 technical fouls to break his own league record.

stop him," said Milwaukee point guard Sam Cassell. "But, man, what a wonderful player."

Despite the encouraging crop of young stars, it was the comeback of one of the league's veterans that provided the most satisfying story of the season. Alonzo Mourning, 31, the Miami Heat's 6' 10" center and one of the best-conditioned athletes in the league, learned in October 2000 that he had a form of focal glomerulosclerosis, a debilitating kidney disease that would sideline him for the season and threaten his career. Mourning sat out most of the season to receive treatment but made an unexpected and stirring return to the Heat on March 27. His play was rusty, and his stamina wasn't up to its usual level, but he provided his teammates with a solid presence at center. "We've had to get used to playing without 'Zo, and now we have to get used to having him in there," said forward Brian Grant. "It's a good problem to have, but you can't expect everything to click right away." Indeed, almost nothing clicked right away, and Pat Riley's team made its fourth consecutive early exit from the playoffs, getting swept by Charlotte in the first round.

Unfortunately, it remains to be seen if Mourning will be able to continue playing. He is

not cured. To treat his condition, which attacks the filters in the kidneys that remove waste from the blood, he takes as many as 14 pills a day. There's no guarantee that the medication will continue to work. "I know the future isn't promised," he said. "Every time I step on the court I'm scared."

While there was plenty of good news for the league, there was also no disguising the truth that the NBA was struggling on several fronts. Television ratings continued to decline, in part because fans seemed put off by the sheer number of boors now plying their wares in the league. To wit, Trail Blazers forward Rasheed Wallace averaged one technical foul every two games; Jason Williams, the point guard for Sacramento (now with the Grizzlies), made offensive comments to an Asian fan; and Knicks point guard Charlie Ward was quoted in *The New York Times Magazine* saying that Jews are "stubborn" and persecute Christians. And, of course, there was Iverson's repugnant rap.

Also troubling was the league's conviction that fans were mostly fed up with a game that has lost some of its zip, stifled by half-court, man-to-man defenses and the stand-around offenses they engender. To remedy the situation the NBA took steps at the end of the year to try to speed up play. Beginning next season teams will be able to play zone defense, and the time a team can take to cross half-court has been reduced, from 10 seconds to eight. "It's important to be willing to make the change, understanding that you don't know exactly how it's going to turn out," said Suns owner Jerry Colangelo, the chairman of the committee that recommended the changes. "This is a work in progress. It's something we're going to continue to monitor. It may need to be tweaked here and there as it's put into practice."

If the new rules have the desired effect, and the league makes a return to its Jordan-era glory days, things could get interesting for the reigning world champions. Still, it's hard to imagine that the Lakers won't be able to stage a repeat of their repeat. Of course, that will be up to Shaq and Kobe.

PHOTO GALLERY

Tall Dirk and No Play: Dallas's
seven-foot center Dirk Nowitzki
of Germany (above, middle) was
stopped cold by San Antonio's
Sean Elliott (left) and Malik Rose
(right) as he drove to the hoop
during Game 4 of the Western
Conference semifinals. The
Mavericks won the game 112–108
but lost the series 4–1.

The Marbury Man: New Jersey's Stephon
Marbury (right, with ball) soared to the rim
against Indiana's Zan Tabak (middle) and
Jermaine O'Neal during the Nets' 97–92
early-season victory over the Pacers in New
Jersey. Marbury finished the 2000–01
season as the only player in the Top 10 in both
scoring and assists, but the Nets suffered
through another woeful year, finishing 26–56.

Fancy Dish: Miami guard Eddie Jones (left, 6) flipped a nifty pass out of a double-team by Toronto's Keon Clark and Vince Carter during the Heat's 103–83 drubbing of the Raptors in January. Jones and the Heat would go 50–32 and finish second to Philadelphia in the Atlantic Division— only to make an early exit from the playoffs for the fourth consecutive season.

Hands Up: New Jersey's Jamie Feick (left, 14) battled Toronto's Antonio Davis (33) and Keon Clark (7) under the backboard during the Nets' 113–111 victory in February. Davis, who led his team in rebounding and blocked shots, was instrumental in the Raptors' rise as they finished second in the Central Division and bounced the New York Knicks out of the playoffs in the first round.

L.A. Story: Sparks center Lisa Leslie (right, 9) outreached three Charlotte players for a rebound during Game 2 of the WNBA Finals, which Los Angeles won 82–54 to complete a sweep of the Sting and join its NBA brethren, the Lakers, as champions. Leslie made WNBA history by being named MVP of the regular season, the All-Star Game and the Finals.

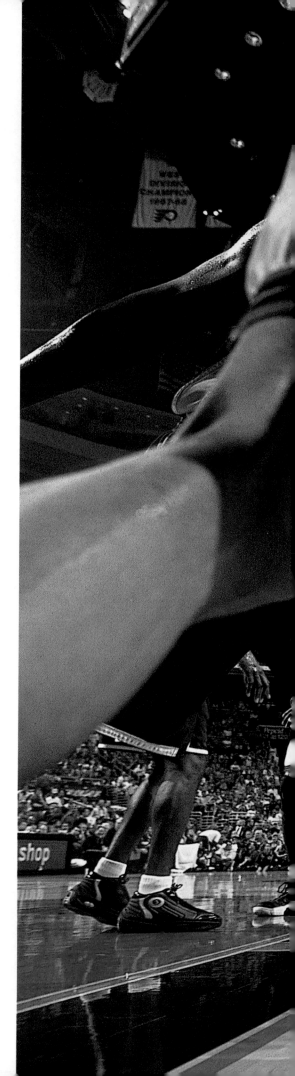

The Lakers' Kobe Bryant (above right) sailed to the basket past San Antonio center David Robinson during L.A.'s 111–72 trouncing of the Spurs in Game 3 of the Western Conference finals. Bryant scored 36 points, corralled nine rebounds and made eight assists in the game. The next night Los Angeles would complete the sweep—its third straight of the playoffs.

After helping his team to a split of the first two games in Los Angeles, the 76ers' Allen Iverson (above, receiving an inbounds pass from Matt Geiger) scored 35 points in Game 3 of the NBA Finals in Philadelphia but could not offset the outstanding performances of the Lakers' two stars, Shaquille O'Neal and Kobe Bryant, who scored 30 and 32 points, respectively, as Los Angeles won 96–91.

PROFILES

Predrag Stojakovic

The world's tallest grocery store manager—isn't that what he should be? Look at 6' 9" Sacramento Kings forward Predrag (Peja) Stojakovic, surrounded by hip-hop-listening, tattoo-covered, American-born basketball players, standing there with that goofy smile and that dorky sweater and those too-snug blue jeans. What's he doing here, a square European peg jammed into a FUBU-wearing circle? Shouldn't he be working in produce? Hey, bud, where's the grapefruit? How much is the cabbage?

He appears lost, and, in truth, he sort of is. Stojakovic (STOY-ak-O-vich) may well be in the U.S., but the U.S. definitely isn't in Stojakovic (above). How

many 23-year-old millionaires do you know who still live with their parents? How many NBA players do you know who don't rush to embrace the dunk? And—C'mon, Peja!—those pants? The NBA is Armani, not Wrangler. "Peja has a nickname," says Kings forward Lawrence Funderburke with a laugh. "It's T.J., for Tight Jeans." Maybe it should be W.K., for Weird Karma. Stojakovic is, by his own humble account, the luckiest man in the long history of lucky men. He was supposed to take over the family grocery. Nothing more. His dad, Miodrag, and mom, Branka, owned such a store in Pozega, a town of 28,000 in eastern central Croatia. Growing up, Peja and his

older brother, Nenad, would round up friends after school and, with empty stomachs and open palms, stealthily scavenge the shelves. This was entertainment in Pozega.

Young Peja was something of an athlete—he enjoyed volleyball and soccer—but the town's sports facilities were scanty. He played basketball once or twice a week and only for fun. "I saw some tapes," he says in the fluent English he learned from TV and teammates. "Magic Johnson, Michael Jordan. That's what I knew of the NBA. Not anything else."

The family business was where Stojakovic was destined to end up. Not in Belgrade, playing professional basketball at 15. Not in Greece, living the life of a European superstar. Not in Sacramento, averaging 20.4 points and 5.8 rebounds as a blossoming star for the high-flying Kings. He was supposed to run the family store. That's how it should have gone.

It's June 26, 1996—NBA draft day. You are a Sacramento fan. You have lived this before. You wish for amnesia. From 1985 to 1993, your team made 21 first- and second-round selections without netting a single impact player.

Maybe, just maybe, things are changing. There's a new general manager in town, Geoff Petrie, who has done some pretty good picking: Brian Grant, Michael Smith and Funderburke in 1994; Corliss Williamson and Tyus Edney a year later. "I want you to know that we're picking a person I really believe in," says Petrie to the arena crowd just before the team's '96 choice is announced in Continental Airlines Arena. "He's a good young player named Predrag Stojakovic. I think he'll be a fantastic pro, and...."

Hello? Anyone?

"It wasn't heavy booing, but there was certainly no celebration," recalls Troy Hanson, the Kings' media-relations director. "If you had to sum up the reaction in one word, it'd be: Who?"

Virtually nobody in Sacramento not employed by the Kings had heard of Stojakovic. If only Sacramento fans had known then what they know now. Stojakovic has become the player Petrie envisioned—an inside-outside threat with Baryshnikov's grace and one of the game's sweetest three-point strokes. While Stojakovic quickly established himself as a long-range specialist, in 2000–01 he has also been driving with increased confidence.

"I honestly believe Peja's the best shooter in the league," says Kings All-Star forward Chris Webber. "He can hit from anywhere at any time, he's a great athlete, and he cuts the hardest without the ball of anyone I've seen—like he's from Princeton. He just loves that orange ball. He's the first to pick it up, the last to put it down."

In his first two seasons Stojakovic would lose sleep over missed jumpers and tough losses. This year he has taken his bad games and amazing ones in the same easygoing stride. "Peja's mature for his age," says Sacramento coach Rick Adelman. It is, Stojakovic acknowledges, harder to view an athletic event as a question of life or death when life or death matters have been part of your everyday existence.

The grocery managerial position never came his way. Peja was 13, lying in bed, when he first heard the gunfire that became a nightly occurrence. He would walk down the street and see walls sprayed with bullet holes. His family, which is Serbian, and his Serbian friends were no longer welcome in Pozega. This was civil war in Yugoslavia. "Suddenly, you didn't talk to the neighbors," he recalls. "During the night, the Croatians would try and scare the Serbian people. We lost everything—the house, the business, our possessions."

Within months Miodrag, Branka and their two sons loaded the car and drove 150 miles east to Belgrade, the hoops capital of Yugoslavia and home to the country's two elite clubs, Partizan and Red Star. When he was 14, Peja auditioned for Red Star's junior team. He was raw but athletic, unsure but 6'4". "They kept me, and I go from playing twice a week to practicing twice a day," he says. "I learned that I could be very good."

After one season Stojakovic was promoted to Red Star's professional team. When the season ended, Red Star offered Stojakovic a six-year contract. He refused to sign for more than four. The team insisted on six. He wouldn't budge. Finally, with the blessing of his parents, Peja shocked Red Star by agreeing to a five-year deal with PAOK, the Greek Professional League power. He and the rest of his family moved to Thessaloniki. It was their first step toward America.

"He was 18, holding his own against Xavier McDaniel and Dominique Wilkins," says Funderburke, one of Stojakovic's PAOK teammates in 1995–96. "Back then he would ask me if he had what it takes to make it in the NBA. I told him the truth: Yes. He was the best young player in Europe. The only thing he needed to work on was not backing down from players, not giving in if a guy pushed or shoved. It took time,

but he got it. Peja became a tough kid."

Soon he was doing more than hold his own: in 1997–98, he was named MVP of the Greek League. When he finally arrived in Sacramento, Stojakovic was a polished offensive weapon—who wasn't expecting to come off the bench and play a meager 21.4 minutes per game. Although he averaged a solid 8.4 points in 1998–99, he was frustrated and ornery. "In Greece, I was a star," Stojakovic says. "Here, I sat and watched."

In 1999–2000, as Stojakovic impressed Adelman with improved defense and surprisingly rugged rebounding, his playing time increased. Although Williamson was the starting small forward, Stojakovic averaged 11.9 points in 23.6 minutes and was usually on the court for the fourth quarter. In September the Kings sent Williamson to the Toronto Raptors for guard Doug Christie. "Corliss was a good player for us," says Adelman, "but after two seasons, it was obvious: Peja was ready to start."

Stojakovic has fit in beautifully with the Kings. His wardrobe is frequently the butt of teammates' jokes—"They don't understand," Peja says. "Fashion is coming from Europe to America"—but he takes the ribbing with a smile. "He's funny, and he's smart," says Webber. "He's a cool guy to hang with."

In the off-season Stojakovic, a Greek citizen, is a regular on the club scene in Thessaloniki, where he still owns a house. His favorite beverage? Cold coffee. "It tastes best that way," he says. "Very Greek."

Sacramento is a long way from Pozega, far removed from the simple life of Stojakovic's youth and the dangerous one of his early teens. Sometimes, when the game is an hour away and he's sitting in the locker room, Stojakovic recalls his boyhood. It's a strange thing—the idea that the same war that killed so many people also started his journey to the American dream. What if it had never happened? What if his parents had never had to move the family?

Peja thinks this one over. "I would work in the family supermarket," he says. "And I would probably be happy."

—Jeff Pearlman
excerpted from SI, Jan. 8, 2001

Allen Iverson

I'm going to bring an NBA legend into the room, and I want you to close your eyes while I describe him.

Compared with the rest of today's superstars, he's small—mostly heart and scabs—but as tough as a '48 pickup. In his prime he was a wind-up toy who never stopped moving without the ball, busting through picks and elbows and knees as though he was trying to break the world record for bruises. He'd go 48 minutes most every game, usually nursing more injuries than an ER episode. He was a Nintendo-type scorer with a gorgeous jumper who considered being knocked to the floor part of his follow-through. You're thinking Jerry West, right?

Wrong.

This guy was electric. He could carry an offense, a team, a city by himself. One night he would torch an opponent for 50 points and the next decide to beat the opposition with assists. He was unpredictable, unguardable and unforgettable. He had moves that could make your pupils dilate. He was the idol of millions around the world, one of the three greatest players of his day.

You're thinking Michael Jordan, right?

Wrong.

This guy seemed to be appreciated only by the fans who saw him night after night. He was shy with the press, yet honest as a Sunday confessional. He dressed the same every day and was mocked for it. He was the same man whether in front of the camera or in the line at the deli. He stayed true to his high school friends. He was a family man whose first move after he left the locker room was to sweep up his two small kids. He never let the fame or the money or the trophies change him.

You're thinking John Stockton, right?

Wrong.

This guy had the 100,000-watt smile of a lotto winner. He had the joy of the game in his blood, and he knew how to spread it. He would hug his coach only slightly less than he hugged his mom, which was constantly. He had the courage to dive into the crowd at least once a game, and the sense of humor to hug the fan who caught him. He had the game to win the shiniest awards, yet the humility to share credit with everybody else in the room.

You're thinking Magic Johnson, right?

Wrong.

Now open your eyes and look at him.

He's Allen Iverson (opposite, and right).

That changes everything, doesn't it? Now you see the cornrows and the tattoos and the pierce-holes dripping gold, and they bug you, right? You think *thug* and *rapper* and *criminal*. SPORTS ILLUSTRATED put the NBA's soon-to-be MVP on the cover of its April 23, 2001, issue, posed as himself, nearly naked, hip-hop to his heart, and suddenly you're mad. West and Jordan and Stockton and Magic, they're welcome on your coffee table, but not this guy. We're up to our clavicles in hate mail (a sampling of which appears on page 14 of the May 28, 2001 issue).

"Christ!" wrote a subscriber in Tucson. "Don't you have enough tattooed, body-pierced, earring- [and] necklace-wearing, corn-rowed freaks on the inside [of the magazine] that you have to put them on the cover?"

"The cover with Allen Iverson made me sick to my stomach," read one e-mail. "I feel the magazine has sent a poor message to young readers."

From Richardson, Texas: "Those preening idiots barely belong to the human race."

Montgomery, Ala.: "Iverson is just another reason why our country is in such bad shape."

Adams, N.Y.: "His angry young oppressed black-man image is b------ ….I am white and not prejudiced, but I

do not feel sorry for Allen Iverson."

Another e-mail: "[The] stare, tattoos and pants to the waist showing his jockstrap sum up the reason I have not watched an NBA game in years."

San Diego: "The picture of Allen Iverson is revolting."

Lindon, Utah: "I object to this grotesque and irreverent picture."

Hundreds of people were obsessed by what's on the outside of the man, not the inside. Not a word about will and loyalty and effort. Not a word of praise for a young superstar who has stuck with one team, one woman his whole career. You see him, but you don't see him.

And he lives with this crap every freaking day.

I'm canceling *their* subscriptions.

—Rick Reilly
SI, May 28, 2001

Iverson did win the NBA's regular-season MVP award, and he topped the league in scoring (31.1 ppg) and steals (2.51 spg). He also led the 76ers (56–26) to the Atlantic Division title and their first NBA Finals appearance since 1983. —Ed.

Ray Allen

Ray Allen (opposite) feels your pain, disenchanted NBA fans. The Milwaukee Bucks' All-Star shooting guard has heard your complaints. Whether or not you're being narrow-minded, he knows that you feel little or no connection to many of today's new-jack players, and he's here to help. Because if you can't relate to him, it's hopeless. You'll never love this game again.

For starters, just look at him. He's an unimposing 6'5" and 205 pounds with none of those totems that so many of you find so off-putting: no tattoos, no cornrows, none of that anvil-sized jewelry. He's strikingly handsome, and with no slang in his lexicon, he speaks in the soothing voice of a pilot pointing out sites of interest below. The worst curse word you'll hear him use is *durn*, which he picked up only since moving to the Midwest five years ago. You like golf? Allen has a 10 handicap. Want to talk art? Funny, Allen does too. He counts among his legion of friends Milwaukee gallery owner Michael Lord, who has lent Allen works by Miro and Chagall and recently sold him a Warhol lithograph. In February Allen had a wooden sculpture delivered to his sprawling home in suburban Mequon, Wis., to see if it "resonated" (his word) with him. He plays the piano, just finished reading *Chicken Soup for the Soul* and gets gooey when he talks about his eight-year-old daughter, Tierra, who lives with her mother in Connecticut.

What's that? You're one of those fans who doesn't mind NBA players in the mold of Allen Iverson? You're partial to stars with flavor, players who embrace hip-hop culture? No problem, the 25-year-old Allen can accommodate you, too. He knows Jay-Z's lyrics as well as any of his teammates do, and you'd be hard-pressed to find a player who donates more time and money to inner-city causes. "Ray's definitely one of the guys," says Milwaukee point guard Sam Cassell.

Allen, however, is not merely a modern-day Zelig, endowed with an uncanny ability to insert himself seamlessly into any social situation. He got game, too. A member of the Dream Team in Sydney and the past two Eastern Conference All-Star teams, Allen plays with a smoothness and efficiency that make everything he does on the court look effortless.

With a blinding first step and hops worthy of Milwaukee's finest brewery, he's among the league's most explosive players. His skill at dropping in floaters and finger rolls makes him more dangerous still. Give him a step and he'll bury a medium-range jumper. Give him two steps and he'll hit the three-pointer, as he did during 2001 All-Star weekend, when he sank 33 of 50 attempts to win the Long Distance Shootout.

"Ray has great range, but he can also penetrate," says Charlotte Hornets coach Paul Silas. "When you use that combination effectively, the way he does, you're impossible to defend."

Hard as it is for defenders to get a hand on Allen, it may be more difficult to get a handle on him. He admits that his interests are all over the map, but he figures it's because that's where he spent his childhood. Ray's father, Walter, was a mechanic for the Air Force, and the family moved from base to base with the frequency of Bedouins. Before Ray's three seasons at UConn—he had a 3.6 GPA and majored in communication sciences—he had lived in Merced, Calif.; Ramstein, Germany; Altus, Okla.; Suffolk, England; Rosamond, Calif.; and rural Dalzell, S.C., where he graduated from Hillcrest High. Instead of fostering a sense of displacement, Allen's itinerant upbringing exposed him to a wide range of people and places, imbuing him with a worldliness unknown to most of his peers.

"I feel like I can go anywhere, which gives me total confidence," he says. "I can take it to the streets, or I can take it to the boardroom. The trick is to allow people to feel they can relate to you. The more people—white, black, young, old—who can say, 'I know where he's coming from,' the more successful you'll be."

This prompts an obvious question: Why is Allen still on the B-list of NBA stars? Why isn't he on the front lines of the league's marketing offensive, scooping up endorsements by the handful? Allen is as recognized for his role as hoops prodigy Jesus Shuttlesworth in the 1998 Spike Lee flick *He Got Game* as he is for any of his noncelluloid basketball feats. He doesn't mind at all: Allen is well-enough known that he has an endorsement deal with Nike and is a bona fide All-Star, but he relishes walking into a Blockbuster or going bowling—now hooked on the local passion, he claims to have a 180 average—without being accosted.

"If you try to please everyone, you can end up pleasing no one," says Bob Williams, president of Burns Sports & Celebrities, Inc., a firm based in Evanston, Ill., that matches athletes with endorsement opportunities. "Ray is hard to pin down, and he ends up being nondescript."

Milwaukee coach George Karl wonders if Allen isn't too polished and image-conscious for his own good. "I call him Barbie Doll because he wants to be pretty," says Karl. "He's a great player, but he cares too much about having style. Basketball isn't about being cool. It's a tough, competitive game, and to win you have to be mean, you have to be an assassin, and that's not Ray."

Karl was especially irked by Allen's play in the two games following the 2001 All-Star break. On successive nights he surrendered 49 and 35 points, respectively, to Iverson and the Atlanta Hawks' Jason Terry. From Karl's vantage point, those defensive performances didn't seem to bother Allen. "Two guys drop 84 points on your ass, and I'm thinking, Where's the pissed-off competitor?" Karl says. "I look at Ray, he's out there *smiling*. Tell me what that's all about."

Allen shrugs. "George is a passionate guy, but I can't bring myself to see basketball as life or death," he says. Allen is sufficiently self-aware to recognize that his game could benefit from a dose of intensity. Still, as accommodating and flexible as he is in everyday life, he is unwilling to change his essential nature. Sure, he wants to win and gets competitive playing pool, Ping-Pong and even Yahtzee with friends. "But I have to be myself," Allen says. "I can't be all things to all people."

Perhaps not. But he comes durn close.

—L. Jon Wertheim
excerpted from SI, Feb. 26, 2001

THE NUMBERS

NBA Final Standings

EASTERN CONFERENCE
Atlantic Division

TEAM	W	L	PCT	GB
Philadelphia	56	26	.683	—
Miami	50	32	.610	6
New York	48	34	.585	8
Orlando	43	39	.524	13
Boston	36	46	.439	20
New Jersey	26	56	.317	30
Washington	19	63	.232	37

Central Division

TEAM	W	L	PCT	GB
Milwaukee	52	30	.634	—
Toronto	47	35	.573	5
Charlotte	46	36	.561	6
Indiana	41	41	.500	11
Detroit	32	50	.390	20
Cleveland	30	52	.366	22
Atlanta	25	57	.305	27
Chicago	15	67	.183	37

WESTERN CONFERENCE
Midwest Division

TEAM	W	L	PCT	GB
San Antonio	58	24	.707	—
Utah	53	29	.646	5
Dallas	53	29	.646	5
Minnesota	47	35	.573	11
Houston	45	37	.549	13
Denver	40	42	.488	18
Vancouver	23	59	.280	35

Pacific Division

TEAM	W	L	PCT	GB
LA Lakers	56	26	.683	—
Sacramento	55	27	.671	1
Phoenix	51	31	.622	5
Portland	50	32	.610	6
Seattle	44	38	.537	12
LA Clippers	31	51	.378	25
Golden State	17	65	.207	39

NBA Individual Leaders

SCORING

	GP	PTS	AVG
Allen Iverson, Phil	71	2207	31.1
Jerry Stackhouse, Det	80	2380	29.8
Shaquille O'Neal, LA Lakers	74	2125	28.7
Kobe Bryant, LA Lakers	68	1938	28.5
Vince Carter, Tor	75	2070	27.6
Chris Webber, Sac	70	1898	27.1
Tracy McGrady, Orl	77	2065	26.8
Paul Pierce, Bos	82	2071	25.3
Antawn Jamison, GS	82	2044	24.9
Stephon Marbury, NJ	67	1598	23.9

ASSISTS

	GP	ASSISTS	AVG
Jason Kidd, Phoe	77	753	9.8
John Stockton, Utah	82	713	8.7
Nick Van Exel, Den	71	600	8.5
Mike Bibby, Van	82	685	8.4
Gary Payton, Sea	79	642	8.1
Andre Miller, Clev	82	657	8.0
Mark Jackson, Tor/NY	83	661	8.0
Sam Cassell, Mil	76	580	7.6
Stephon Marbury, NJ	67	506	7.6
Terrell Brandon, Minn	78	583	7.5

FREE THROW PERCENTAGE

	FTA	FTM	PCT
Reggie Miller, Ind	348	323	.928
Allan Houston, NY	307	279	.909
Doug Christie, Sac	312	280	.897
Steve Nash, Dall	258	231	.895
Mitch Richmond, Wash	160	143	.894
Steve Smith, Port	347	309	.890
Ray Allen, Mil	392	348	.888
Darrell Armstrong, Orl	249	220	.884
Eric Piatkowski, LA Clippers	181	158	.873
Terrell Brandon, Minn	224	195	.871

STEALS

	GP	STEALS	AVG
Allen Iverson, Phil	71	178	2.51
Mookie Blaylock, GS	69	163	2.36
Doug Christie, Sac	81	183	2.26
Jason Kidd, Phoe	77	166	2.16
Baron Davis, Char	82	170	2.07
Terrell Brandon, Minn	78	161	2.06
Ron Artest, Chi	76	152	2.00
Darrell Armstrong, Orl	75	135	1.80
Steve Francis, Hou	80	141	1.76
Antoine Walker, Bos	81	138	1.70

REBOUNDS

	GP	REB	AVG
Dikembe Mutombo, Atl/Phil	75	1015	13.5
Ben Wallace, Det	80	1052	13.2
Shaquille O'Neal, LA Lakers	74	940	12.7
Tim Duncan, SA	82	997	12.2
Antonio McDyess, Den	70	845	12.1
Kevin Garnett, Minn	81	921	11.4
Chris Webber, Sac	70	777	11.1
Shawn Marion, Phoe	79	848	10.7
Antonio Davis, Tor	78	787	10.1
Elton Brand, Chi	74	746	10.1

FIELD GOAL PERCENTAGE

	FGA	FGM	PCT
Shaquille O'Neal, LA Lakers	1422	813	.572
Bonzi Wellls, Port	726	387	.533
Marcus Camby, NY	580	304	.524
Kurt Thomas, NY	614	314	.511
Wally Szczerbiak, Minn	920	469	.510
Darius Miles, LA Clippers	630	318	.505
John Stockton, Utah	651	328	.504
Donyell Marshall, Utah	849	427	.503
Corliss Williamson, Det	647	325	.502
Clarence Weatherspoon, Clev	692	347	.501
Rasheed Wallace, Port	1178	590	.501

THREE-POINT FIELD GOAL PERCENTAGE

	FGA	FGM	PCT
Brent Barry, Sea	229	109	.476
John Stockton, Utah	132	61	.462
Shammond Williams, Sea	133	61	.459
Hubert Davis, Wash	171	78	.456
Danny Ferry, SA	156	70	.449
Toni Kukoc, Phil/Atl	157	70	.446
Pat Garrity, Orl	224	97	.433
Ray Allen, Mil	467	202	.433
Rashard Lewis, Sea	285	123	.432
Dell Curry, Tor	145	62	.428

BLOCKED SHOTS

	GP	BS	AVG
Theo Ratliff, Phil/Atl	50	187	3.74
Jermaine O'Neal, Ind	81	228	2.81
Shawn Bradley, Dall	82	228	2.78
Shaquille O'Neal, LA Lakers	74	204	2.76
Dikembe Mutombo, Atl/Phil	75	203	2.71
Adonal Foyle, GS	58	156	2.69
Raef LaFrentz, Den	78	206	2.64
David Robinson, SA	80	197	2.46
Tim Duncan, SA	82	192	2.34
Ben Wallace, Det	80	186	2.33

NBA Awards

ALL-NBA TEAMS

First Team	Second Team	Third Team
G Allen Iverson, Philadelphia	Tracy McGrady, Orlando	Gary Payton, Seattle
G Jason Kidd, Phoenix	Kobe Bryant, LA Lakers	Ray Allen, Milwaukee
C Shaquille O'Neal, LA Lakers	Dikembe Mutombo, Philadelphia	David Robinson, San Antonio
F Chris Webber, Sacramento	Kevin Garnett, Minnesota	Karl Malone, Utah
F Tim Duncan, San Antonio	Vince Carter, Toronto	Dirk Nowitzki, Dallas

NBA ALL-DEFENSIVE TEAMS

First Team	Second Team
G Gary Payton, Seattle	Kobe Bryant, LA Lakers
G Jason Kidd, Phoenix	Doug Christie, Sacramento
C Dikembe Mutombo, Philadelphia	Shaquille O'Neal, LA Lakers
F Tim Duncan, San Antonio	Bruce Bowen, Miami
F Kevin Garnett, Minnesota	P.J. Brown, Charlotte

ALL-ROOKIE TEAMS (CHOSEN WITHOUT REGARD TO POSITION)

First Team	Second Team
Mike Miller, Orlando	Hidayet Turkoglu, Sacramento
Kenyon Martin, New Jersey	Desmond Mason, Seattle
Marc Jackson, Golden State	Courtney Alexander, Washington
Morris Peterson, Toronto	Marcus Fizer, Chicago
Darius Miles, LA Clippers	Chris Mihm, Cleveland

2001 NBA Playoffs

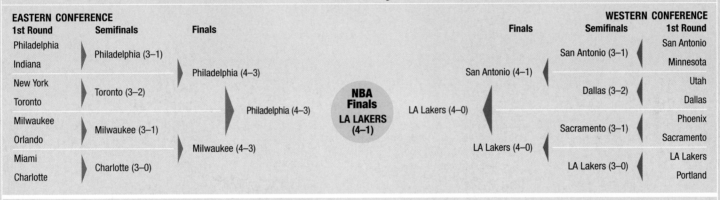

EASTERN CONFERENCE

1st Round	Semifinals	Finals
Philadelphia	Philadelphia (3–1)	
Indiana		Philadelphia (4–3)
New York	Toronto (3–2)	
Toronto		Philadelphia (4–3)
Milwaukee	Milwaukee (3–1)	
Orlando		Milwaukee (4–3)
Miami	Charlotte (3–0)	
Charlotte		

NBA Finals — LA LAKERS (4–1)

LA Lakers (4–0)

WESTERN CONFERENCE

Finals	Semifinals	1st Round
San Antonio (4–1)	San Antonio (3–1)	San Antonio / Minnesota
	Dallas (3–2)	Utah / Dallas
LA Lakers (4–0)	Sacramento (3–1)	Phoenix / Sacramento
	LA Lakers (3–0)	LA Lakers / Portland

NBA Finals Composite Box Score

PHILADELPHIA 76ERS

PLAYER	GP	FIELD GOALS FGM	FIELD GOALS PCT	3-PT FG FGM	3-PT FG FGA	FREE THROWS FTM	FREE THROWS PCT	REBOUNDS OFF	REBOUNDS TOTAL	A	STL	TO	BS	AVG	HI
Iverson	5	66	40.7	11	39	35	72.9	5	28	19	9	12	1	35.6	48
Mutombo	5	33	60.0	0	0	18	69.2	20	61	2	2	5	11	16.8	23
Snow	5	22	40.7	0	3	19	73.1	11	22	30	8	14	1	12.6	14
McKie	5	15	31.3	4	9	6	66.7	7	27	30	6	14	3	8.0	14
Hill	5	13	39.4	0	0	7	77.8	7	33	2	0	5	6	6.6	18
Geiger	5	12	66.7	0	0	2	100.0	2	5	2	1	3	0	5.2	10
Bell	5	4	30.8	0	3	5	50.0	2	9	4	10	4	0	2.6	6
MacCulloch	5	5	41.7	0	0	3	75.0	5	7	0	0	2	0	2.6	13
Jones	5	4	40.0	2	4	0	—	2	10	1	1	2	2	2.0	4
Ollie	5	1	33.3	0	0	3	100.0	1	1	1	0	0	0	1.0	3
Lynch	2	1	33.3	0	0	0	—	2	5	1	2	0	0	1.0	2
Buford	3	1	16.7	0	1	0	—	2	6	0	0	1	0	0.7	2
Totals	**5**	**177**	**42.4**	**17**	**59**	**98**	**71.5**	**66**	**214**	**92**	**39**	**65**	**23**	**93.8**	**107**

LOS ANGELES LAKERS

PLAYER	GP	FIELD GOALS FGM	FIELD GOALS PCT	3-PT FG FGM	3-PT FG FGA	FREE THROWS FTM	FREE THROWS PCT	REBOUNDS OFF	REBOUNDS TOTAL	A	STL	TO	BS	AVG	HI
O'Neal	5	63	57.3	0	0	39	51.3	31	79	24	2	20	17	33.0	44
Bryant	5	44	41.5	3	9	32	84.2	5	39	29	7	18	7	24.6	32
Fisher	5	17	43.6	10	19	5	83.3	1	6	10	8	6	1	9.8	18
Fox	5	14	44.1	7	15	12	92.3	3	23	19	6	14	2	9.8	20
Horry	5	14	56.0	8	13	6	100.0	10	25	6	4	2	7	8.4	15
Grant	5	10	29.4	0	0	6	75.0	12	28	3	2	2	7	5.2	8
Harper	3	5	62.5	1	3	2	66.7	0	5	3	1	0	1	4.3	8
Lue	5	7	58.3	4	6	0	—	1	4	7	7	5	1	3.6	6
Shaw	5	6	30.0	3	10	3	60.0	3	16	14	4	7	0	3.6	7
Madsen	2	0	00.0	0	0	0	—	1	1	0	0	0	1	0.0	—
Totals	**5**	**181**	**46.5**	**36**	**75**	**105**	**67.7**	**67**	**226**	**115**	**41**	**75**	**44**	**100.6**	**108**

Oh, Happy Ray!

After 22 years in the league and several near misses, Colorado defenseman Ray Bourque finally lifted the Stanley Cup

B.J. SCHECTER

This was the moment Raymond Bourque had waited for his entire career, his entire life. The Stanley Cup, the most revered trophy in North American sports, had been within Bourque's reach on several occasions but had always eluded his grasp. He had spent more than 20 seasons with the Bruins, and in March 2000, when it became apparent that Boston wouldn't contend for the Cup before the end of his career, Bourque asked for a trade to a championship-caliber team. The Bruins graciously granted his wish, sending him to Colorado, and from the day Bourque pulled on the Avalanche sweater, everybody wanted him to win a Cup.

Colorado made it to the brink of the Stanley Cup finals that year, losing to the Dallas Stars in Game 7 of the Western Conference finals, but then, a year later, they did it: With a 3–1 victory over New Jersey in Game 7, they won their second NHL title in six years, but more importantly, they delivered the Stanley Cup to the 40-year-old Bourque, ending the legendary defenseman's 22-year quest. Soon after the final whistle blew, Avalanche captain Joe Sakic accepted the Cup from NHL commissioner Gary Bettman, skipped the traditional captain's spin around the rink with the fabled trophy and literally handed it to Bourque, whose eyes began to well up with tears. The crowd at the Pepsi Center went wild when Bourque lifted the 34½-pound piece of silver over his head. "Maybe it's because I'm old or I was tired, but it felt really heavy," Bourque said.

You could search from Saskatoon to St. Petersburg without finding a hockey fan, or player, who dislikes Ray Bourque. He is the quintessential old-school team player, a superbly skilled defenseman of unerring consistency. Even in Boston, where fans are notoriously provincial and treat players who leave Beantown as traitors, Bourque's name ranks with Williams's and Russell's. The television ratings were higher in Boston for the Stanley Cup than they were in the

New York area, home of the New Jersey Devils.

After Colorado clinched the Cup, Avalanche goalie Patrick Roy, who won the Conn Smythe Trophy as the playoff MVP for a record third time, said, "A name was missing from that thing. And today it's back to normal. [It was so special] seeing Ray raise that Cup, seeing his eyes, seeing how excited he was."

Bourque played in 1,826 games in 22 seasons, starting in 1979 and playing through the '80s, '90s and into the 21st century. He played in two Stanley Cup finals with Boston, but each time the Bruins were thwarted by Wayne Gretzky's Edmonton Oilers. Though Bourque had two years left on his contract when the season began, most observers assumed that this would be his final season, win or lose. So from the time the Avalanche opened training camp their goal was clear: win it for Ray.

The Avalanche ripped through the regular season, winning the Western Conference points race with a 52-16-10 record and establishing a few milestones along the way. In October, Roy, whose 2.21 goals-against average was the lowest in his 17-year career, surpassed Terry Sawchuk as the goalie with the most career victories (448). In February, just before the trading deadline, the Avalanche acquired the final piece of their championship puzzle when they obtained defenseman Rob Blake from the Los Angeles Kings. "[Now] they're the overwhelming favorite to win the Stanley Cup," said Detroit general manager Ken Holland.

On March 24 the high-flying Avalanche traveled to Boston, where Bourque faced his old team for the first time since the trade. With Bruins fans cheering his every move, he played marvelously, assisting on two goals in a 4–2 Colorado victory. "I was very happy I had an opportunity at the end to thank the fans, who have been so good to me," Bourque said. "They treated me very well today, and I want to thank them. I certainly appreciate that. It was a very nice day, and I had a lot of fun."

Led by Bourque (opposite, left of trophy), playoff-MVP Roy (right of trophy) and leading scorer Sakic (in front of Roy), the Avalanche celebrated its 3–1 victory over the Devils in Game 7 of the Stanley Cup finals. The triumph was Colorado's second NHL title in six years.

Hands-on Owner: In December 2000, Lemieux returned from a three-and-a-half-year retirement to take a more active interest in the Penguins, the team he owns. Super Mario scored 35 goals and made 41 assists in 43 regular-season games, then led Pittsburgh to the Eastern Conference finals, where it fell to New Jersey.

Now Bourque & Co. were ready to begin their drive for a championship. In the first round of the playoffs the Avalanche faced Vancouver and former Colorado coach Marc Crawford, who had a bitter parting from the team in 1998. The inspired Canucks put up a valiant fight, losing 5–4 and 2–1 in the first two games in Colorado. With two more tough victories in Vancouver the Avalanche swept the Canucks out of the playoffs and earned the respect of their former coach. "Our three-hundred-thousand-dollar players were trying to corral million-dollar players," said Crawford. "But the superstars won out. I told the guys there's no shame in losing to a team that is great. And Colorado is a great team."

In the conference semifinals it was Blake's turn for an emotional homecoming—though the emotions were not as tender as those that greeted Bourque in Boston. The Avalanche met the upstart Kings, who had shocked the Red Wings in the first round. While Blake was so well respected on the ice that the Kings didn't name another captain after he left, he didn't fare as well in the stands. Kings fans were unforgiving, vigorously booing Blake during three games at the Staples Center. Los Angeles stole Game 1 in Colorado and hung on despite losing the next three games. They took Game 5, 1–0, then won a 1–0 double-overtime thriller to force a Game 7, but the Avalanche wouldn't be denied. Blake, who scored a key goal in Colorado's clinching 5–1 win, was relieved it was

over. "You build your friendships through battles you've gone through over the years, and a month later you have to put all of that aside and battle your old team," said Blake. "It's very difficult."

More difficulty awaited the Avalanche in the Western Conference finals, where it met the St. Louis Blues. Shortly after the Los Angeles series, Colorado center Peter Forsberg felt a searing pain in his abdomen, the result of a ruptured spleen that would require emergency surgery, ending his season then and there. Without Forsberg, Colorado battled its way past St. Louis in five games, the last three of which went into overtime. Roy, who had some shaky moments early in the playoffs, was the stalwart, making big save after big save. "I don't care what I accomplished yesterday," said Roy, who is also the NHL's alltime leader in playoff wins. "Your next game makes everything disappear."

The 2000–01 regular season will be best remembered for the reappearance of one of the greatest players in NHL history. In 1997 Mario Lemieux retired from hockey, his prodigious powers still very much intact. When Gretzky called it quits two years later, hockey was left without a true superstar. At the same time, the Pittsburgh Penguins went into a financial tailspin and filed for bankruptcy. Lemieux bought a stake in the team (35%) in September 1999 and proved almost as adept in the front office as he had been on the ice, turning a loss of $16 million the previous season into a profit of $47,000 in his first year of ownership. But the Penguins, who possessed two top-shelf offensive threats in Jaromir Jagr and Alexei Kovalev, were struggling in the win-loss columns.

No ivory-tower owner, Lemieux opted for a hands-on approach to that problem: On Dec. 27, 2000, he restored himself to the Penguins' lineup, ending a 44-month retirement. It was as if he never left. He set up a goal in the first minute of the game and would score one and set up another during the 5–0 victory over Toronto. His performance was 21 minutes of awe-inspiring, nature-defying brilliance. "Mario is the bright color of the game," said Detroit Red Wings center Igor Larionov. "People want to see a Monet, a Rembrandt at work. Whenever he's on the ice, he's capable of producing a masterpiece or at least the unpredictable or unexpected. It's art, hockey performed at its highest skill level. If people are appreciating him more now, it's like an artist who gains proper recognition only after he passes away. But he lives again."

Lemieux finished the regular season with 35 goals and 41 assists in 43 games, leading the Penguins to a sixth-place finish in the Eastern Conference and single-handedly revitalizing the franchise, which regularly sold out its home games.

Pittsburgh made a strong playoff run as well, reaching the conference finals, where it fell to the New Jersey Devils. "This is the best time of my life," said Lemieux. "I had a lot of great moments in the early 1990s, but to be back and have a chance to play one more time has been great, especially with me playing well and the team playing well."

While Lemieux rejoined his team in 2000–01, two other stars, Eric Lindros of Philadelphia and Michael Peca of Buffalo, left theirs because of contract disputes. Lindros—a restricted free agent whose history of concussions has dimmed his once-bright star considerably—turned down Philadelphia's $8.5 million offer, and the Flyers were unable to move him before the March 13 trading deadline. Peca, also a restricted free agent, turned down the Sabres' four-year, $11.5 million deal, and Buffalo let him sit all year, finally trading him after the season. He accused the Sabres and the league of trying to punish him, a charge Buffalo's brass steadfastly denied. But like Alexei Yashin, a holdout in 1999, Peca was shipped to the Islanders, who were in rebuilding mode.

There were two notable ownership changes in 2000–01. On Feb. 15 a group headed by Gretzky purchased the Phoenix Coyotes. And though Gretzky talked about building a championship team and took an active role early on, firing general manager Bobby Smith two days after buying the team, the Coyotes narrowly missed the playoffs.

In Montreal, an American—*sacré bleu!*—bought the Canadiens, winners of a record 24 Stanley Cups. The $184 million that George Gillett Jr., a ski resort developer from Vail, Colo., spent for the team was a bargain when you consider that Molson Inc. spent $190 million to build the Molson Centre, which Gillett also acquired in the deal. Gillett had his work cut out for him, though, as the Habs finished dead last in the Northeast Division at 28-40-8.

The league, too, has work to do (still) in the area of on-ice violence. The playoffs were marred by an ugly incident in Game 4 of the Eastern Conference semifinals between New Jersey and Toronto. In the waning seconds of the Leafs' 3–1 victory, Toronto tough guy Tie Domi blindsided Devils defenseman Scott Niedermayer with a flying elbow to the skull. The cheap shot left Niedermayer with a concussion that sidelined him for four games and recast a shadow over the NHL, which claims it wants to shed the image that it allows gratuitous violence. That's a claim the toothless punishment handed down to Domi would seem to refute: He was suspended for 11 games, eight at the beginning of the 2001–02 season. To make matters worse, Toronto coach Pat Quinn plunged the NHL image to WWF depths when he grabbed a photographer

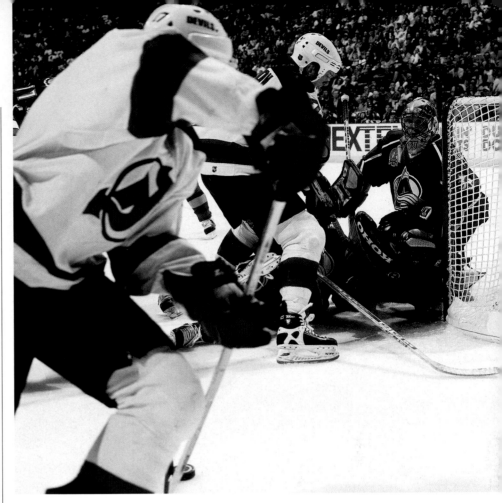

around the neck and pushed him aside as the man attempted to take pictures of Domi entering league offices to hear his punishment.

But ugly incidents could not take away from Bourque's shining moment. While Bourque was no longer the player he had been during his peak Boston years, when he routinely racked up 80 points a year, he was certainly still a valuable contributor. He scored the game-winning goal in Game 3 of the finals, and he played 29 minutes and 35 seconds in Game 7, which would be the last game of his Hall of Fame career. Seizing the chance to end his career in storybook fashion, Bourque announced his retirement a few weeks after finally lifting the Cup.

He felt the gravity of the moment as the national anthem was played before Game 7. "I couldn't breathe the last 30 seconds, and it wasn't because I was tired," he said. "It was just too much, and I was trying to hold back the tears, the emotions. All night long it was tough to stay focused, from the national anthem on. I had tears in my eyes on the bench a few times. You kind of just let your mind drift for a couple of seconds, and then you have to regroup and just hold it and wait and wait."

As he left the ice in tears you got the sense that Ray Bourque was the happiest man in the world. For his teammates it was a fitting retirement gift. "Just seeing Ray carry that cup around the ice makes you want to cry," said Colorado forward Dan Hinote.

Colorado's Roy (above, right) produced another superb season, allowing a career-low 2.21 goals a game while leading his team to a league-best 118 points. In October he secured the 448th victory of his career to surpass Terry Sawchuk as the alltime wins leader among goalies, and in June he won a record third Conn Smythe Trophy.

PHOTO GALLERY

Devils goalie Martin Brodeur (left) got knocked sideways by Colorado right wing Dan Hinote, who went barreling into the net in Game I of the Stanley Cup finals. Hinote wasn't the only thing to get past the usually stingy Brodeur as the Avalanche took the series opener 5–0.

Snowed In: Edmonton right wing Mike Grier (above, right) got a frosty reception from Flyers defenseman Chris Therien during Philadelphia's 2–0 victory over the Oilers at the First Union Center in November. Both teams would make the playoffs in April only to be eliminated in the first round.

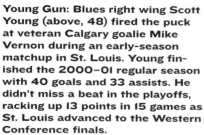

Young Gun: Blues right wing Scott Young (above, 48) fired the puck at veteran Calgary goalie Mike Vernon during an early-season matchup in St. Louis. Young finished the 2000–01 regular season with 40 goals and 33 assists. He didn't miss a beat in the playoffs, racking up 13 points in 15 games as St. Louis advanced to the Western Conference finals.

In the 2000–01 season opener against Dallas, Colorado's Ray Bourque (right, 77) hustled after a loose puck like it was Game 7 of the Stanley Cup finals. That would come eight months later, on June 9, and Bourque and the Avalanche would be there. They defeated the Devils 3–1 to win the Cup and fulfill the only unrealized dream of Bourque's 22-year career, a span in which he won five Norris Trophies as the NHL's top defenseman and was named to 19 All-Star games.

PROFILES

Ray Bourque

When it came to getting traded, the guy sitting next to Ray Bourque (right) was an old hand. Dave Andreychuk, flying across North America in a chartered jet in March 2000, was on his way to his fifth team in an 18-year NHL career. Bourque, on the other hand, had been monogamous for 20 years, a Boston Bruin for better (two trips to the Stanley Cup finals) or worse (in '97 the Bruins missed the playoffs for the first time in 30 years); richer (he was the NHL's highest-paid defenseman at age 24) or poorer (as a homesick rookie he spent $185 a month talking to his dad on the phone); in sickness (Detroit's Denis Polonich broke his jaw with a punch in a 1980 fight) and in health (he regularly played more than 30 minutes a game). But as he and Andreychuk headed out to join their new team, the Avalanche, Bourque leaned heavily on his well-traveled teammate to sort out the emotions that being traded evoked. Bourque had broken into the NHL with Boston in 1979—the same year Larry Bird debuted with the Celtics. In the Hub he had been an 18-time All-Star and won a Calder Trophy and five Norris Trophies. Yet for all those achievements, the city never conferred upon him the mythic status of Bird or another Bruins defenseman, Bobby Orr, who led Boston to its last two Stanley Cups, in '70 and '72. "Ray Bourque has never gotten his due in this town," said Bruins general manager Harry Sinden after Bourque became the team's alltime leading scorer in 1997. "And he probably never will."

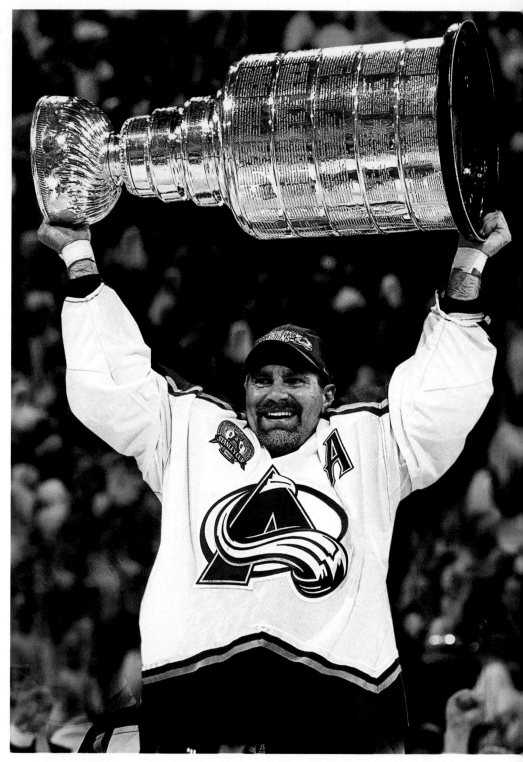

The consummate team player, Bourque was far more interested in getting a Stanley Cup than in getting his due. But by late February 2000 it was clear that he wasn't going to get either. With the Bruins in disarray—they had missed the playoffs for only the second time in 33 years the season before—Bourque asked Sinden for a trade. The general manager obliged, shopping him to five teams with reasonable shots at the Cup. The best offer came from the Avalanche: Brian Rolston, two prospects and a first-round draft pick for Bourque and Andreychuk, a 36-year-old forward.

Bourque gave two reasons for asking out: "To challenge for the Cup and to see what is left in Ray Bourque." Not that challenging for the Cup was a given with the underachieving Avs, who when the deal was made were two points shy of ninth place in the Western Conference. There was going to have to be plenty left in Ray Bourque if Colorado was going to make a strong push for the Cup.

Bourque estimated that during his last days in Boston, he was playing well in three of every five games. "The atmosphere wasn't good," he said during the 1999–2000 season. "I wasn't as consistent, wasn't as sharp. That was mental. To get the best out of myself, I needed a different environment." Which isn't to say that leaving Boston, let alone asking to leave Boston, was easy. Bourque has a way of becoming attached to things—like the beat-up yellow pillow he slept with as a kid, the one he made his dad bring to him in Trois-Rivières during his Junior A days. But just as he did when he was 15, he put his emotions aside, went out on the ice and excelled. The day after the trade he made his Colorado debut, in Calgary. Though he pulled a muscle in warmups, he didn't say anything until after the second period, when the game was in hand. Bourque was +4 and had an assist in the Avs' 8–3 win. He wasn't the only one on the ice to feel rejuvenated. "He gave us so much life," defenseman Aaron Miller said. "You see the energy in that game? It was almost like guys were trying to impress Ray. Like, Look at me! See what I can do!"

When the trade was made, Edmonton Oilers president Glen Sather said of the Avalanche, "There are so many stars there now, they'll be bumping into one another." If anything, though, the Avs' big shots fell over each other trying to appease the new guy. Fifteen minutes

after the deal was consummated, Patrick Roy, Adam Foote and Dave Reid phoned Bourque from the team's Calgary hotel. Joe Sakic offered to give up his captain's C, and Adam Deadmarsh, whose pregame ritual required him to be the first player onto the ice after that night's starting goalie, offered to cede that honor to Bourque, who held the same superstition. Ever the team player, Bourque graciously declined both offers.

Colorado went 12-2-1 after the trade, won the Northwest Division and advanced to the conference finals, losing to Dallas in seven games. Though Bourque could have become a free agent on July 1, he signed a one-year deal with the Avs. "I think people who know me well enough know that when I am happy and trustful, I will be there," he said. "We competed for the Stanley Cup, and it rejuvenated my game. I feel we've got some unfinished business."

This season proved to be the 40-year-old Bourque's best since '95–96, as he led the Avs in minutes played and went to his 19th straight All-Star Game. Meanwhile, back in Boston, little had changed in the wake of his departure. By unloading Bourque and Andreychuk, the Bruins had freed up millions, but they squandered most of it on over-the-hill defenseman Paul Coffey. When Colorado made its only trip of the season to Boston, on

March 24, the B's were nearly as rudderless as when Bourque had left.

The fans hadn't changed much, either: They still adored number 77. Ten thousand of them were in their seats for the pregame skate at the Fleet Center, and signs reading EVERBODY LOVES RAYMOND were scattered throughout the rink. Bourque kept his emotions in check and assisted on two goals in a 4–2 win. "In a lot of ways I'll always be a Bruin," he said. Boston would narrowly miss the playoffs, while the Avs finished with the league's best record, meaning they would have home ice advantage throughout their run at Bourque's elusive Cup.

Bourque was as solid in the playoffs as he had been in the regular season, winning Game 3 of the finals with a slap shot past New Jersey goalie Martin Brodeur. After the Avs clinched Game 7, Sakic, in his role as captain, received the Stanley Cup from commissioner Gary Bettman. Without pausing, he handed it like a hot potato to Bourque, allowing him to be the first to hoist and kiss it. As the old man and the trophy made their way around the ice, some 2,000 miles west of the city where he had toiled for 20 years, it was clear that Ray Bourque had finally found his due.

—Mark Bechtel
excerpted from SI *PRESENTS*,
June 20, 2001

John Madden

The weak November sun barely camouflages the Toronto winter lurking around the corner. The Black Square—a basketball court that earned its nickname years ago when a city worker would flood it with a fire hose and John Madden and his friends would play hockey from four till frostbite—will soon be ready for Canada's game once more. Not much has changed here at the Parma Court housing projects since Madden was a boy. Laundry is drying over balcony railings, and a volleyball game is winding down in the community center next door. The projects, built as Ontario public housing in the 1960s, remain a study in brown: chocolate-colored bricks, autumn grass the color of coffee-stained teeth, the pockmarks of thou-

sands of hockey pucks on the door of the maintenance building. Since he was a baby, Madden lived in the Parma Court projects, a complex of houses off busy Victoria Park Avenue, in which the smell of marijuana would perfume the stairwells at night. When he was 14 or 15, Madden would look out his bedroom window and see men selling narcotics on the street, wearing ski masks to hide their identity. Madden says. "They kept the drugs in their jackets," he says. "Cars would pull up. They'd run up to the cars and make the exchange. My mom and I were like, Wow, this isn't good."

These days life for Madden is deliriously good. The boy who had next to nothing now has everything—or at least

he will once the New Jersey Devils finally hand out their Stanley Cup rings. The boy who had to settle for a bowl of cereal for dinner because cereal was the only thing in the cupboard now dines out with his wife, Lauren, whenever they like. The boy who was called Welfare Case by classmates owns a town house in New Jersey and a house on a lake in Connecticut.

Madden lived in the projects until he was 16, when he moved an hour away to Barrie to reside with his father, also named John (his parents divorced before he was 10), and to play Tier II junior hockey. The only clues that an NHL player grew up at Parma Court are three newspaper clippings displayed under Plexiglas on a weathered bulletin board

an NCAA career record with 23 short-handed goals, played second-line center behind 1993 Devils third-round draft pick Brendan Morrison (now with the Vancouver Canucks), won one national championship ('96) and left school 15 credits short of a degree in sports management and communications.

After his final college game, Wolverines coach Red Berenson delivered the same lecture to Madden that he had given to scores of players—get your B.A. and prepare for life after hockey—but all Madden heard was Berenson's seeming lack of faith in him. "At the time Johnny was upset that no NHL teams were calling about him," Berenson says. "Look, he wasn't drafted in the NHL. He was a blue-collar kid, a hardworking kid, but no one could have predicted he would make it in the NHL. I told him, 'You don't want to be a minor leaguer at 32 when you could have gone into management training and done something substantial.' I felt I owed him that."

New Jersey president Lou Lamoriello kept coming to Ann Arbor to scout Morrison and kept leaving with a warm feeling about the fireball on the Wolverines' second line. He signed Madden as a free agent in June 1997. Three years later Madden scored the winning goal in Game 4 of the Stanley Cup finals.

Madden didn't miss the swell shin pads, the new sticks or anything else in the minivan life of a young hockey player. Looking back on his days in Parma Court, he says the thing he wanted most and didn't have was family dinners. In his new world, gilded by designer suits and well-appointed homes and a four-year, $7 million contract, Madden is going to take care of the most important things. There will be family dinners. There probably will be summer school to earn his degree, and years from now, when his one-year-old son, Tyler, takes his first trip to a hockey tournament, Madden will be behind the wheel. On that day, he says, he'll find whichever of Tyler's teammates might not have the newest or the nicest of everything, whose family's budget might be a little tight, and he will treat that kid like a god.

—Michael Farber
excerpted from SI, Dec. 4, 2000

on the lawn. Other than the articles, nothing is left of Little Johnny Madden in Parma Court. There is, however, a lot of Parma Court left in Madden.

"He plays with a chip on his shoulder, and it isn't a small one," Devils center Bobby Holik says. "It's what makes him successful. He has to play with attitude. When you don't have size"—Madden is 5'11" and 195 pounds—"you have to make up for it another way."

Madden (above) has taken his defiant attitude and has constructed a blossoming career, proving himself a master architect at working not with mortar or bricks but with slights, real and perceived. Madden is the NHL's most dangerous penalty killer, if not the best, having led the league with six shorthanded goals as a rookie in 1999–2000. His quickness and positioning could turn him into the premier defensive forward in the game once he curbs his tendency to gamble on loose pucks in hopes of a counterattack....

There were five friends from Parma Court—Madden, Sheldon Burke and his brother Shawn, Mike Bella and Jimmy Warner—and they had maybe two full

bags of equipment among them. They saved money on tape by using old skate laces to attach their shin pads. "We'd see kids in the dressing room with straps on their shin pads," Madden says, "and we'd go, 'Whoa, that kid has straps!' "

Madden may have had little money, but he had a fabulous support system, most notably his mother, Lily, who often worked two jobs. His friends, too, were like family. Burke, five years older, kept telling Madden that he was the best hockey player in the world. "You could see it," says Warner, 33, a manager for a mechanical contractor. "Ten years old, playing ball hockey on the Black Square, he's making all of us look like nobs."

Soon enough hockey people began to see what the kids in Parma Court saw. A youth coach picked up all of Madden's expenses one year because Madden couldn't afford to play and the coach couldn't afford to have him not play. In high school Madden was recruited by U.S. colleges, and after two disastrous 690 efforts on the SAT, he cobbled together a score of 950 that earned him a scholarship to Michigan. Madden stayed in Ann Arbor for four seasons, set

Adam Oates

Adam Oates is steering his Mercedes through morning traffic on the Beltway. He drives much the way he plays for the Washington Capitals, moving opportunistically from lane to lane, occasionally making a well-calculated pass. "So did you hear that some guy gave $360 million to my alma mater?" says Oates, who has a degree from Rensselaer Polytechnic Institute. "It's the largest donation ever by an individual to a university, but get this—the guy gave the money anonymously. So he sets this record, but nobody knows who he is. Kind of mysterious."

Oates (right), who is the least recognized of the certain Hall of Famers in the NHL today, knows from mystery. How is it, for example, that Oates, whom RPI coach Mike Adessa once affectionately called "a stumpy, heavy-footed, poor-skating, no-shooting kid," is in his 16th NHL season and through April 1, 2001, had 961 career assists (ninth alltime) and 1,277 career points (22nd)? How is it that at 38, Oates, who's still a slow skater, was tied for the league lead with 67 assists?

Where does he get the energy, at his age, to center Washington's top line, play more than 21 minutes a night and dominate on face-offs? How does he do any of it with that sawed off, misshapen stick he uses? And who, behind that aloof exterior, is Adam Oates, anyway?

"Whenever I go to a new team, a lot of guys ask me what it's like to play with Adam Oates," says Phoenix Coyotes center Joe Juneau, a former teammate of Oates's. "But they really want to know what's up with his sticks. Those things are the ugliest in the league."

Oates runs through four dozen black Sher-Woods a month, and the ones he tosses away after a single heft (about half, simply because he doesn't like their feel) are spared his indelicate touch. "There's no science to it," Oates says of how he shapes his sticks. "I take each one, go to work on it and hope I can make it feel how I want it to feel."

The way Oates goes to work on his stick would get Bob Vila jazzed. First he

chops off the toe of the blade to square it (a unique, superstitious practice he began 10 years ago), then he sands the base of the blade until it's flat ("When you're in the corner and your stick is against the wall, you can still keep a lot of blade on the ice," Oates explains), and then he saws, bends, twists, massages and burns the blade until it feels the way he wants it to. The process takes Oates about 15 minutes per stick.

"That's just another example of how he's always trying to do whatever he can to get an edge," says Caps coach Ron Wilson. "If Adam notices something in a game, he adjusts right away. He takes the information, processes it and puts it to use."

Oates's processing skills, as well as his sure hands, have made him the second-best passer of his time and the player most commonly compared with the best, Wayne Gretzky. Like other on-ice visionaries, Oates changes speeds and uses subtle shifts in movement and positioning to put defenders off balance....

As Washington's captain, Oates doesn't slap bottoms or organize player lunches or invite the new guys over for a beer. After games he ducks into the

shower before the media arrive in the dressing room, leaving the spokesman's role to players such as goalie Olaf Kolzig. "I got named captain before last season because of how I do things," says Oates. "I'm not going to change. I hope younger guys see that I treat this game with a lot of care and attention."

Players can glean lasting lessons from Oates's manner in practice, the way he executes each drill, no matter how routine, with meticulousness. One of Oates's best friends is pro golfer Mike Weir, and last summer Oates accompanied Weir to the British Open, where they stayed in a rented house near St. Andrews. "We're in the driveway one day, whacking balls into a field across the road," Weir recalls. "The whole time Adam is saying things like, 'Weirsy, how's my grip? How's my posture?'" Weir would give him a suggestion or two, and then Oates would get quiet. He'd stare off for a few moments, angling his face the way he does, and then step back in and address the ball. He hit it better and better as the day went on.

—Kostya Kennedy
excerpted from SI, April 9, 2001

THE NUMBERS

NHL Final Standings

EASTERN CONFERENCE
Northeast Division

	GP	W	L	T	RT	GF	GA	PTS
Ottawa	82	48	21	9	4	274	205	109
Buffalo	82	46	30	5	1	218	184	98
Toronto	82	37	29	11	5	232	207	90
Boston	82	36	30	8	8	227	249	88
Montreal	82	28	40	8	6	206	232	70

Atlantic Division

	GP	W	L	T	RT	GF	GA	PTS
New Jersey	82	48	19	12	3	295	195	111
Philadelphia	82	43	25	11	3	240	207	100
Pittsburgh	82	42	28	9	3	281	256	96
NY Rangers	82	33	43	5	1	250	290	72
NY Islanders	82	21	51	7	3	185	268	52

Southeast Division

	GP	W	L	T	RT	GF	GA	PTS
Washington	82	41	27	10	4	233	211	96
Carolina	82	38	32	9	3	212	225	88
Florida	82	22	38	13	9	200	246	66
Atlanta	82	23	45	12	2	211	289	60
Tampa Bay	82	24	47	6	5	201	280	59

WESTERN CONFERENCE
Central Division

	GP	W	L	T	RT	GF	GA	PTS
Detroit	82	49	20	9	4	253	202	111
St. Louis	82	43	22	12	5	249	195	103
Nashville	82	34	36	9	3	186	200	80
Columbus	82	28	39	9	6	190	233	71
Chicago	82	29	40	8	5	210	246	71

Pacific Division

	GP	W	L	T	RT	GF	GA	PTS
Dallas	82	48	24	8	2	241	187	106
San Jose	82	40	27	12	3	217	192	95
Los Angeles	82	38	28	13	3	252	228	92
Phoenix	82	35	27	17	3	214	212	90
Anaheim	82	25	41	11	5	188	245	66

Northwest Division

	GP	W	L	T	RT	GF	GA	PTS
Colorado	82	52	16	10	4	270	192	118
Edmonton	82	39	28	12	3	243	222	93
Vancouver	82	36	28	11	7	239	238	90
Calgary	82	27	36	15	4	197	236	73
Minnesota	82	25	39	13	5	168	210	68

RT=regulation ties—games lost in overtime; worth 1 pt.

Individual Regular-Season Leaders

SCORING
Points

PLAYER AND TEAM	GP	G	A	PTS	+/−	PM
Jaromir Jagr, Pitt	81	52	69	121	19	42
Joe Sakic, Col	82	54	64	118	45	30
Patrik Elias, NJ	82	40	56	96	45	51
Alexei Kovalev, Pitt	79	44	51	95	12	96
Jason Allison, Bos	82	36	59	95	-8	85
Martin Straka, Pitt	82	27	68	95	19	38
Pavel Bure, Fla	82	59	33	92	-2	58
Doug Weight, Edm	82	25	65	90	12	91
Zigmund Palffy, LA	73	38	51	89	22	20
Peter Forsberg, Col	73	27	62	89	23	54
Alexei Yashin, Ott	82	40	48	88	10	30
Luc Robitaille, LA	82	37	51	88	10	66
Bill Guerin, Edm/Bos	85	40	45	85	7	140
Mike Modano, Dall	81	33	51	84	26	52
Alexander Mogilny, NJ	75	43	40	83	10	43
Pierre Turgeon, StL	79	30	52	82	14	37
Adam Oates, Wash	81	13	69	82	-9	28
Peter Bondra, Wash	82	45	36	81	8	60
Petr Sykora, NJ	73	35	46	81	36	32
Robert Lang, Pitt	82	32	48	80	20	28

SCORING (CONT.)
Goals

PLAYER AND TEAM	GP	G
Pavel Bure, Fla	82	59
Joe Sakic, Col	82	54
Jaromir Jagr, Pitt	81	52
Peter Bondra, Wash	82	45
Alexei Kovalev, Pitt	79	44

Game-Winning Goals

PLAYER AND TEAM	GP	GW
Joe Sakic, Col	82	12
Jaromir Jagr, Pitt	81	10
Alexei Yashin, Ott	82	10
Alexei Kovalev, Pitt	79	9
Milan Hejduk, Col	80	9

Assists

PLAYER AND TEAM	GP	A
Jaromir Jagr, Pitt	81	69
Adam Oates, Wash	81	69
Martin Straka, Pitt	82	68
Doug Weight, Edm	82	65
Joe Sakic, Col	82	64

SCORING (CONT.)
Power Play Goals

PLAYER AND TEAM	GP	PP
Peter Bondra, Wash	82	22
Joe Thornton, Bos	72	19
Joe Sakic, Col	82	19
Pavel Bure, Fla	82	19
Paul Kariya, Ana	66	18
Markus Naslund, Van	72	18

Short-Handed Goals

PLAYER AND TEAM	GP	SHG
Steve Sullivan, Chi	81	8
Theoren Fleury, NYR	62	7
Wes Walz, Minn	82	7
Pavel Bure, Fla	82	5
Five tied with four.		

Plus/Minus

PLAYER AND TEAM	GP	+/−
Joe Sakic, Col	82	45
Patrik Elias, NJ	82	45
Scott Stevens, NJ	81	40
Petr Sykora, NJ	73	36
Brian Rafalski, NJ	78	36

Goaltending

Goals Against Average (Minimum 25 games)

PLAYER AND TEAM	GP	MINS	GA	AVG
Marty Turco, Dall	26	1266	40	1.90
Roman Cechmanek, Phil	59	3431	115	2.01
Manny Legace, Det	39	2136	73	2.05
Dominik Hasek, Buff	67	3904	137	2.11
Brent Johnson, StL	31	1744	63	2.17

Save Percentage (Minimum 25 games)

PLAYER AND TEAM	GP	GA	SA	PCT	W	L	T
Marty Turco, Dall	26	40	532	.925	13	6	1
Mike Dunham, Nash	48	107	1381	.923	21	21	4
Sean Burke, Phoe	62	138	1766	.922	25	22	13
Dominik Hasek, Buff	67	137	1726	.921	37	24	4
R. Cechmanek, Phil	59	115	1464	.921	35	15	6

Wins

PLAYER AND TEAM	GP	MINS	W	L	T
Martin Brodeur, NJ	72	4297	42	17	11
Patrick Roy, Col	62	3585	40	13	7
Dominik Hasek, Buff	67	3904	37	24	4
Olaf Kolzig, Wash	72	4279	37	26	8
Arturs Irbe, Car	77	4406	37	29	9

Shutouts

PLAYER AND TEAM	GP	MINS	SO	W	L	T
Dominik Hasek, Buff	67	3904	11	37	24	4
Roman Cechmanek, Phil	59	3431	10	35	15	6
Martin Brodeur, NJ	72	4297	9	42	17	11
Ed Belfour, Dall	63	3687	8	35	20	7
Tommy Salo, Edm	73	4364	8	36	25	12

NHL Awards

AWARD	PLAYER AND TEAM
Hart Trophy (MVP)	Joe Sakic, Col
Calder Trophy (top rookie)	Evgeni Nabokov, SJ
Vezina Trophy (top goaltender)	Dominik Hasek, Buff
Norris Trophy (top defenseman)	Nicklas Lidstrom, Det
Lady Byng Trophy (for gentlemanly play)	Joe Sakic, Col
Adams Award (top coach)	Bill Barber, Phil
Selke Trophy (top defensive forward)	John Madden, NJ
Jennings Trophy (goaltender on club allowing fewest goals)	Dominik Hasek, Buff
Conn Smythe Trophy (playoff MVP)	Patrick Roy, Col

2001 Stanley Cup Playoffs

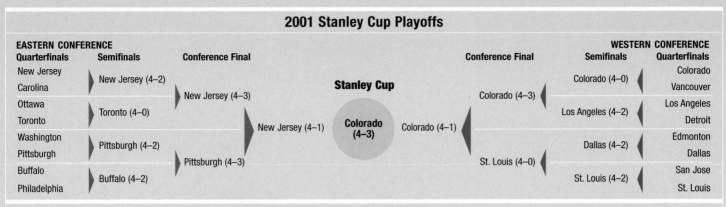

EASTERN CONFERENCE						WESTERN CONFERENCE	
Quarterfinals	Semifinals	Conference Final			Conference Final	Semifinals	Quarterfinals
New Jersey	New Jersey (4–2)					Colorado (4–0)	Colorado
Carolina		New Jersey (4–3)			Colorado (4–3)		Vancouver
Ottawa	Toronto (4–0)					Los Angeles (4–2)	Los Angeles
Toronto			New Jersey (4–1)	Colorado (4–1)			Detroit
Washington	Pittsburgh (4–2)					Dallas (4–2)	Edmonton
Pittsburgh		Pittsburgh (4–3)			St. Louis (4–0)		Dallas
Buffalo	Buffalo (4–2)					St. Louis (4–2)	San Jose
Philadelphia							St. Louis

Stanley Cup
Colorado (4–3)

Stanley Cup Championship Box Scores

GAME 1

New Jersey	0	0	0	0
Colorado	1	2	2	5

First Period
Scoring: 1, Colorado, Sakic 10 (Hejduk, Blake), 11:07. Penalties: White, NJ (holding) 4:28; Podein, Col (elbowing), 13:46.

Second Period
Scoring: 2, Colorado, Drury 9 (Hinote, Nieminen), 9:35. 3, Colorado, Sakic 11 (Blake, Skoula), 15:06. Penalties: De Vries, Col (boarding), 7:01; Tanguay, Col (tripping), 10:46; Daneyko, NJ (boarding), 14:16; Nieminen, Col (goalie int.), 14:16.

Third Period
Scoring: 4, Colorado, Blake 5 (pp) (Tanguay, Sakic), 5:36. 5, Colorado, Reinprecht 2 (Dingman, Reid), 17:36. Penalties: Hinote, Col (holding), 3:30; Stevenson, NJ (goalie int.), 4:45; White, NJ (roughing), 8:04; Sykora, NJ (charging), 8:04; Foote, Col (double roughing minor), 8:04; Daneyko, NJ (slashing, roughing), 9:43; O'Donnell, NJ (roughing), 11:34; Podein, Col (tripping), 11:34; De Vries, Col (tripping), 13:20; O'Donnell, NJ (served by Gomez) (instigator, fighting major, game misconduct) 17:36; Dingman, Col (fighting major), 17:36; Hinote, Col (roughing), 18:20.
Shots on goal: NJ—7-11-7—25. Colorado—14-7-9—30. Power-play opportunities: NJ 0-of-6, Col 1-of-5. Goalies: NJ, Brodeur (30 shots, 25 saves); Col, Roy (25 shots, 25 saves). A: 18,007.
Referees: Devorski, Marouelli.
Linesmen: Schachte, Lazarowich.

GAME 2

New Jersey	2	0	0	2
Colorado	1	0	0	1

First Period
Scoring: 1, Colorado, Sakic 12 (pp) (Hejduk, Blake), 5:58. 2, New Jersey, Corkum 1 (Rafalski), 14:29. 3, New Jersey, Stevenson 1 (Niedermayer, Mogilny), 17:20. Penalties: Niedermayer, NJ (cross-checking), 1:43; Brylin, NJ (int.), 4:53; Elias, NJ (slashing) 12:28; Messier, Col (roughing), 14:46; Foote, Col (holding stick), 15:17; Holik, NJ (slashing), 19:39.

Second Period
Scoring: None. Penalties: De Vries, Col (int.), 9:11; Madden, NJ (diving), 9:11; Skoula, Col (holding), 14:47.

Third Period
Scoring: None. Penalties: Daneyko, NJ (cross-checking), 1:28; White, NJ (roughing), 2:58; Nieminen, Col (roughing), 2:58; Mogilny, NJ (high sticking), 4:26.
Shots on goal: NJ—12-6-2—20. Col—8-4-8—20. Power-play opportunities: NJ 0-of-3; Col 1-of-6. Goalies: NJ, Brodeur (20 shots, 19 saves); Col, Roy (20 shots, 18 saves). A: 18,007.
Referees: McCreary, Shick.
Linesmen: Wheler, Lazarowich.

GAME 3

Colorado	1	0	2	3
New Jersey	1	0	0	1

First Period
Scoring:1, NJ, Arnott 8 (pp) (Holik, Elias), 3:16; 2, Colorado, Skoula 1 (Podein, Messier), 10:38. Penalties: Foote, Col (tripping), 1:29; Yelle, Col (int.), 6:28; Brylin, NJ (int.) 14:29; Tanguay, Col (hooking), 15:03; Nieminen, Col (boarding), 16:29.

Second Period
Scoring: None. Penalties: O'Donnell, NJ (cross-checking), 2:40; O'Donnell, NJ (holding), 8:25; Foote, Col (tripping), 14:52; Arnott, NJ (boarding), 19:02.

Third Period
Scoring: 3, Colorado, Bourque 4 (pp) (Sakic). 0:31. 4, Colorado, Hinote 2 (Nieminen, Drury), 6:28. Penalties: Klemm, Col (holding), 8:22.
Shots on goal: Col—5-11-5—21. NJ—8-3-11—22. Power-play opportunities: Col 1-of-4; NJ 1-of-6. Goalies: Col, Roy (22 shots, 21 saves); NJ, Brodeur (21 shots, 18 saves). A: 19,004.
Referees: Fraser, Marouelli.
Linesmen: Collins, Schachte.

GAME 4

Colorado	1	1	0	2
New Jersey	0	1	2	3

First Period
Scoring: 1, Colorado, Blake 6 (Tanguay), 3:58. Penalties: Stevenson, NJ (int.), 1:36; Gomez, NJ (goalie int.), 4:42; Yelle, Col (diving), 7:15; Sykora, NJ (hooking), 7:15; Stevens, NJ (hooking), 7:42; Sakic, Col (hooking), 8:26.

Second Period
Scoring: 2, New Jersey, Elias 8 (sh) (Sykora), 3:42. 3, Colorado, Drury 10 (Dingman,

Second Period *(Cont.)*
Hinote), 13:54. Penalties: White, NJ (roughing), 2:18; Skoula, Col (int.), 10:16; Stevenson, NJ (tripping), 16:42.

Third Period
Scoring: 4, New Jersey, Gomez 5 (Pandolfo, Corkum), 8:09. 5, New Jersey, Sykora 9 (Elias, Holik), 17:23. Penalties: None.
Shots on goal: Col—4-4-4—12. NJ—8-11-16—35. Power-play opportunities: Col 0-of-5; NJ 0-of-2. Goalies: Col, Roy (35 shots, 32 saves), NJ, Brodeur (12 shots, 10 saves). A: 19,040.
Referees: Devorski, McCreary.
Linesmen: Collins, Schachte.

GAME 5

New Jersey	2	1	1	4
Colorado	1	0	0	1

First Period
Scoring: 1, New Jersey, Elias 9 (Sykora, Rafalski), 3:09. 2, Colorado, Tanguay 3 (pp) (Sakic, Bourque), 10:09. 3, New Jersey, Mogilny 5 (Gomez, Rafalski), 18:47. Penalties: Holik, NJ (tripping), 8:56; NJ bench (served by Gomez) (too many men on ice), 19:24.

Second Period
Scoring: 4, New Jersey, Brylin 3 (pp) (Mogilny, Niedermayer), 4:38. Penalties: Blake, Col (int.), 3:53; Niedermayer, NJ (int.), 16:33.

Third Period
Scoring: 5, New Jersey, Madden 4 (Stevenson, Brylin), 18:05. Penalties: McKenzie, NJ (holding), 12:54; Sutton, NJ (roughing), 20:00; Hinote, Col (roughing), 20:00.
Shots on goal: NJ—6-10-10—26. Col—6-9-8—23. Power-play opportunities: NJ 1-of-1; Col 1-of-4. Goalies: NJ, Brodeur (23 shots, 22 saves); Col, Roy (26 shots, 22 saves). A: 18,007.
Referees: Fraser, Shick.
Linesmen: Wheler, Lazarowich.

GAME 6

Colorado	1	2	1	4
New Jersey	0	0	0	0

First Period
Scoring: 1, Colorado, Foote 3 (unassisted), 18:02. Penalties: Reid, Col (obstruction), 5:22; Foote, Col (high sticking), 7:20; Mogilny, NJ (hooking), 9:12; Skoula, Col (hooking) 11:08.

Second Period
Scoring: 2, Colorado, Nieminen 4 (pp) (Skoula, Foote), 2:26. 3, Colorado, Drury 11 (Reinprecht, Foote), 18:27. Penalties: Holik, NJ (roughing), 0:29; Colorado bench (served by Nieminen) (too many men on ice), 8:35; Niedermayer, NJ (holding), 11:10; Bourque, Col (obstruction), 13:01.

Third Period
Scoring: 4, Colorado, Tanguay 4 (Reid, Sakic), 13:46. Penalties: Podein, Col (int.), 3:24; Niedermayer, NJ (slashing), 8:26; White, NJ (slashing), 17:27; Hinote, Col (fighting major), 18:19; Sutton, NJ (roughing, fighting major), 18:19; White, NJ (high sticking), 19:43; Dingman, Col (fighting major), 19:48; Daneyko, NJ (fighting major), 19:48.
Shots on goal: Col—5-7-6—18; NJ—12-7-5—24. Power-play opportunities: Col 1-of-7; NJ 0-of-6. Goalies: Col, Roy (24 shots, 24 saves); NJ, Brodeur (18 shots, 14 saves). A: 19,040.
Referees: Marouelli, McCreary.
Linesmen: Collins, Lazarowich.

GAME 7

New Jersey	0	1	0	1
Colorado	1	2	0	3

First Period
Scoring: 1, Colorado, Tanguay 5 (Hinote), 7:58. Penalties: Brylin, NJ (boarding), 3:20; Gomez, NJ (holding), 16:06.

Second Period
Scoring: 2, Colorado, Tanguay 6 (Sakic, Foote), 4:57. 3, Colorado, Sakic 13 (pp) (Hejduk, Tanguay), 6:16. 4, New Jersey, Sykora 10 (pp) (Elias, Arnott), 9:33. Penalties: O'Donnell, NJ (high sticking), 5:51; Messier, Col (high sticking), 9:22; Messier, Col (holding), 12:23; Arnott, NJ (tripping), 12:23.

Third Period
Scoring: None. Penalties: Blake, Col (int.), 4:59; White, NJ (high sticking), 10:32; Foote, Col (holding stick), 12:11; Stevens, NJ (tripping), 14:42.
Shots on goal: NJ—9-12-5—26; Col—10-7-5—22. Power-play opportunities: NJ 1-of-3; Col 1-of-5. Goalies: NJ, Brodeur (22 shots, 19 saves); Col, Roy (26 shots, 25 saves). A: 18,007.
Referees: Fraser, Marouelli.
Linesmen: Collins, Schachte.

Blue Angels

Unlike their predecessors in Durham, who antagonized more fans than they inspired, the 2000—01 champs were difficult not to like

B.J. SCHECTER

For the past decade and a half, Duke has been college basketball's version of the New York Yankees—the team everyone loves to hate. The Blue Devils are arrogant, their critics charge; they get all the breaks and all the calls. They also win with maddening consistency, having reached nine Final Fours since 1986. Nothing engenders enmity like success—just ask the Yankees—but it was awfully hard to hate the 2000–01 Duke team.

Sure, the Blue Devils won 29 of their first 33 games, were ranked No. 1 most of the way and caught their share of breaks, but the way the Blue Devils carried themselves on and off the court made this team unique. They weren't the spoilsports of the Bobby Hurley–Christian Laettner era or the prima donnas of the William Avery–Corey Maggette year. This team was, dare we say, likable.

The credit for this development can be shared by coach Mike Krzyzewski, whose steady guiding hand led the Blue Devils to their third national title, and the team's undisputed leader on the court, forward Shane Battier. Battier's route through college basketball is increasingly becoming the road less traveled: He was a star who stayed four years, who excelled on the hardwood and in the classroom. Indeed, Battier may have a brighter future off the court than on it, though he went sixth overall in the NBA draft. He is the selfless player every coach wishes he had, a natural leader whose court sense is second to none. Sophomore point guard Jason Williams scored more and usually had the ball in his hands when the game was on the line, but Battier did all the little things to put the Blue Devils in position to win games. He might draw a charge at a crucial time, make an out-of-nowhere block (his come-from-behind stuff of North Carolina's Joseph Forte in March was one of the highlights of the season), grab a key rebound or make a nifty pass; whatever Duke needed, Battier seemed to supply it every time out.

Confident but humble, respectful yet not without a killer instinct, Battier was almost too good to be true. His stature as the ultimate gentleman of the game was not lost on opponents. Before Duke's 82–72 victory over Arizona in the national championship game, Arizona's Richard Jefferson wryly summed up what Battier had accomplished in 2000–01. "He's the Player of the Year, Defender of the Year, Academic of the Year, Man of the Year," said Jefferson. "He's all-everything. Some people rank Shane Battier right below Jesus Christ."

To get a clear picture of Duke's season one need look no further than its four epic games with Maryland, of which the Blue Devils won three. In their first meeting in January, Duke was thoroughly outplayed in College Park, Md. Williams had one of his worst performances of the season, while Maryland played like a Final Four team—until the game's final minute, that is. Duke trailed by 10 points with 54 seconds remaining. Suddenly Williams came alive, scoring eight points in 13 seconds to help Duke tie the stunned Terrapins and send the game into overtime. The Blue Devils won 98–96. The shock of the loss sent Maryland reeling—the Terps lost four of their next five games and didn't regain their status as a title contender until the rematch at Cameron Indoor Stadium in February.

Few pundits gave Maryland a chance to win the second game. For one thing, Duke was playing extremely well, having won six of its last seven games. For another, it was senior night at Duke, and the Cameron Crazies were sure to be in full voice. But the Terps played their best game of the year, outplaying and outmuscling Duke and silencing the legendarily boisterous Duke faithful with a 91–80 victory. Worse for Duke was that center Carlos Boozer suffered a stress fracture in his right foot, a potentially season-ending injury. Duke's only weakness was its lack of depth, especially

After Arizona rallied to within three points of Duke late in the national championship game, Battier (opposite, 31) willed the Blue Devils to victory with two offensive rebounds that led to Duke baskets. The senior forward finished with 18 points and was named the Final Four's Most Outstanding Player.

Notre Dame's Ruth Riley (above, right) grabbed 13 rebounds during her team's 68–66 win over Purdue in the NCAA title game. Though she scored only one point in the first eight minutes as the Irish fell behind by as many as 12 points, Riley recovered to score the game's last four points, clinching the title for Notre Dame.

inside, and the loss of Boozer sorely taxed the Blue Devils' bench.

After the game a cake that was supposed to celebrate Battier's 122nd victory sat untouched in a corner of the locker room. Some Blue Devils hung their heads, others cried, and Krzyzewski went into a bunker. A former Army cadet who played for Bobby Knight at West Point, Krzyzewski stayed up all night with his assistants, kicking around ideas and plotting strategies to recover from both Boozer's injury and the devastating loss to the Terps.

Some fans wondered if Duke's chances for a national title had been quashed, but Krzyzewski took a proactive approach to keep them alive. He gave the players a day off, and then he and his staff established a training-camp-like environment to get the team to refocus. He scheduled 6:30 a.m. practices for the next two days. "When Coach starts calling 6:30 a.m. practices,

you know it's serious," said senior J.D. Simpson.

Instead of becoming more regimented, however, Krzyzewski decided to loosen the reins. The Blue Devils didn't watch any tape or do any drills in their first practice after the Maryland loss; they scrimmaged for 45 minutes. "I was trained for that," said Krzyzewski. "Next play, let's go. Whether it's muddy or sunny, let's figure out a way to win."

They did, and how: The Blue Devils wouldn't lose another game all season. After the Maryland loss Duke beat North Carolina by 14 in Chapel Hill, and things started rolling from there. "We don't have a system, a triple-post offense or anything like that," said sophomore forward Mike Dunleavy. "We just kind of play basketball. When you have that confidence that everybody on the floor can stick it, the other team knows it."

Duke's third game with Maryland came in the semifinals of the ACC tournament and proved that the Blue Devils were still the favorites to win it all—with or without Boozer. When Maryland guard Steve Blake drilled a three-pointer to tie the game at 82 with 8.1 seconds remaining, Williams drove the length of the floor and missed a layup in traffic. But senior swingman Nate James, who had recently lost his starting spot, tipped in the game-winner.

"When Carlos went down, the tendency would've been to bottle them up and overcoach them," Krzyzewski said. "Instead we let them grow wild."

The fourth meeting between Duke and Maryland came at the Final Four, in Minneapolis. Boozer had returned to the Blue Devils' lineup, and both teams were playing extremely well. The Terps jumped out to a 22-point lead late in the first half and appeared well on their way to a rout. Krzyzewski called his first desperation timeout of the season; it came only nine seconds before the first scheduled television timeout. He reminded his team what had turned around their season. "You can't play any worse," Krzyzewski told his players. "What are you worried about? That you're going to lose by 40? We're already losing by 20, so will you just play?"

The Blue Devils cut the lead to 11 by halftime, caught the Terps early in the second half and then broke the game open, winning 95–84. Two nights later Arizona stayed with Duke for most of the championship game, but the Blue Devils used their poise and superb three-point shooting to pull away in the closing stages. Battier and Williams had stellar games as usual, but it was the previously struggling Dunleavy who made the biggest difference, sinking five three-pointers and scoring 18 of his 21 points in the second half. When Arizona clawed its way back into the game, Dunleavy killed the Wildcats' momentum with three three-pointers.

Afterward Battier found Krzyzewski and thanked his coach for showing so much faith in the team. As they hugged on the court, Battier told Coach K that the Blue Devils won this title for him. "It was really special for us to separate Coach from the pack," Battier said later. "A bunch of coaches have won two. Getting three makes you a legend."

The NCAA tournament has made many a legend, and this year was no different, as a few teams and several players made names for themselves. Marvin O'Connor, a junior guard from St. Joseph's, produced the best individual performance at the Big Dance, scoring 37 points in a second-round loss to Stanford. When O'Connor fouled out late in the game he was given a stand-

ing ovation by the partisan Stanford crowd, and Cardinal All-America Casey Jacobsen pulled him aside and said, "It was a pleasure being on the same court with you today."

Gonzaga, a Jesuit school in Spokane, Wash., with an enrollment of 4,500, made it to the Sweet 16 for the third consecutive year; and banged-up Temple, with only nine healthy players, reached the Elite Eight. Though the 2001 tournament had the greatest number of higher seeds eliminated in the first round since the tournament expanded to 64 teams in 1985 (13 of 32), it was still a tough tournament for the little guys. That's because few small or mid-major schools were invited. The six power conferences received an unprecedented 35 bids, and in an effort to accommodate an additional automatic bid (expanding the field to 65 teams), the powers that be made Winthrop and Northwestern State compete in a play-in game for the right to play No. 1–seeded Illinois.

Williams (above), Duke's superb sophomore guard, led the ACC in scoring and averaged 25.7 points a game in the NCAA tournament. He scored 16 points and made three steals in the final against Arizona.

There was the usual array of mammoth upsets, to be sure. Hampton, the 15th seed in the West region, knocked off second-seeded Iowa State, only the fourth time a 15 has dropped a two (a 16th seed has never beaten a No. 1 seed); 12th-seeded Utah State upended fifth-seeded Ohio State in the East; No. 13 seed Indiana State eliminated fourth-seed Oklahoma in the South region; and Kent State, a 13, bounced fourth-seed Indiana out of the West. But no little guy, except 12th-seeded Gonzaga, made it past the second round. While the NCAA tournament is famous for its David-versus-Goliath upsets, the cream usually rises; low seeds in the later rounds are rarer than Louisville fans in Lexington. The 2001 Final Four featured two No. 1 seeds, Duke and Michigan State, a No. 2, Arizona, and a three-seed, Maryland.

It was quite a season for Arizona, filled with Grand Canyon–esque highs and lows. Loaded with talent, the Wildcats were the consensus preseason No. 1, and all five starters were candidates for the John Wooden award that goes to the nation's top player. Center Loren Woods may have gone too far when he predicted that Arizona could be one of the best teams ever, but few observers doubted that the Wildcats would contend for the title. Yet after winning the Maui Invitational, Arizona lost three of its next five games and suddenly looked vulnerable. Then coach Lute Olson's wife, Bobbi, who was very close to many of the players, passed away after a long battle with cancer. Coach Olson took a leave of absence, and the team descended further into its funk. But Olson returned after five games, and Arizona rallied and knocked off Stanford in March to earn the second seed in the Midwest region of the NCAAs. Clearly peaking at the right time, the Wildcats were scarcely threatened as they cruised through the region, defeating top-seed Illinois in the final. That victory vaulted Arizona into the Final Four and a meeting with defending champion Michigan State, which had reeled off a 24–4 regular-season record and was making its third consecutive appearance in the Final Four. The rugged Spartans would not repeat, though, as Arizona, firing on all cylinders, trounced them 80–61.

In the Big East, two teams surprised their conference peers, one by how well it played and the other by how poorly. Seton Hall was supposed to be a national title contender with a blue-chip freshman class that included the No. 1 recruit in the nation, 6' 11" Eddie Griffin. The Pirates lived up to their billing early, rising as high as No. 7 in the national polls. But after a loss to Georgetown in January, Griffin and guard Ty Shine got into a fight in the locker room, irrevocably poisoning the team's chemistry. The Pirates finished 16–15 and settled for an NIT bid. The Big East overachiever was Boston College, which went 11–19 (3–13) in 1999–2000 and had been picked to finish at the bottom of the conference again. But sensational sophomore point guard Troy Bell helped catapult BC from worst to first; the Eagles won the Big East and grabbed a No. 3 seed in the NCAA tournament, where they were upset by USC in the second round. Despite the early exit from the Big Dance, the Eagles had to be pleased with BC's surprising turnaround.

Injuries to three players on the nation's two best teams provided the women's basketball season with some late-season drama. Connecticut and Tennessee had won five of the last six national titles between them, and both teams continued to be loaded with talent in 2000–01. Surely one of them would win the national title. But UConn lost All-Americas Svetlana Abrosimova and Shea Ralph in February and March, respectively, while Tennessee had to do without Tamika Catchings, the reigning player of the year, who blew out her knee in January. Suddenly the race for the championship was wide open.

Jackie Stiles and Southwest Missouri State were more than happy to seize the opportunity. Stiles, a flashy guard from Claflin, Kans. (pop. 700), could have gone to any of the big-time basketball schools but chose Southwest Missouri in part because the Bears began recruiting her when she was 12. She became the NCAA women's alltime career leading scorer during this, her senior season. In tournament wins over Rutgers, top-seeded Duke and Washington, Stiles averaged 35 points a game and led the Bears to the Final Four in St. Louis. The Bears fell to Purdue, but not before winning legions of new fans.

Notre Dame, which announced its status as a contender by beating UConn and grabbing the No. 1 ranking in January, overcame a 16-point first-half deficit to defeat the Huskies again in the national semifinal. That set the stage for an all-Indiana championship and cued Notre Dame center Ruth Riley, who took over. The NCAA player of the year, Riley poured in 28 points in the final—including the game-winning free throws with 5.8 seconds left—grabbed 13 rebounds and made seven blocks. The Irish won 68–66. "I can't even describe it," Riley said. "We worked so hard that it was fitting to end the season this way."

Thus the 2000–01 season ended with one team reaching the mountaintop for the first time and another planting its third flag at the summit. No doubt they both enjoyed the view.

PHOTO GALLERY

When the final buzzer sounded to end the women's NCAA final, Ruth Riley (00) and her Notre Dame teammates celebrated their first national championship while Purdue guard Kelly Komara (sitting) felt the sting of her team's narrow defeat.

North Carolina's sophomore forward Julius Peppers and Duke's backup center Casey Sanders (20) formed a four-point star as Peppers drove to the hoop and Sanders guarded it during the Blue Devils' 95–81 victory in the final game of the regular season. The win gave Duke a share of the ACC title.

Double Trouble: Stanford's Jason Collins (above, center) and his twin brother, Jarron, (above, right) were too much for Loren Woods (above, left) and Arizona during the Cardinal's 85–76 road victory in January. The Collins twins combined for 41 points and 21 rebounds as Stanford improved to 13–0 and took the top spot in the polls.

Butler Did It: Brandon Miller (right, dark jersey) typified his team's desire, diving for a loose ball against Wake Forest forward Darius Songaila during 10th-seeded Butler's 79–63 upset of the seventh-seeded Demon Deacons in the first round of the NCAA tournament.

Sophomore forward Henry Domercant of Eastern Illinois (right, middle) boxed out Austin Peay's Trenton Hassell— the Ohio Valley Conference Player of the Year—during the Panthers' 84–83 victory in the conference title game. A goaltending call against Austin Peay in the game's final second provided the winning margin and a berth in the NCAA tournament for Eastern Illinois.

Kentucky sophomore Marquis Estill (above, 50) bounded over, and through, Tennessee center Charles Hathaway en route to a thunderous dunk during the Wildcats' 84–74 home victory over the fourth-ranked Volunteers in January.

Duke forward Mike Dunleavy (far right) drained one of his five three-pointers— including three in less than a minute early in the second half—in the NCAA championship game against Arizona. Dunleavy finished with 21 points as Duke won 82–72.

PROFILES

Shane Battier

At the stroke of midnight on Jan. 1, 1993, Shane Battier, then 14, began writing on an index card 10 goals he wanted to accomplish in the next year. Adopting an idea from a motivational speaker he'd heard at a basketball camp, Shane pinned the card to the wall next to his bed in his family's house in Birmingham, Mich., so that it was the first thing he would see every morning and the last thing he would see at night. His goals ranged from building a giant city out of Legos to saving a human life. He also aspired to start as a ninth grader on the varsity at Detroit Country Day School. When he was

named to the starting five the following fall, he went home, stared at the card and said, "Wow, this really works!"

On every New Year's Eve since, Battier (below), now a senior forward at Duke, has filled out a new card, recycling some of his unachieved goals and replacing those attained with fresh ones. In a good year he knocks off seven out of 10 goals. These days he keeps the card on the desk in his apartment at Duke, and among his goals are to win his first national title, become a first-team All-America and an Academic All-America, and earn a national player of the year award. He didn't attain any of

these in 2000, so they'll be back on the list for 2001.

Battier's goal cards provide much needed insight into a personality that even he described, in filling out a Duke sports information department questionnaire, as "Complex and pseudo-intellectual yet laid-back and simple." Welcome to the enigma that is Shane Battier. …

As an 11th grader Shane delivered the commencement speech to the graduating seniors at another area high school. He conducted part of his interview with Duke admissions director Christoph Guttentag in German. The Blue Devils'

associate athletic director, Chris Kennedy, recalls returning home after his first encounter with Battier, in 1996, and when his wife asked him about his day, he responded, "I just met a kid who's going to be president someday."…

Battier acknowledges that he strives to be different, and he believes that stems from the time when he would have given anything to be like every other kid. Battier's father, Ed, the manager of a small trucking company, is black. His mother, Sandee, a corporate secretary, is white. Each brought a child from a previous marriage to their union, and Shane is the oldest of the two sons and a daughter they've had together. In Birmingham, an affluent white suburb of Detroit, Battier was the only child of African-American descent at Harlan Elementary School…. When he moved to multicultural Country Day in 1991, he tried to fit in with both his black and white schoolmates, and as a seventh grader he overheard a black female classmate call him "a sellout."

"That was the first time I thought, Who am I?" Battier says. "I didn't want to hang out with my white friends because I'd be perceived as a sellout, and I didn't want to hang out with my black friends because I'd be rejecting my white side. For the first time I felt alone, and I really didn't like myself. My saving grace was basketball, because on the court it didn't matter what color you were."…

Once the games began, he displayed a clinical, old-school style. "Shane's game has absolutely no soul," Kurt Keener, Battier's coach at Country Day says. "He has an ego you can fit in a thimble, and he doesn't think in creative terms on the court because he's never been interested in making the highlights."

In fact, Battier's calling card is drawing charges. He holds the Duke record with 85, and in 2000 was named the National Association of Basketball Coaches (NABC) defensive player of the year for the second straight season (sharing the honor with Cincinnati's Kenyon Martin). In Durham he's billed as the Minister of Defense; the rest of the ACC sees him as Eddie Haskell. "Most of his charges are really flops, but he's a charmer who can do no wrong in the refs' eyes," says North Carolina forward Kris Lang. "He gets away with murder."…

Battier led Country Day to three consecutive state Class B championships, including one his senior season, when the Yellow Jackets were 24–0 with him in the lineup and 1–3 when he sat out with a broken right elbow suffered while drawing a charge—in practice. He lost only 11 games in high school and 11 during his first three seasons at Duke….

Battier even aspires to be the nation's top player after the game. He has vowed to conduct an entire season's worth of interviews without uttering a cliché. "One of Shane's great joys in life is shattering stereotypes," former Duke assistant coach Quin Snyder says….

After having spent the previous two summers doing internships on Wall Street and at a Chicago advertising firm, Battier remained in Durham last summer to work on his ball handling and shooting off the dribble. He will try to maintain his 3.5 average despite a torrent of interview requests that have led to his granting more than 100 before this season has

started. Ed and Sandee worry about Shane's burning out, and his calendar is distressingly packed. But he did reject a personal appeal from Bill Bradley to work on his presidential campaign, and no matter how busy he is, he never fails to sit down for a weekly dinner with his younger brother, Jeremy, who's now a freshman wide receiver at Duke.

Juggling all his responsibilities as the poster boy for college basketball isn't as simple as Battier makes it look. "Those closest to me know my life isn't that easy," he says. "I've gone home every night for four years and said, 'Whew, I made it through this day. What will tomorrow be like?' One of my biggest faults is that I'm often looking ahead to the next day rather than watching the sunset today."…

Still, he has his index card to attend to. He hopes to be confirmed as player of the year and wants to scratch a line through his goals of winning an NCAA title and being drafted into the NBA.

There is nothing on Battier's card, however, that suggests what he might do after his basketball career. But he does relish the times when he meets a stranger who inquires about his major and almost inevitably follows up by asking, "Religion? What are you going to do with that?"

Battier stares back expressionless, and says, "I'm going to rule the world."

—Tim Crothers
excerpted from SI, Nov. 20, 2000

Battier crossed three significant goals off of his list after the 2000–01 season as the Blue Devils won the national title, he won the Naismith Award as player of the year and the Memphis Grizzlies drafted him with the sixth pick of the 2001 NBA draft. —Ed.

Eddie Griffin

The griffin of classical mythology was part lion and part eagle, a hybrid of strength and wisdom. Six-foot-nine-inch, 229-pound Seton Hall freshman Eddie Griffin is no mythical creature—not yet, anyway, even if followers of the 18th-ranked Pirates suspect otherwise—but finding a balance between strength and wisdom has been the central tension of his young life.

Griffin has long possessed strength out of proportion to his age, and he hasn't always shown wisdom in its deployment. As a child, Eddie's outbursts of temper—scraps with kids in school and at home with his older brother, Jacques—alarmed his single mother, Queen Bowen. When Eddie was 10, she decided that he needed to have more male supervision and sent him from

their home in Philadelphia to live with his adult half-brother, Marvin Powell, in East Hartford, Conn.

Eddie rejoined his mom 3 ½ years later and a year after that enrolled at Philly's Roman Catholic High. Last March, three days after leading the Cahillites to the city's Catholic League title for the second straight time, he was expelled for fighting. The Archdiocese

Catholic High, over a game of cards.

A teammate had wanted into the game. Griffin insisted on playing one more hand. The teammate urged him again to surrender his chair. His mother describes the incident's beginnings as "roughhousing," but it escalated into more, and under Roman Catholic's zero-tolerance policy against fighting, the school had no choice but to order the two students to leave. Only by the grace of an exception for second-semester seniors did he even have the option of earning his diploma with the help of a tutor. "Eddie wasn't thrilled with the solution," says the Reverend Paul Brandt, Roman Catholic's president. "We weren't thrilled with it, either. But life can be that way. And for all of that, I never saw him lose his cool on the court. Trust me, with all the attention he was getting, there wasn't an opponent who wasn't trying to provoke him."…

Griffin's mere presence at Seton Hall is proof that he's tough to predict. "A lot of people thought I would take the easy way out and go to the NBA," he says. "But it wouldn't have been best for me."

To find vindication for his decision, all Griffin has to do is turn on the TV. On Nov. 27 he was as wide-eyed as any 18-year-old would be when *SportsCenter* screened two of his dunks in a victory over St. Peter's. Around that time, in a clip from an NBA game, he caught a glimpse of what might have been his fate: DeShawn Stevenson, a Fresno high school star from last season who chose to skip college, vegetating on the end of the Utah Jazz's bench. "I thought, I'm glad that's not me," Griffin says.

He believes college will serve him well if he continues to build strength (he has already added 17 pounds) and improve his ball handling skills. "In high school he told me, 'I don't believe in skipping steps,'" says Seton Hall coach Tommy Amaker. "The goal is to get there, but also to make use of every moment."

One challenge for the Pirates will be to savor each moment, knowing that their star freshman could leave after one season. Griffin is nonetheless at least envisioning what a sophomore year might be like. He talks of his mother

of Philadelphia permitted him to graduate only after he finished the last six weeks of his course work at home, underwent anger-management counseling and accepted that he'd be barred from walking at commencement.

Griffin took his punishment and brought his ample talent to Seton Hall. But following a 78–66 loss to Georgetown on Jan. 6, the Pirates' locker room remained closed for more than an hour, for reasons school officials have refused to divulge. When the doors finally opened, junior guard Ty Shine walked out with a bandage under his right eye, and the school announced that Griffin had been suspended for the Pirates' next game. It didn't take a Detective Sipowicz to find out what had happened.…

For his loss of temper in high school Griffin paid a far steeper price than a

one-game suspension, and in penitence he seemed to find some wisdom. Isolated with a tutor, Griffin turned in a string of A's after having done B– work over the previous five semesters. Instead of writing off school entirely and leaving for the NBA, an option pro scouts agree was his, he earned his diploma and honored a commitment to enroll at Seton Hall.…

After a practice in early January 2001, Griffin sat on the edge of the stage at one end of Seton Hall's Walsh Gym. This was Eddie the eagle, poised and perched, thoughtfully answering questions from a half-dozen reporters. Visible on his left biceps was a tattoo of four aces that he got almost four years ago. The image now serves as an ironic reminder that Griffin nearly cut short his amateur career, in the cafeteria at Roman

making the trip to Hawaii for next year's Maui Invitational and invokes his favorite class at Roman Catholic, business law, to explain why he'd like to be a criminal justice major. Just the same, says Amaker, "if the right thing for Eddie is to go pro, I'm driving him to the airport."

Amaker's other challenge will be to keep the Roughhouse in the Clubhouse from further opening a schism between the Pirates' newcomers and their upperclassmen, most of all Shine, who had a terrific NCAA tournament in 2000 only to return in the fall to a campus in full swoon over the incoming freshmen.... After a mid-January win over Notre Dame, Shine bolted from the Meadowlands' Continental Airlines Arena without saying a word to the press....

The lesson for Griffin is that he could certainly benefit from less lion and more eagle. But so could all the Pirates—lest, come March, they go out like a lamb.

—Alexander Wolff
excerpted from SI, January 22, 2001

On March 21 Powell, 34 and the father of three, died of a heart attack. The next week Amaker accepted the head coaching job at Michigan. On April 3 Griffin announced that he would enter the NBA draft. The New Jersey Nets selected him with the seventh pick overall then traded him to Houston. —Ed.

Jackie Stiles

Once one had heard a few of the Jackie Stiles stories circulating at the 2001 Women's Final Four in St. Louis, it wasn't all that absurd to imagine the ponytailed, 5'8" guard from Claflin, Kans., (pop. 700) carrying underdog Southwest Missouri State to the national title. There was one about how, as a junior, she had single-handedly won the Kansas state 1A track and field meet for Claflin High by winning the 400, 800, 1,600 and 3,200 in one day, and another about how she had broken her right (shooting) wrist early in her sophomore season but still averaged 20 points a game by shooting with her left.... Didn't someone of such heroic will and accomplishment deserve to win an NCAA championship?

By choosing Southwest Missouri State, a mid-major school in Springfield that started recruiting her when she was 12, instead of a bigger program like Connecticut, Stiles seemed to have eliminated that possibility and confined her legend to the Midwest forever. Then on March 1 she broke the NCAA Division I women's career scoring record by dropping in her 3,123rd point, against Creighton. Suddenly her fame took flight, and people living beyond the prairies started hearing about her.... In tournament games against Rutgers and top-seeded Duke and Washington that followed, she averaged 35.0 points with a combination of pull-up jumpers, driving layups and long-range bombs.

The Savvis Center in St. Louis, a 3½-hour drive from Springfield, offered Stiles a home court advantage but no respite from the media and fan frenzy her performances had inspired. Stiles traveled to Minneapolis on March 28 to receive the Wade Trophy as the nation's outstanding player and then returned to St. Louis the next day to face interviews, autograph sessions, awards ceremonies, a banquet welcoming the Final Four teams and practice. After Stiles received her Kodak All-America award, her handlers whisked her behind a curtain just long enough for her to catch her breath. "I can't believe I'm still talking," she said. "Am I even making any sense any-more?"

In the end fatigue wouldn't dull her mental acuity, but it would compromise something equally important: her legs. Purdue held Stiles to one of her worst shooting nights, limiting her to seven of 21 shots in an 81–64 loss. "They made me work so hard to get the ball the first half, in the second half I kind of ran out of gas," a teary-eyed Stiles said afterward.

It was a dismal ending to a glorious college career, but it wasn't the end of Stiles's story. "I can't imagine getting paid to play," she said when asked about moving on to the WNBA. "Please, someone in the WNBA, take me so this won't be my last game."

She needn't worry. As former WNBA coach Nancy Lieberman-Cline had said earlier in the week, "I'd hate to be the one to pass on her."

—Kelli Anderson
excerpted from SI, April 9, 2001

Drafted fourth by Portland, Stiles averaged 14.9 points a game during her rookie season —Ed.

THE NUMBERS

2001 NCAA Basketball Men's Division I Tournament

WEST

1st Round		2nd Round	Regionals
1 Illinois	24–7	Illinois 96–54	
16 N'western St	19–12		Illinois 79–61
8 Tennessee	22–10	Charlotte 70–63	
9 Charlotte	21–10		Illinois 80–64
5 Syracuse	24–8	Syracuse 79–69	
12 Hawaii	17–13		Kansas 87–58
4 Kansas	24–6	Kansas 99–75	
13 Cal St–N'Ridge	22–9		Arizona 87–81
6 Notre Dame	19–9	Notre Dame 83–71	
11 Xavier	21–7		Mississippi 59–56
3 Mississippi	25–7	Mississippi 72–70	
14 Iona	22–10		Arizona 66–56
7 Wake Forest	19–10	Butler 79–63	
10 Butler	23–7		Arizona 73–52
2 Arizona	23–8	Arizona 101–76	
15 Eastern Illinois	21–9		Arizona 80–61

MIDWEST

1st Round		2nd Round	Regionals
1 Michigan St	24–4	Michigan St 69–35	
16 Alabama St	22–8		Michigan St 81–65
8 California	20–10	Fresno St 82–70	
9 Fresno St	25–6		Michigan St 77–62
5 Virginia	20–8	Gonzaga 86–85	
12 Gonzaga	24–6		Gonzaga 85–68
4 Oklahoma	26–6	Indiana St 70–68 (ot)	
13 Indiana St	21–11		Michigan St 69–62
6 Texas	25–8	Temple 79–65	
11 Temple	21–12		Temple 75–54
3 Florida	23–6	Florida 69–56	
14 Western Ky.	24–6		Temple 84–72
7 Penn St	19–11	Penn St 69–59	
10 Providence	21–9		Penn St 82–74
2 N Carolina	25–6	N Carolina 70–48	
15 Princeton	16–10		

NATIONAL CHAMPIONSHIP

DUKE 82
ARIZONA 72

EAST

Regionals	2nd Round	1st Round	
	Duke 94–81	Duke 95–52	
Duke 76–63		1 Duke	29–4
		16 Monmouth	21–9
	Missouri 70–68	8 Georgia	16–14
		9 Missouri	19–12
UCLA 75–50	Utah St 77–68 (OT)	5 Ohio St	20–10
		12 Utah St	27–5
Duke 79–69	UCLA 61–48	4 UCLA	21–8
		13 Hofstra	26–4
	Southern Cal 69–54	6 Southern Cal	21–9
Southern Cal 74–71		11 Oklahoma St	20–9
	Boston Coll 68–65	3 Boston College	26–4
Southern Cal 80–76		14 Southern Utah	25–5
	Iowa 69–56	7 Iowa	22–11
Kentucky 92–79		10 Creighton	24–7
	Kentucky 72–68	2 Kentucky	22–9
Duke 95–84		15 Holy Cross	22–7

SOUTH

Regionals	2nd Round	1st Round	
	Stanford 89–60	1 Stanford	28–2
Stanford 90–83		16 NC–Greensboro	19–11
	St. Joseph's 66–62	8 Georgia Tech	17–12
Stanford 78–65		9 St. Joseph's	25–6
	Cincinnati 84–59	5 Cincinnati	23–9
Cincinnati 66–43		12 BYU	24–8
	Kent St 77–73	4 Indiana	21–12
Maryland 87–73		13 Kent St	23–9
	Georgia St 50–49	6 Wisconsin	18–10
Maryland 79–60		11 Georgia St	28–4
	Maryland 83–80	3 Maryland	21–10
Maryland 76–66		14 George Mason	18–11
	Georgetown 63–61	7 Arkansas	20–10
Georgetown 76–57		10 Georgetown	23–7
	Hampton 58–57	2 Iowa St	25–5
		15 Hampton	23–5

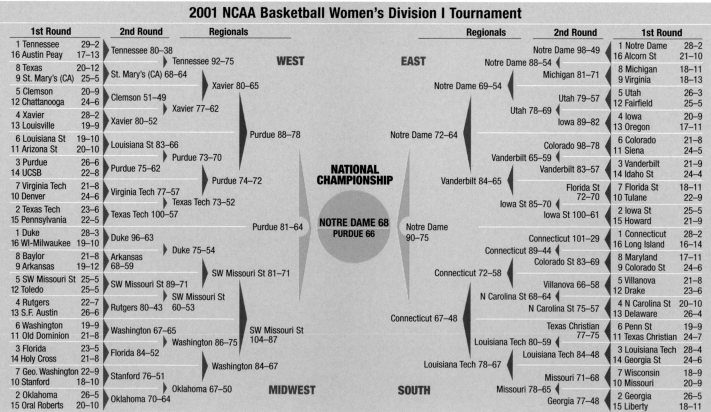

2001 NCAA Basketball Women's Division I Tournament

WEST

1st Round		2nd Round	Regionals
1 Tennessee	29–2	Tennessee 80–38	
16 Austin Peay	17–13		Tennessee 92–75
8 Texas	20–12	St. Mary's (CA) 68–64	
9 St. Mary's (CA)	25–5		Xavier 80–65
5 Clemson	20–9	Clemson 51–49	
12 Chattanooga	24–6		Xavier 77–62
4 Xavier	28–2	Xavier 80–52	
13 Louisville	19–9		Purdue 88–78
6 Louisiana St	19–10	Louisiana St 83–66	
11 Arizona St	20–10		Purdue 73–70
3 Purdue	26–6	Purdue 75–62	
14 UCSB	22–8		Purdue 74–72
7 Virginia Tech	21–8	Virginia Tech 77–57	
10 Denver	24–6		Texas Tech 73–52
2 Texas Tech	23–6	Texas Tech 100–57	
15 Pennsylvania	22–5		

MIDWEST

1st Round		2nd Round	Regionals
1 Duke	28–3	Duke 96–63	
16 WI–Milwaukee	19–10		Duke 75–54
8 Baylor	21–8	Arkansas 68–59	
9 Arkansas	19–12		SW Missouri St 81–71
5 SW Missouri St	25–5	SW Missouri St 89–71	
12 Toledo	25–5		SW Missouri St 60–53
4 Rutgers	22–7	Rutgers 80–43	
13 S.F. Austin	26–6		SW Missouri St 104–87
6 Washington	19–9	Washington 67–65	
11 Old Dominion	21–8		Washington 86–75
3 Florida	23–5	Florida 84–52	
14 Holy Cross	21–8		Washington 84–67
7 Geo. Washington	22–9	Stanford 76–51	
10 Stanford	18–10		Oklahoma 67–50
2 Oklahoma	26–5	Oklahoma 70–64	
15 Oral Roberts	20–10		

NATIONAL CHAMPIONSHIP

NOTRE DAME 68
PURDUE 66

EAST

Regionals	2nd Round	1st Round	
	Notre Dame 98–49	1 Notre Dame	28–2
Notre Dame 88–54		16 Alcorn St	21–10
	Michigan 81–71	8 Michigan	18–11
Notre Dame 69–54		9 Virginia	18–13
	Utah 79–57	5 Utah	26–3
Utah 78–69		12 Fairfield	25–5
	Iowa 89–82	4 Iowa	20–9
Notre Dame 72–64		13 Oregon	17–11
	Colorado 98–78	6 Colorado	21–8
Vanderbilt 65–59		11 Siena	24–5
	Vanderbilt 83–57	3 Vanderbilt	21–9
Vanderbilt 84–65		14 Idaho St	24–4
	Florida St 72–70	7 Florida St	18–11
Iowa St 85–70		10 Tulane	22–9
	Iowa St 100–61	2 Iowa St	25–5
Notre Dame 90–75		15 Howard	21–9

SOUTH

Regionals	2nd Round	1st Round	
	Connecticut 101–29	1 Connecticut	28–2
Connecticut 89–44		16 Long Island	16–14
	Colorado St 83–69	8 Maryland	17–11
Connecticut 72–58		9 Colorado St	24–6
	Villanova 66–58	5 Villanova	21–8
N Carolina St 68–64		12 Drake	23–6
	N Carolina St 75–57	4 N Carolina St	20–10
Connecticut 67–48		13 Delaware	26–4
	Texas Christian 77–75	6 Penn St	19–9
Louisiana Tech 80–59		11 Texas Christian	24–7
	Louisiana Tech 84–48	3 Louisiana Tech	28–4
Louisiana Tech 78–67		14 Georgia St	24–6
	Missouri 71–68	7 Wisconsin	18–9
Missouri 78–65		10 Missouri	20–9
	Georgia 77–48	2 Georgia	26–5
		15 Liberty	18–11

NCAA Men's Championship Game Box Score

DUKE 82		FG	FT	REB			
PLAYER	MIN	M–A	M–A	O–T	A	PF	TP
Battier	40	7–14	3–6	4–11	6	1	18
Dunleavy	32	8–17	0–1	2–3	0	3	21
Sanders	10	0–1	0–0	0–2	1	1	0
Duhon	39	3–5	2–3	1–4	6	2	9
Williams	29	5–15	4–6	0–3	4	4	16
Boozer	30	5–9	2–3	1–12	1	3	12
James	20	2–3	2–3	1–3	0	3	6
Totals	200	30–64	13–22	9–38	18	17	82

Percentages: FG—.469, FT—.591. 3-pt goals: 9–27, .333 (Battier 1–5, Dunleavy 5–9, Duhon 1–1, Williams 2–11, James 0–1). Team rebounds: 4. Blocked shots: 5 (Battier 2, Boozer 2, James). Turnovers: 11 (Williams 6, Boozer 2, James 2, Duhon). Steals: 5 (Williams 3, James, Sanders).

ARIZONA 72		FG	FT	REB			
PLAYER	MIN	M–A	M–A	O–T	A	PF	TP
Wright	28	5–9	0–1	4–11	0	4	10
Jefferson	35	7–13	1–3	2–8	3	2	19
Woods	37	8–15	6–8	4–11	1	4	22
Arenas	34	4–17	2–3	2–4	4	1	10
Gardner	40	2–11	3–4	1–3	2	2	7
Wessel	2	0–0	0–0	0–0	0	0	0
Edgerson	8	0–0	0–0	0–1	0	4	0
Walton	16	2–6	0–0	2–3	4	3	4
Totals	200	28–71	12–19	15–41	14	20	72

Percentages: FG—.394, FT—.632. 3-pt goals: 4–22, .182 (Jefferson 4–8, Woods 0–1, Arenas 0–4, Gardner 0–8, Walton 0–1). Team rebounds: 4. Blocked shots: 7 (Woods 4, Wright 2, Jefferson). Turnovers: 9 (Jefferson 5, Arenas, Walton, Woods, Wright). Steals: 5 (Arenas, Gardner, Jefferson, Woods, Wright).

Halftime: Duke 35, Arizona 33.   A: 45,994.
Officials: Thornley, Boudeaux, Corbett.

Final AP Top 25

Poll taken before NCAA tournament.

1. Duke	29–4	5. Arizona	23–7	9. Kentucky	22–9	13. Oklahoma	26–6	17. Syracuse	24–8
2. Stanford	28–2	6. N Carolina	25–6	10. Iowa St	25–5	14. Mississippi	25–7	18. Texas	25–8
3. Michigan St	24–4	7. Boston College	26–4	11. Maryland	21–10	15. UCLA	21–8	19. Notre Dame	19–9
4. Illinois	24–7	8. Florida	23–6	12. Kansas	24–6	16. Virginia	20–8	20. Indiana	21–12

21. Georgetown	23–7
22. St Joseph's	25–6
23. Wake Forest	19–10
24. Iowa	22–11
25. Wisconsin	18–10

NCAA Men's Division I Individual Leaders*

SCORING

			FIELD GOALS			3-PT FG		FREE THROWS				
	CLASS	GP	FG	FGA	PCT	FG	FGA	FT	FTA	PCT	PTS	AVG
Ronnie McCollum, Centenary	Sr	27	244	592	41.2	85	252	214	236	90.7	787	29.1
Kyle Hill, Eastern Illinois	Sr	31	250	527	47.4	86	198	151	180	83.9	737	23.8
DeWayne Jefferson, Mississippi Valley	Sr	27	216	500	43.2	107	285	98	122	80.3	637	23.6
Tarise Bryson, Illinois St	Sr	30	208	447	46.5	62	174	207	252	82.1	685	22.8
Henry Domercant, Eastern Illinois	So	31	256	519	49.3	79	179	115	141	81.6	706	22.8
Rashad Phillips, Detroit	Sr	35	232	536	43.3	136	329	185	202	91.6	785	22.4
Brandon Wolfram, Texas–El Paso	Sr	32	251	425	59.1	6	18	206	250	82.4	714	22.3
Rasual Butler, LaSalle	Jr	29	231	574	40.2	97	272	82	97	84.5	641	22.1
Brandon Armstrong, Pepperdine	Jr	31	240	537	44.7	76	198	128	155	82.6	684	22.1
Marvin O'Connor, St. Joseph	Jr	32	240	516	46.5	99	265	127	188	67.6	706	22.1

FIELD GOAL PERCENTAGE

	CLASS	GP	FG	FGA	PCT
Michael Bradley, Villanova	Jr	31	254	367	69.2
Nakiea Miller, Iona	Sr	27	163	244	66.8
Kimani Ffriend, Nebraska	Sr	28	144	231	62.3
Andre Hutson, Michigan St	Sr	32	173	278	62.2
George Evans, George Mason	Sr	30	233	380	61.3
Carlos Boozer, Duke	So	32	160	265	60.4

FREE THROW PERCENTAGE

	CLASS	GP	FT	FTA	PCT
Gary Buchanan, Villanova	So	31	97	103	94.2
Brent Jolly, Tennessee Tech	So	29	95	102	93.1
Ryan Mendez, Stanford	Sr	34	94	101	93.1
Rashad Phillips, Detroit	Sr	35	185	202	91.6
Ronnie McCollum, Centenary	Sr	27	214	236	90.7
Titus Ivory, Penn St	Sr	33	125	139	89.9

REBOUNDS

	CLASS	GP	REB	AVG
Chris Marcus, Western Kentucky	Jr	31	374	12.1
Reggie Evans, Iowa	Jr	35	416	11.9
J.R. VanHoose, Marshall	Jr	27	299	11.1
David West, Xavier	So	29	316	10.9
Eddie Griffin, Seton Hall	Fr	30	323	10.8

ASSISTS

	CLASS	GP	A	AVG
Markus Carr, Cal St–Northridge	Jr	32	286	8.9
Omar Cook, St. John's	Fr	29	252	8.7
Sean Kennedy, Marist	Jr	27	219	8.1
Tito Maddox, Fresno St	So	25	200	8.0
Ashley Robinson, Mississippi Valley	Jr	27	201	7.4

THREE-POINT FIELD GOAL PERCENTAGE

	CLASS	GP	FG	FGA	PCT
Amory Sanders, SE Missouri St	Sr	24	53	95	55.8
David Falknor, Akron	Jr	22	47	87	54.0
Cary Cochran, Nebraska	Jr	30	78	165	47.3
Casey Jacobsen, Stanford	So	34	84	178	47.2
Tim Erickson, Idaho St	Sr	28	82	177	46.3

THREE-POINT FIELD GOALS MADE PER GAME

	CLASS	GP	FG	AVG
DeWayne Jefferson, Mississippi Valley	Sr	27	107	4.0
Rashad Phillips, Detroit	Sr	35	136	3.9
Brian Merriweather, TX–Pan Am	Sr	29	108	3.7
Cory Schwab, Northern Arizona	Sr	29	105	3.6
Demond Mallet, McNeese St	Sr	31	107	3.5

BLOCKED SHOTS

	CLASS	GP	BS	AVG
Tarvis Williams, Hampton	Sr	32	147	4.6
Eddie Griffin, Seton Hall	Fr	30	133	4.4
Wojciech Myrda, Louisiana-Monroe	Jr	28	123	4.4
Kris Hunter, Jacksonville	Sr	28	114	4.1
Ken Johnson, Ohio St	Sr	31	125	4.0
Hondre Brewer, San Francisco	Jr	30	114	3.8

STEALS

	CLASS	GP	S	AVG
Greedy Daniels, Texas Christian	Jr	25	108	4.3
Desmond Cambridge, Alabama A&M	Jr	28	107	3.8
Senecca Wall, Sam Houston St	Sr	29	103	3.6
John Linehan, Providence	Jr	26	81	3.1
Fred House, Southern Utah	Sr	31	93	3.0
Andy Woodley, Northern Iowa	Jr	27	80	3.0

Reversals of Fortune

While the U.S. national team saw its World Cup fate take hairpin turns, San Jose went from worst to first in MLS

HANK HERSCH

Bruce Arena kept saying it over and over, but no one believed him because no one wanted to. After the U.S. national team's incendiary start in the final round of qualifying for the 2002 World Cup—four victories and a tie, including a 2–0 defeat of archrival Mexico—its fans were gaga, speculating on how their side stacked up against soccer's international superpowers and scanning eBay to size up the cheapest flights to Japan and South Korea. The Americans had never looked better, attacking with flair, defending with fervor. Who cared about Arena's cautionary words, utterances to be expected from any coach in the catbird seat? "We're only halfway through this round," Arena repeatedly said. "We haven't done anything yet."

Mounting injuries were the first sign of trouble. The offense was gradually crippled, as midfield maestro Claudio Reyna (groin) and forward Brian McBride (blood-clot disorder) were sidelined along with up-and-coming strikers Clint Mathis (torn right ACL) and Josh Wolf (broken left foot). Midfielders John O'Brien and Ben Olsen also struggled with injuries. After the plague of injuries came a storm of miscues by the normally solid backline, which had allowed only one goal in the first five matches. But now it began to buckle under the pressure. After a 1–0 defeat at Mexico came a devastating 3–2 loss to Honduras on Sept. 1 at RFK Stadium in Washington, where the visitors' supporters seemed to outnumber the home side's. Another blanking at Costa Rica (2–0) gave the U.S. its longest losing streak in qualifying in 44 years. Only three of the six teams left from the region—North America, Central America and the Caribbean—would advance to the 2002 Cup. The Yanks stood fourth.

World Cup qualifying has alway been an arduous process. After 1950 the U.S. failed to advance to the next nine Cups—a streak that ended with what remains arguably the most important goal in U.S. soccer history. In 1989, as the Americans

struggled to secure a berth for the '90 tournament, FIFA, which had awarded the '94 World Cup to the U.S., considered moving its prized event to a more soccer-worthy country. With the U.S. needing a victory at Trinidad & Tobago in its last match to qualify, midfielder Paul Caligiuri launched a looping, left-footed shot from 30 yards that found the upper right corner. That 31st-minute goal held up, and the U.S. advanced to Italia '90 while holding on to the rights to host USA '94.

"It was completely instinctive, no thought whatsoever," recalls Caligiuri, who scored only four other times in his 13-year, 114-match career for the national team. "A gift from the gods."

The gift kept on giving. The slew of sold-out venues from Boston to Los Angeles at World Cup '94 prompted investors to bankroll Major League Soccer, which began play in 1996. In April, MLS entered its sixth season, and it continues to make progress. Attendance improved by 9% in 2001, and more important, the quality of play picked up as well. In particular, the Miami Fusion showed plenty of flair, leading the league with a 16-5-5 record and 2.2 goals per game. Making that achievement all the more remarkable was the team's woeful history. After losing for three straight years and having the league's worst attendance, the Fusion had reportedly considered moving to Winston-Salem, N.C.

But with 22-year-old Nick Rimando's goalkeeping, 38-year-old Preki's playmaking and the finishing touches of MLS's top two scorers—Alex Pineda Chacon, the league MVP, and Diego Serna—crowds in Miami swelled to 14,274 a game. Former NASL midfielder and Fusion TV analyst Ray Hudson, in his first full season as Miami's coach, encouraged an aggressive approach on the field by challenging his troops. Hudson, 46, compared players to a ballpoint pen, saying, "If it doesn't work, you shake it; if it doesn't work, you shake it again; and if it still doesn't work, you get rid of it."

Donovan (opposite) made the most of his return to U.S. shores, drawing a game-deciding penalty in the national team's crucial qualifying win over Jamaica on Oct. 7, and leading San Jose in scoring in the playoffs as the Earthquakes rumbled to the MLS title.

Chastain (above, 6) and Venturini (crouching) celebrated with their CyberRays teammates after Julie Murray's penalty kick hit the net to give Bay Area a shootout victory over Atlanta in the inaugural WUSA championship game in Foxboro, Mass. The teams had played to a 3–3 tie after 90 minutes of regulation and 15 minutes of extra time.

Miami easily won the Eastern Division, but its run ended in the semifinals of the playoffs when it was beaten by a team even more resurgent. After finishing with the league's worst record in 2000, the San Jose Earthquakes marched into the 2001 title game against the Los Angeles Galaxy behind rookie coach Frank Yallop; former D.C. United stalwart Jeff Agoos, the defender of the year; and striker Landon Donovan. A 19-year-old from Redlands, Calif., Donovan was loaned to MLS after a year and a half with the German power-house Bayer Leverkusen, which recognized his sparkling talent when he was 16, signing him to a four-year, $400,000 deal in 1999. But Donovan languished on the Leverkusen amateur team, pining for home.

With the Earthquakes, he quickly came of age. On Aug. 8 he led San Jose to a 5–1 rout of New England with two goals and two assists. He fin-

ished with seven goals and 10 assists in the 17 games he started, and in MLS Cup 2001, he pounced on a cross from Richard Mulrooney in the 45th minute, rocketing a volley from 12 yards into the upper corner to tie the game at one. "It was just one of those times when you know you've hit it well," Donovan said.

When reserve forward Dwayne DeRosario collected the ball on the left flank six minutes into overtime, cut inside on defender Danny Califf and curled a shot from 16 yards into the far corner, the Quakes had a 2–1 victory and a completed journey from worst to first. That play also completed Caligiuri's journey as a pro: The title game was the last MLS match for the 37-year-old Galaxy defender whose left foot, it could be said, had kick-started the league.

Just as the '94 World Cup provided the impetus for MLS, the 1999 Women's World Cup yielded the Women's United Soccer Association (WUSA) in the summer of 2001. The eight-team league included stars from around the globe as well as most of the top U.S. players—most notably Mia Hamm. Though her Washington Freedom tied for last place, Hamm's star power attracted an average of 12,748 fans to Freedom matches, helping WUSA to draw 8,133 per game and exceed its modest attendance goal of 7,500. Hamm was supplanted as the world's top player, however, by the New York Power's Tiffeny Milbrett, who led the league with 16 goals and won its first MVP award.

Goals were scarce early in the season, but offenses improved as the season progressed. The two playoff semifinals produced high drama, and the final, the Founders Cup, between the Bay Area CyberRays and the Atlanta Beat, was a thriller. After Bay Area's Tisha Venturini made it 3–3 with a goal in the 86th minute, the teams played two overtimes without breaking the deadlock. Like their co-tenants at San Jose's Spartan Stadium, the CyberRays had known difficulty, starting the season 1-4-1. And also like the Earthquakes, the Bay Area side prevailed, with the clinching penalty coming from Australian midfielder Julie Murray, the Founders Cup MVP. As fireworks boomed above the crowd of 21,078, CyberRays defender Brandi Chastain, who scored Bay Area's first goal in the game, pronounced this victory sweeter than the U.S. team's in '99. "The World Cup happens every four years," Chastain said. "This league will be going every summer, and there will be a champion every year. To me, it is so important for young girls to be able to come to the stadium on a regular basis, not just every four years."

The prospect of going *eight* years between World Cup appearances weighed heavily on the U.S. men as they prepared to face Jamaica at Foxboro on Oct. 7. Victories in the Americans' final two matches would assure them a berth; anything less and the U.S. would need considerable help from the soccer gods to make it to Japan/South Korea 2002.

Reyna's return to health was a huge boost. "When you get Claudio in the mix, you get players forward and create chances," Arena said. "We've sorely missed that." Only four minutes into the match Reyna sent a free kick to the near post, where a diving Joe-Max Moore flicked a header into the net.

But Jamaica equalized 10 minutes later, and the Americans were once again on Uneasy Street—until Donovan, in only his seventh national-team appearance, streaked onto a pass in the box from Reyna, stopped on a dime and

was cleaned out by defender Tyrone Marshall. The referee immediately pointed to the spot, without protest from Jamaica. Moore drilled the penalty kick, and the U.S. escaped with a 2–1 win.

Minutes later, when the other matches in the region had ended, it became clear that the Yanks had won much more. A tie between visiting Mexico and Costa Rica, and Trinidad & Tobago's stunning upset of Honduras in Tegucigalpa meant that the U.S. hadn't merely kept its hopes of qualifying alive—it had clinched a spot in the field of 32. Officials had to hunt down four bottles of champagne in the stadium's catering supply room. Said Agoos, "Nobody in our locker room thought we would qualify today."

The Yanks could look ahead to May, when the World Cup will begin and more unexpected turns can be expected.

The Fusion's Serna (above, 17) battled Richie Williams of the MetroStars during New York/New Jersey's 3–0 win in Miami on July 7. Despite three losses to the MetroStars, the Fusion finished with the league's best record (16-5-5) and advanced to the semifinals of the MLS playoffs.

PHOTO GALLERY

Los Angeles's Cobi Jones (above, right) eluded Ryan Suarez of Dallas during the teams' 0–0 draw at the Rose Bowl in May. The Galaxy would enhance its reputation as the Buffalo Bills of MLS, losing the championship game for the third time in six years.

Bay Area's Kelly Lindsey (right, 5) shielded the ball from Atlanta's Homare Sawa during the Founders Cup, the inaugural WUSA title game, on Aug. 25. Lindsey assisted on the CyberRays first goal in the exciting, back-and-forth affair that would require overtime and penalty kicks to determine a champion.

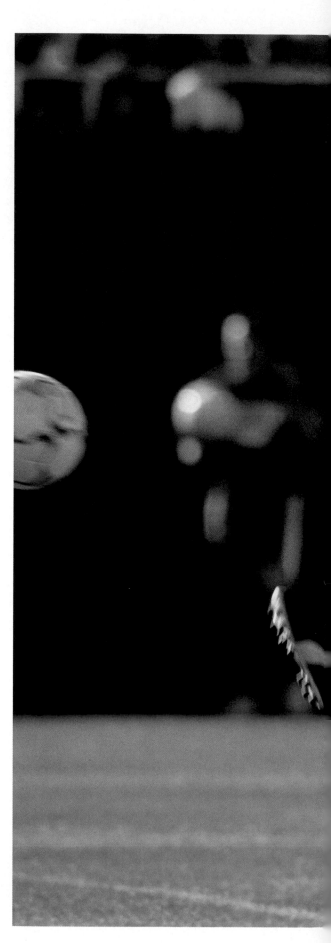

Clint Mathis of the U.S. (above, 5) beat Costa Rica's Reynaldo Parks to a header in the box during a World Cup qualifier in Kansas City on April 25. Mathis nodded the ball down to the far post, where his teammate Josh Wolff poked it into the goal to give the Americans a 1–0 victory. The loss would be Costa Rica's only defeat in 10 games of qualifying as they finished first in the group, followed by Mexico and the U.S.

U.S. Air: Joe-Max Moore (right, in white) of the United States went airborne in pursuit of the ball during the second half of a World Cup qualifier against Jamaica on Oct 7. Moore was the star of the game, scoring both goals in a 2–1 victory that booked the Americans' tickets to the 2002 World Cup—their fourth straight berth in the world's most popular sporting event.

George Weah

Jack the Rebel came calling in May of that year, as the rainy season began and the civil war spun into endgame. The streets of Liberia's capital, Monrovia, bore the latest bad fruit of Charles Taylor's seven-year drive for power: boy soldiers killing for fun, 3,000 dead within the previous two months, U.S. Marines evacuating thousands of foreigners, and warlords and their armies looting the city in a final spasm of greed. Jack the Rebel pulled up at George Weah's house in a convoy consisting of one military transport and five pickup trucks, some 70 men spilling out the sides. Jack the Rebel stood with a piece of paper in hand and shouted, "Everybody out! Get your asses out!" When the dozen or so men and 17 women in the house—friends, relatives and employees of Weah's—emerged and saw the waiting troops, they began to

tremble like leaves in a howling wind, because they assumed it was time to die.

The men were told to line up with their hands on a wall that shielded the house from the street. The women were sent back inside. Jack the Rebel waved the piece of paper and said, "George Weah has written a letter saying he wants to be president of this country. He doesn't want to play football anymore. He's getting into politics." Then the troops began beating the men. One soldier proclaimed, "Each woman will receive seven men here tonight! If anybody shakes, we'll kill every one of you!" The air echoed with the cocking of automatic weapons. A pack of soldiers went into the house. The screams began not long after....

The troops began sacking Weah's home, emptying it of everything of value: furniture, clothing, crockery, cam-

eras, someone's pet crocodile, a prized album of photos from Weah's brilliant career. The soldiers also took two of Weah's cars: a Mercedes and a Land Rover. Then they splashed the house with gasoline and set it on fire.

Weah (above) was in Italy, starring for the European soccer power AC Milan, when he heard that his house had been burned and that all the women inside, including two of his teenage cousins, had been raped. Only four months earlier the international soccer federation (FIFA) had named Weah World Player of the Year for 1995; he was the greatest soccer talent Africa had produced, Liberia's proudest export. Being a national hero, however, did not make him untouchable. On May 20, 1996, three days before the assault on his house and family, *The New York Times* had quoted Weah as saying the

U.N. should move into Liberia, supplant the battling warlords and teach his country democratic ways.

Later Taylor, a former government minister who would be elected president of Liberia in July 1997, insisted that he had not ordered the attack on Weah's house, but who believed him?

The soccer player was now seen as a political threat....Still, he has returned to Liberia time and again in the last five years, believing that a man who burns the bridge to his past is lost. If someone else does the burning, "you build a bridge and go across," he says. "You always have to come back."

This time, a late night in February 2001, Weah flies to Liberia from France, where he now plays for the team Olympique Marseilles. As he strides across the tarmac in Monrovia, people rush out of the darkness to touch him. A huge crowd waits at one end of the runway, some members waving a banner of welcome....George Weah is home when he doesn't have to be; when he could be in the U.S. with his wife and three children; when he could be in Marseilles, where the water actually flows out of faucets and the buildings aren't pocked by gunfire. The people cheer because as Liberia sinks further into the ranks of pariah states, Weah not only returns but also comes bearing the ultimate gift: distraction. For this week, at least, there's a chance for Liberians to obsess about the national team and drink a bit and forget that, after 11 years of unrelenting misery, their world is still going straight to hell....

Not long ago Weah—name and fortune made over two decades with his dazzling play for AS Monaco, for Paris-St. Germain and, especially, for the 1996 and '99 Italian league champion, AC Milan—had resigned himself to retiring without representing country and continent in the World Cup. Playing for his third professional team in 10 months, he seemed sure to become the greatest player since Northern Ireland's George Best to miss out on sport's greatest event. Then, handed one last chance, Weah began to concoct a sporting miracle.

Since June 2000, when he took over as the technical director, coach and star player of the national team [nicknamed the Lone Star], Weah has set up goal after goal and led Liberia to nine wins in 10 games, including upsets of Ghana and Nigeria....

No one has given more of himself to Liberia over the last decade than Weah, who earned more than $15 million during his prime years with AC Milan, and paid close to $2 million out of his own pocket to keep the Lone Star alive after the civil war began in 1990. He became a one-man football association, supplying jerseys, cleats and equipment and paying the players' salaries....In October '96, Weah bought tickets to fly in 10 Liberian players from Europe, chartered a plane for $47,000 to fly the team to a game in Zaire and paid everyone in the 27-man delegation a per diem. Of the 25 players on the current Lone Star, 10 landed overseas contracts because Weah recommended them and paid for their flights to tryouts.

Then there are the stories about how Weah sent one Liberian he had never met to the U.S. for medical treatment; how he kept handing money to patients in the hospital in Abidjan, the capital of Ivory Coast ($1,000 here, $1,000 there); and how, whenever Weah returned to Liberia for Christmas, he would withdraw $20,000 from the bank in $20s and $50s. Then he would stand at the front door of his house, and, Clar says, "people would come, and George would give them Christmas."

"He's been designated by God," says Liberian striker Frank Seator. "George has assisted millions of people, indirectly and directly. We have ministers here who have money, and they don't give anybody one cent. But he takes his time, his money, to go out to the people. I'm telling you: He's designated. You can't get over how he lives his life."

Hoover Amos, one of Weah's security men, agrees. "My father says George has the spirit of Jesus Christ," Amos says. "He calls George 'Wonderful.' Anytime George is about to come to the country, my father says, 'Oh, Lord, Jesus Christ is coming. Wonderful is coming.'"

—S.L. Price
excerpted from SI, April 16, 2001

Liberia narrowly missed qualifying for the 2002 World Cup, finishing one point behind Nigeria in Africa's Group B. —Ed.

Clint Mathis

When Clint Mathis was seven years old, his older brothers, Phil and Andy, made a rule: Young Clint could play soccer with them in their Conyers, Ga., neighborhood, but only if he used his left foot exclusively. "They didn't want me to grow up playing just right-footed," says Clint, the new It boy of American soccer. Those days yielded comical scenes, as the towheaded kid in the blue-and-white-striped Diego Maradona jersey scampered madly to use his left. "Right foot!" his brothers would say when Clint cheated, followed by, "Sit down!"

Lately those lessons have been paying off as Mathis, 24, has fast become the first MLS-bred American star, an ambipedal forward whose growing collection of highlight-reel goals has inspired adoring New York/New Jersey MetroStars supporters to worship him with religious fervor (his fan club is called the East Rutherford Mathodist Church) and to break out in rapturous song (to the tune of *Guantanamera*): *There's only one Clint Mathis!/There's only one Clint Mathis!/Only one Clint Maaaaa-this!*

As of May 6, Mathis was leading MLS with six goals in five matches, and he's always a threat to score in bunches; in 2000 he set a league single-game record with five goals against the Dallas Burn. He scored three on May 2 in a 4–1 victory over the Kansas City Wizards. Mathis also has two goals and four assists in four World Cup qualifying games....

Just as important, the quality of Mathis's goals matches their quantity. On April 28 he embarked on a breathtaking 60-yard slalom run past three Burn defenders for one of the most electrifying strikes in U.S. soccer history. The goal, replays of which were aired worldwide, evoked heady comparisons to Maradona.

Says MetroStars captain Tab Ramos,

"Taking people on with the ball at your feet is the hardest thing in the game. Clint has the full package—the flair, the ability to change speeds; I don't think any American player has had that at age 24."

What's more, Mathis (below) has a sense of the dramatic, often disappearing for stretches of games, only to swoop in like a superhero when he's most needed. During a Cup qualifier in Honduras in March, he played so poorly that coach Bruce Arena let loose a stinging philippic at halftime. "One of my worst games ever," says Mathis. "I might have made two good passes." In the dying minutes, though, he curled a world-class free kick over the Honduran wall and into the net, giving the U.S. a stunning 2–1 victory.

When Mathis left the field that night, Arena could only shake his head and smile. "As a coach you pull your hair out," he says. "Clint underperforms in a lot of areas except the one that matters

most: He's involved in the plays that make a difference. That's called genius. He has a lot of creative ideas out there, and you have to allow that to blossom."

Mathis can throw a football 60 yards, but his brothers decided the sport was too dangerous for him, so he stuck with soccer instead, developing his instincts in youth leagues.... Though Mathis spent time with various U.S. youth teams and played four seasons at South Carolina (three of them with current national team striker Josh Wolff), he was hardly expected to explode onto the American pro scene. As a part-time starter for two seasons with the Los Angeles Galaxy, he never scored more than seven goals.

His break came last season when L.A. signed Mexico's Luis Hernandez and, as a result, the then last-place MetroStars picked up Mathis in a dispersal draft. With 13 goals and 13 assists for the

Metros, Mathis finished second in the league's MVP voting and drew Arena's attention for international duty. In fact, when Mathis and Wolff came on as substitutes during a World Cup qualifier against Mexico in February, Clint's mom, Pat, called her friend Sandy Wolff, Josh's mom, seconds before Mathis's pinpoint pass set up Wolff for the first goal in the 2–0 win.

As the MetroStars have embraced Mathis, he has grown equally fond of Gotham. In 2000 he wore under his uniform jersey an I LOVE NY T-shirt, which he exposed whenever he scored, and he has been a regular at Broadway musicals and the WWF theme restaurant in Times Square. "Everything has happened at the right time for me," he says.

Still, you can never take the South completely out of the boy. Mathis likes to wear black leather Harley-Davidson boots with his black Harley shirt with his backward-turned black Harley baseball cap. (His contract, alas, prevents him from actually riding a Harley.) Small wonder that, with a nod to Mathis's mischievous side and his down-home *yes sir*'s, Arena gave him the nickname Eddie Haskell.

How MLS reacts to Mathis's newfound star power could have a long-term impact on the six-year-old league. Will MLS be a seller's league, peddling its homegrown American stars to wealthy European clubs, a policy that could drive away potential fans? Or will it take the financial leap of faith required to keep those players? "Playing in Europe has always been a dream," he says, "but I'm happy here now and I want to win a title with the MetroStars. The reason Americans want to go to Europe is financial. For MLS to move to the next level, it has to step up for an American player who has developed here, to show this is a league that can compete in the world market."

Though he may soon be pulled in many directions, there's only one Clint Mathis—and, as his growing legions of fans would attest, that's a shame.

—Grant Wahl
excerpted from SI, May 14, 2001

Mathis's 2001 season was cut short on June 5, when he tore his right ACL during training with the national team. —Ed.

Santino Quaranta

Thomas Quaranta is a big fan of *The Godfather*. So big that when his son Thomas Jr. had his first child, Senior suggested that the boy be called Santino, after James Caan's character in the movie. Santino's parents couldn't have known it at the time, but it was fitting that they named him for the Corleone known as Sonny. A 16-year-old forward for D.C. United, Quaranta is the youngest pro athlete in a major U.S. team sport. (The similarities between Santino Quaranta and Santino Corleone end with the nickname. Quaranta is no hothead, and he regularly navigates his Infiniti SUV, which he bought shortly after he signed his contract, through toll booths without getting gunned down.)

Quaranta grew up in Highlandtown, a blue-collar neighborhood in Baltimore. He learned the game on a sandy pitch behind a school across the street from his house, and he was often the smallest and youngest player. That helped develop his toughness as well as his flair, a combination that has served him well in his rookie season in MLS. Through Aug. 5 he had netted five goals in 13 games, been named Player of the Week in mid-July and started the All-Star Game.

The 6-foot, 165-pound Quaranta is the youngest member of a youth movement that's sweeping the league. His teenage cohorts include Landon Donovan, a 19-year-old striker for the San Jose Earthquakes, who scored four goals in the All-Star Game; the Chicago Fire's DaMarcus Beasley, another 19-year-old All-Star starter and one of the league's top attacking midfielders; Quaranta's 18-year-old teammate, midfielder Bobby Convey, who was elected to start the All-Star Game but missed the match because of a hernia; and Edward Johnson, a 17-year-old striker who has given the Dallas Burn a lift off the bench.

MLS's brass is doing its best to bring in only teens with a bona fide chance of thriving on and off the field....By the time he was a sophomore at Archbishop Curley Prep, Quaranta had caught the attention of scouts from the U.S. Soccer Federation, which footed the bill to move him to Bradenton, Fla., where he trained with the rest of the national Under-17 team. Quaranta and his 17 teammates went to school every morning, practiced every afternoon and did their homework every evening, all the while living at Nick Bollettieri's tennis academy. Such soccer academies are commonplace around the world, and it's hard to argue with the results. The second U.S. U-17 team to pass through the academy finished fourth in the 1999 world championship....

Being selected by D.C. has allowed Quaranta to live with his family in Baltimore, where, from the comfort of familiar surroundings, he can focus on the prospect of playing alongside men twice his age. "I was worried," he says. "I didn't have a clue what to expect. How were the guys going to treat me?" Quaranta got his answer after his first practice. As he stood at his locker conducting an interview, [D.C. goalkeeper Mike] Ammann took a coffee filter, filled it with shaving cream and tossed the makeshift pie in his face. Quaranta went along with the gag, which endeared him to the veterans.

"He gravitates to the older guys because they want to teach him the ropes, and he's eager to learn," says D.C. coach Thomas Rongen. On the road Quaranta no longer rooms with Convey, recently bunking with Abdul Thompson Conteh, a 31-year-old forward from Sierra Leone. In May the older guys went to bat for Quaranta when he wanted to go to his girlfriend's junior prom, which was scheduled the night before a road game. After defender Eddie Pope explained the significance of that night for 16-year-old American boys, Rongen, who is Dutch, gave the go-ahead. Quaranta had a blast, caught a plane the next morning, reached Columbus, Ohio, in time for the pregame meal and scored his first MLS goal.

—Mark Bechtel
excerpted from SI, Aug. 13, 2001

T H E   N U M B E R S

Major League Soccer

2001 FINAL STANDINGS

Eastern Division

TEAM	WON	LOST	TIED	PTS
Miami (1)	16	5	5	53
NY/NJ (6)	13	10	3	42
New England	7	14	6	27
D.C.	8	16	2	26

Central Division

TEAM	WON	LOST	TIED	PTS
Chicago (2)	16	6	5	53
Columbus (4)	13	7	6	45
Dallas (8)	10	11	5	35
Tampa Bay	4	21	2	14

Western Division

TEAM	WON	LOST	TIED	PTS
Los Angeles (3)	14	7	5	47
San Jose (5)	13	7	6	45
Kansas City (7)	11	13	3	36
Colorado	5	13	8	23

*League canceled all regular-season games after Sept. 11, 2001. Note: Three points for a win. One point for a tie. Number in parentheses is playoff seed.

Scoring Leaders

PLAYER, TEAM	GP	G	A	PTS
Alex Pineda Chacon, Miami	25	19	9	47
Diego Serna, Miami	22	15	15	45
John Spencer, Colorado	23	14	7	35
Jeff Cunningham, Columbus	22	10	13	33
John Wilmar Perez, Colum.	25	8	15	31

Goals Leaders

PLAYER, TEAM	GP	G
Alex Pineda Chacon, Miami	25	19
Diego Serna, Miami	22	15
John Spencer, Colorado	23	14
Abdul Thompson Conteh, D.C.	25	14
Ronald Cerritos, San Jose	25	11
Ariel Graziani, Dallas	25	11

Assists Leaders

PLAYER, TEAM	GP	A
Diego Serna, Miami	22	15
John Wilmar Perez, Columbus	25	15
Preki, Miami	24	14
Jeff Cunningham, Columbus	22	13
Ian Bishop, Miami	23	13

Goals-Against-Average Leaders

PLAYER, TEAM	GAA
Zach Thornton, Chicago	1.08
Joe Cannon, San Jose	1.09
Nick Rimando, Miami	1.29
Tim Howard, NY/NJ	1.33
Tom Presthus, Columbus	1.36

2001 Playoffs

Chicago

Dallas

Chicago (7–1)

NY/NJ

Los Angeles* (4–4)

Los Angeles

Los Angeles (7–1)

San Jose 2–1 (ot)

San Jose (6–3)

Miami (6–3)

San Jose (6–0)

Miami

Kansas City

San Jose

Columbus

*Won tiebreaking minigame. Note: Except for the final, which was a single game, scores in parentheses are points earned (three for a win, one for a tie) in a three-game series, the winner being the first team to accumulate five points.

MLS Cup 2001

COLUMBUS, OHIO, OCTOBER 21, 2001

San Jose	1	0	1	—2
Los Angeles	1	0	0	—1

Goals: Hernandez (Vanney) 21; Donovan (Mulrooney) 43; DeRosario (Ekelund) 96.
San Jose—Cannon, Conrad, Dayak, Agoos, Barrett, Russell, Corrales, Mulrooney, Ekelund, Cerritos (DeRosario 85), Donovan.

Los Angeles—Hartman, Hendrickson, Vanney, Caliguri (Frye 53), Califf, Elliott, Cienfuegos, Vagenas, Jones, Victorine (Mullan 75), Hernandez.
Att: 21,626.

Women's United Soccer Association

2001 FINAL STANDINGS

TEAM	GP	W	L	T	PTS	GF	GA	DIFF.	HOME	ROAD
†Atlanta	21	10	4	7	37	31	21	+10	5-2-4	5-2-3
*Bay Area	21	11	6	4	37	27	23	+4	6-3-1	5-3-3
*New York	21	9	7	5	32	30	25	+5	4-3-3	5-4-2
*Philadelphia	21	9	8	4	31	35	28	+7	5-3-2	4-5-2
San Diego	21	7	7	7	28	29	28	+1	4-3-4	3-4-3
Boston	21	8	10	3	27	29	35	-6	4-6-1	4-4-2
Washington	21	6	12	3	21	26	35	-9	3-6-1	3-6-2
Carolina	21	6	12	3	21	28	40	-12	4-5-2	2-7-1

†Regular-season champion. *Clinched playoff berth.

SCORING LEADERS

PLAYER, TEAM	GP	G	A	PTS
Tiffeny Milbrett, New York	20	16	3	35
Shannon MacMillan, San Diego	20	12	6	30
Charmaine Hooper, Atlanta	19	12	3	27
Dagny Mellgren, Boston	19	11	4	26
Danielle Fotopoulos, Carolina	21	9	5	23
Maren Meinert, Boston	17	8	7	23

GOALS-AGAINST-AVERAGE LEADERS

PLAYER, TEAM	GAA
Briana Scurry, Atlanta	0.82
LaKeysia Beene, Bay Area	0.97
Melissa Moore, Philadelphia	1.01
Gao Hong, New York	1.11
Jaime Pagliarulo, San Diego	1.40

2001 PLAYOFFS
Semifinals
Atlanta 2, Philadelphia 2
Bay Area 3, New York 2

2001 Founders Cup, August 25, Foxboro Stadium
Bay Area 3, Atlanta 3
Bay Area won 4–2 on penalties.

International Competition

2000–2001 U.S. MEN'S NATIONAL TEAM RESULTS

DATE	OPPONENT	SITE	RESULT	U.S. GOALS
Oct 25, 2000	Mexico	Los Angeles	2–0 W	Donovan, Wolff
Nov 15	Barbados†	St. Michael, Barbados	4–0 W	Mathis, Stewart, Jones, Razov
Jan 27, 2001	China	Oakland	2–1 W	McBride, own goal
Feb 3	Colombia	Miami	0–1 L	—
Feb 28	Mexico†	Columbus, OH	2–0 W	Wolff, Stewart
March 3	Brazil	Los Angeles	2–1 L	Mathis
March 28	Honduras†	San Pedro Sula, Hond.	2–1 W	Stewart, Mathis
April 25	Costa Rica†	Kansas City, MO	1–0 W	Wolff
June 7	Ecuador	Columbus, OH	0–0 T	—
June 16	Jamaica†	Kingston, Jamaica	0–0 T	—
June 20	Trinidad & Tobago†	Foxboro, MA	2–0 W	Razov, Stewart
July 1	Mexico†	Mexico City	0–1 L	—
Sept 1	Honduras†	Washington, D.C.	2–3 L	Stewart (2)
Sept 5	Costa Rica†	San Jose, Costa Rica	0–2 L	—
Oct 7	Jamaica†	Foxboro, MA	2–1 W	Moore (2)

†Qualifying for 2002 World Cup. Record in full internationals from Oct. 25, 2000, through Oct. 7, 2001: 8-5-2.

2000–2001 U.S. WOMEN'S NATIONAL TEAM RESULTS

DATE	OPPONENT	SITE	RESULT	U.S. GOALS
Sept 14, 2000	Norway†	Melbourne, Australia	2–0 W	Milbrett, Hamm
Sept 17	China†	Melbourne, Australia	1–1 T	Foudy
Sept 20	Nigeria†	Melbourne, Australia	3–1 W	Chastain, Lily, MacMillan
Sept 24	Brazil†	Canberra, Australia	1–0 W	Hamm
Sept 28	Norway†	Sydney	2–3 L	Milbrett (2)
Nov 11	Canada	Columbus, OH	1–3 L	Milbrett
Dec 10	Mexico	Houston	3–2 W	Lily, Parlow (2)
Dec 17	Japan	Phoenix	1–1 T	Chastain
Jan 11, 2001	China	Panyu, China	0–1 L	—
Jan 14	China	Hangzhou, China	1–1 T	Lalor
March 7	Italy	Rieti, Italy	0–1 L	—
March 11	Canada#	Lagos, Portugal	0–3 L	—
March 13	Portugal#	Silves, Portugal	2–0 W	Welsh, Rigamat
March 15	Sweden#	Albufeira, Portugal	0–2 L	—
March 17	Norway#	Quartfeira, Portugal	3–4 L	Marquand, Schott, Reddick
June 30	Canada	Toronto	2–2 T	MacMillan, Milbrett
July 3	Canada	Blaine, MN	1–0 W	Milbrett
Sept 9	Germany*	Chicago	4–1 W	Hamm (2), Parlow, Milbrett

Record from Sept. 14, 2000, through Sept. 9, 2001: 7-7-4. †Olympic Games. #Algarves Cup. *U.S. Women's Cup, the remainder of which was canceled after the Sept. 11 terrorist attacks on New York City and Washington, D.C.

U. S. Open Cup

2001 RESULTS

Third Round
Pittsburgh (A-League) 2, El Paso (A-League) 1
Chicago (MLS) 1, Kansas City (MLS) 0
San Jose* (MLS) 0, Milwaukee (A-League) 0
Los Angeles (MLS) 3, Seattle (PDL) 1
New England (MLS) 2, Charleston (A-League) 1
Columbus (MLS) 2, Miami (MLS) 1
Richmond (A-League) 2, Connecticut (A-League) 1
D.C. United (MLS) 3, Hershey (A-League) 0

*Advanced on penalties. Note:MLS: Major League Soccer (1st division); A-League (2nd division); PDL: Premier Development League (Amateur).

Quarterfinals
Chicago 3, Pittsburgh 2 (ot)
Los Angeles* 1, San Jose 1
New England 2, Columbus 1
D.C. United 2, Richmond 1

*Advanced on penalties. Note: MLS: Major League Soccer (1st division); A-League (2nd division); PDL: Premier Development League (Amateur).

Semifinals
Los Angeles 1, Chicago 0 (ot)
New England 2, D.C. United 0

2001 Lamar Hunt U.S. Open Cup Final, October 27, Fullerton, CA

New England	1	0	—1
Los Angeles	0	2	—2

Goals: Harris (unassisted) 30; Hendrickson (Vanney) 70; Califf (Jones) 92.
New England—Fernandez, Franchino, Wright, Cullen, Alvarez, Heaps (sent off, 88), Downing (Chronopolous 78), Cloutier, Cate, Williams (Woods 61), Harris (Sunsing 68).
Los Angeles—Hartman, Vanney, Caliguiri (Mullan 64), Califf, Hendrickson, Elliott, Vagenas, Cienfuegos, Frye, Victorine (Lalas 91), Jones.
Att: 4,195.

Women's Movement

Led by Jennifer Capriati and the Williams sisters, the women's tour outshined the men's for the second year in a row

B.J. SCHECTER

Ranked 267th in the world in 1998, Capriati (opposite) completed an impressive comeback in 2001, winning the Australian and French Opens and seizing the No. 1 spot in the WTA Tour rankings in October.

Perhaps CBS executives sensed the inevitable. Or maybe they were just reacting to the obvious. Whatever the case, by moving the U.S. Open women's final to prime time on a Saturday night, CBS sent the unmistakable message that the women's game had overtaken the men's in popularity. And the women didn't disappoint. Though there was more parity in the men's game—which had four different champions in the Grand Slams—the women provided more intensity and entertainment from baseline to baseline, with a few notable exceptions.

Once again the Williams sisters were lightning rods for history, excitement and controversy. In their ongoing efforts to maintain lives outside tennis, and to simply take a break from the intense world of the WTA, Venus and Serena took significant time off at the beginning of the tennis season, drawing criticism from fans and players alike. They devoted little time to practice during this period, pursued outside interests such as fashion classes, and were noticeably absent from early tournaments.

In the first major of the year, the Australian Open, Martina Hingis dispatched both sisters in succession, defeating Serena 6–2, 3–6, 8–6 in the quarterfinals and routing Venus 6–1, 6–1 in the semis. Afterward Hingis said of the Williams sisters, "They're always saying, 'O.K., we went to school.' Either you go to school or you play tennis. You can't do both. Tennis is a full-time commitment."

Apparently players as supremely talented as the Williamses can get away with part-time commitment. But first, perhaps, they need a wake-up call. Venus got hers in May, when she lost in the first round of the French Open to little-known Barbara Schett. Following that shocking defeat Venus rededicated herself to tennis and was determined to show the world that she could still perform at the championship level. One month later,

with her rocket serve and stunning power and range, she defended her Wimbledon title by beating Justine Henin 6–1, 3–6, 6–0 in the final. Afterward she vowed to make tennis more of a priority. "I'm still a kid, and I don't want to grow up yet," she said, "but I have to in some things, but not everything. So it's a happy medium. Grand Slams definitely are Number 1. Then Number 2, for sure, is Number 1. Oh boy, that sounds like a Dr. Seuss book." She meant, if we can unravel the Seussian construct, that outside of peaking for Grand Slam tournaments, she's going to make sure she's happy and fulfilled—which won't necessarily involve tennis.

The final of the U.S. Open read like a happy bedtime story in the Williams household, one that outspoken papa Richard had been predicting for years. The Williams sisters had met in tournaments before, including in the 2000 Wimbledon semifinals, but they had not yet played each other in the final of a Grand Slam. Their play in the early rounds in New York was so stellar that people started checking the record for the last time two sisters had met in a Grand Slam final. They had to go back to 1884, when Maud Watson downed her sister Lilian at Wimbledon.

Dominating the field with their power and grace, Venus and Serena dispatched some of the world's top players with ease. In the semis, Venus dismantled Jennifer Capriati, winner of the year's first two Grand Slams, and Serena made Hingis, the world's No. 1 player, look like an amateur. The all-Williams final was set.

Based on the sisters' form, Venus versus Serena looked to be the battle of the ages. But it didn't turn out that way. The tennis was uneventful, sloppy at times, and surprisingly emotionless as Venus cruised to a 6–2, 6–4 victory. There were times when it seemed as if neither sister wanted to win. "I was saying, 'Come on, Serena, just do this or do that,'" said Venus. "When I'd find myself

match point the two sisters hugged at the net and Venus said to Serena, "I love you. I feel so bad. I feel like I haven't won."

But arguably both sisters had won; their appearance in a Grand Slam final was a thumping affirmation of the barriers they have obliterated in their careers. The Williams sisters' impact on tennis is similar to Tiger Woods's effect on golf. "Tennis has come to a different level now," said Jeanne Moutoussamy-Ashe, the widow of Arthur Ashe. "Arthur would have liked to have been here for them because we're all beneficiaries. They've done a wonderful job."

The story of the first half of the season, though, was Capriati, who completed an inspiring comeback. Once considered the bright future of the women's game, Capriati crumbled under the immense pressure and disappeared from tennis for several years. She played her first professional match at 13. At age 14 she made it to the semifinals of the French Open and vaulted into the Top 10. By 17, however, Capriati was burned out. In December 1993 she was cited for shoplifting and five months later was arrested for marijuana possession at a Florida motel. She went five years without winning a match in a Grand Slam event, and it was doubtful that she would ever recapture her form.

"There were times when I thought maybe this isn't worth it," Capriati said. "But once I got over the hump and enjoyed the game and stopped worrying about the other stuff, I knew I'd break through eventually."

After an inconsistent season in 2000, Capriati rededicated herself in the off-season, working out daily with a personal trainer, and arrived at the Australian Open in the best shape of her life. She toned the mental side of her game as well. No longer did she let unforced errors or poor line calls affect her. The results were striking indeed. Capriati defeated Monica Seles, Lindsay Davenport and Hingis in successive matches to win the Australian. "Who would have ever thought I would have made it here after so much happened?" said Capriati after beating Hingis 6–4, 6–3 in the final. "Dreams do come true."

And Capriati wasn't done dreaming. At the

Venus Williams started slowly in 2001 but roared back in style, winning Wimbledon and the U.S. Open, in which she and her sister, Serena, squared off in the first all African-American final in Grand Slam history and the first major final between sisters since 1884.

doing that, I'd lose a couple of points. When I'd lose a couple of points, I wasn't sorry [for her] anymore." Lackluster tennis aside, though, this event had the pomp and circumstance befitting its historic status. Arthur Ashe Stadium was chock full of A-list celebrities. "Hey, I wouldn't have missed it either if I knew something so historic was going to happen," Serena said. "I guess a lot of people want to watch us. For me it's really exciting because some of these [celebrities] are really superstars. I didn't think that they would want to watch little me play tennis."

In the end the better player won, as Venus seized her fourth Grand Slam title. Following

French Open she continued her superb play, arriving in Paris as the fourth seed but leaving as the champion. In a remarkable final, she rallied to beat Kim Clijsters 1–6, 6–4, 12–10. "I never thought I'd be standing here 11 years later, after playing my first time here when I was 14 years old," Capriati told the crowd afterward. "Really I'm just waiting to wake up from this dream."

On the men's side of the French Open, Gustavo Kuerten knew he wasn't dreaming when he cruised to the final. A fixture at Roland Garros now, and a master on clay, Kuerten had only one truly tough match en route to the final. There he defeated Alex Corretja to win his third French Open title, then drew a large heart in the clay and lay down inside it as a tribute to the French fans.

There was plenty of heart and desire on display at Wimbledon, where Goran Ivanisevic became the first wild card to win a Grand Slam. Ivanisevic, who was only invited to the event because he had lost in the Wimbledon final three times, came to the All-England having won just nine matches during the season. Down two sets to one in the semis against local favorite Tim Henman, Ivanisevic was spared by a rain delay. Refreshed, he came back the next day and rallied to win.

In the final, which was pushed to Monday due to the weather, Ivanisevic defeated Patrick Rafter in a marvelous five-set match that went 9–7 in the fifth. Contemplating retirement because of a bum shoulder, Ivanisevic knew this might be his last chance to win a Grand Slam. Before the match he said, "If some angel comes tonight in my dreams and says, 'O.K., Goran, you are going to win Wimbledon tomorrow, but you won't be able to touch the racket ever again in your life,' I'd say, 'O.K., I take that.' "

Though the women overshadowed the men at the U.S. Open, one match stood out above all, men's or women's. Andre Agassi and Pete Sampras are more accustomed to meeting in finals, but with Sampras struggling (he was seeded 10th), they met one another in a quarterfinal—one that will rank with the best matches in tennis history. Neither player had his serve broken as Sampras outslugged his fellow legend 6–7, 7–6, 7–6, 7–6.

It's too bad for the men that the tournament couldn't have ended right then and there, because everything that followed was a letdown. Sampras reached the final, where he faced 20-year-old Lleyton Hewitt, but he had nothing left. Looking slow and tired, he lost in straight sets.

Once again, the men could not match the drama of the women's tour.

For Goran Ivanisevic, the name of the game was persistence. At Wimbledon, the 29-year-old Croatian endured a rain-delayed semifinal, a 16-game fifth set in the final and four match points for the championship, his first Grand Slam title in 48 attempts.

PHOTO GALLERY

Feats of Clay: Gustavo Kuerten of Brazil (right) won the French Open for the third time in his career and finished the 2001 season with five clay-court titles under his belt. The crowd-pleasing "Guga" faltered at season's end, however, and dropped to the No. 2 ranking in the ATP Champions Race.

Terms of Service: At the tennis-advanced age of 31, Andre Agassi (left) remained a formidable opponent all year. He won his seventh major—the Australian Open—went toe-to-toe with Pete Sampras in an instant-classic U.S. Open quarterfinal and was in contention for the No. 1 ranking up to the season-ending Masters Cup. The Las Vegas native finished the year ranked third in the world.

Australia's lightning-quick Lleyton Hewitt (opposite) dived into the spotlight in 2001. After a lackluster performance at the Australian Open, the 20-year-old reached the quarters at the French and ran off with his first Grand Slam title at the U.S. Open, defeating Pete Sampras in straight sets. Riding the momentum of his Open victory, Hewitt went on a furious tear late in the year, winning 22 of his last 24 matches and becoming the youngest man to hold the No. 1 ranking.

PROFILES

Jennifer Capriati

It was all going to be so easy. That's what everyone thought back when Jennifer Capriati was young and fresh. Championships seemed inevitable for the Fort Lauderdale schoolgirl, a Chris Evert wannabe who learned the game from Evert's dad, Jimmy, and pounded the hardest ground strokes anyone had seen. She collected wins like Barbie dolls, popping her gum and grinning. In 1990, at age 14, Capriati became the youngest girl ever to be ranked in the top 10, and she cruised into the French Open semifinals, becoming the youngest to advance so far at a Grand Slam tournament. She was going to be the next big American thing.

Everyone said so. Endorsements, magazine covers: All the treasures of the modern age were laid at Capriati's feet. No one bothered to ask if any of it was good for her. For what no one knew about Capriati then—what no one really would know until 4:58 p.m., Paris time, on June 9, 2001—was that at her core, she needs a fight. Capriati responds best to adversity, not ease. So in the 2001 French Open final, at the tennis-old age of 25, Capriati, the onetime troubled teen who in the last two years has clawed her way back to the top, again buried herself in a hole from which to clamber out. After a first set in which she demonstrated little

more than frayed nerves, the heavily favored Capriati righted herself, engaged No. 12 seed Kim Clijsters in a mesmerizing final set and, with a 1–6, 6–4, 12–10 victory in the French Open final, fulfilled the promise she had shown on this same court more than a decade ago.

Then, after becoming the first American woman since Evert in 1986 to win in Paris, Capriati found Evert herself waiting at the podium to present the trophy. "I never thought I'd be standing here 11 years later, after playing my first time here when I was 14 years old," Capriati told the crowd. "Really, I'm just waiting to wake up from this dream."

Capriati's astounding return to form seemed to take the tour's most unpredictable Grand Slam event in a new direction. Love was in the air. By the time the fortnight had ended, TV screens were saturated with shots of Jennifer's divorced parents, Denise and Stefano, sitting side by side and hugging after her wins.… But it was Capriati's victory, and her run over the last two years, that told a tale of things larger than tennis. "What she did is an example for everybody," Stefano said. "All families have [problems], but with love you can always come back."

Well, with love, hard work and Capriati's embrace of a challenge. She battled a bad reputation, being cited for shoplifting in 1993 and arrested for marijuana possession in '94, and she entered drug rehab soon afterward. She lost lucrative endorsement deals and, in 1995, suffered through her parents' divorce. Over the last year Capriati has seen her mother stricken with thyroid cancer, skin cancer and recurring hip ailments that forced Denise to skip the Australian Open and undergo hip-replacement surgery. During the recovery Jennifer was always there, holding up Denise in the shower, helping her dress, keeping her spirits high. "I couldn't do the things I wanted to do," says Denise, "and at times you go on a pity party and say, 'I don't have any more energy.' Jennifer would hear none of it. 'Mom,' she would say, 'we've fought bigger battles than this.'"

By the time she hit Paris, Jennifer had the drill down. Accompanied by her 21-year-old brother, Steven, as well as Denise and Stefano, Jennifer did no sightseeing and kept telling her mother, "Only the strong survive." On the morning of the final Jennifer turned to Steven and said, "Time to do what we came here to do."

After a dismal first set against Clijsters, Capriati willed herself back into the match.… But four times in the final set, Clijsters came within two points of the match, and it was then that Capriati revealed her mettle.…

[On the fourth of those] at 7–8, deuce, Capriati shook off two net cords and fired a service winner. Six games later, on Capriati's second match point, as Clijsters sagged, she whipped the ball past the Belgian teenager with a forehand. Capriati then hopped three times and clenched her hands over her head as if she were the heavyweight champ.…

But for Capriati, tennis is one thing, stardom another. She never had the crossover dreams of Anna Kournikova and the Williams sisters. "She'd be perfectly content with going home after this and watching TV in her bedroom or on the couch or playing with her dogs," says Steven. "That'd make her as happy as going on a shopping spree in Paris."

Capriati still regards the media as the monster that once devoured her and her family. The night before the French final she worried that another Grand Slam title would bring a level of hype she hadn't imagined. "It was pretty quiet after [the Australian Open]," she said following her win on Saturday. "After this one it might get pretty crazy. But I think I've got a good head on my shoulders."

Capriati came to Paris more confident than ever. Rather than mumble and stare at the tablecloth during her press conferences, as had been her habit, she made eye contact with reporters and tossed away most of the "you knows" that had propped up her conversation like so many crutches. She emphasized that she is finally at peace, that she likes the person she sees in the mirror. For the first time, she realizes that fame can be a positive force. Before her quarterfinal showdown against Serena Williams, Capriati held up a sign that read GET WELL SOON, CORINA, for Corina Morariu, a doubles specialist who is battling leukemia. After the final Capriati dedicated her title to Morariu, gave the crowd a composed speech and congratulated her opponent. She seemed perfectly comfortable. "It's just my happiness talking," she said.

This is the Capriati everyone has waited for since she first came to Paris as a pro 11 years ago. She's an adult now, bruised and wary, but at times you can still see a hint of the 14-year-old who captivated America. When the crowd at Court Phillippe Chatrier did the wave before she served the last time for the championship, Capriati stared in openmouthed wonder at the sight of so many grown-ups acting like kids. Her mother, too, sometimes can see the five-year-old who had no idea she'd won her first match and grinned so widely at the news. "I love that smile," Denise said. "She can just light up a room when she smiles."

She did it again on Saturday. After she clenched her hands over her head as the cheers rained down, that smile swept over Capriati's face, and she lit up the biggest room in Paris. It came to her so easily that you'd swear it took no work at all.

—S.L. Price
excerpted from SI, June 18, 2001

The Williams Sisters

Along with her sister, Serena, Venus Williams took the U.S. Open—which is usually tennis's most chaotic and contentious Grand Slam event—and consumed it like an olive off a toothpick. Nothing that happened in New York over the fortnight—not the rise of controversial 20-year-old men's champ Lleyton Hewitt, not the boom and bust of 19-year-old Andy Roddick, not even the stirring rebirth of Pete Sampras—could retard the Williams express. After tearing through the women's draw (Venus and Serena hammered No. 2 Capriati and No. 1 Martina Hingis, respectively, in straight sets in the semis, combining for 61 winners while their opponents had only nine), the Williamses took Saturday's final to prime time for the first time. With a choir singing and celebrities mugging, they brought the women's final its best TV rating (7.7 overnight) in two decades and provided America with a sloppy, tense spectacle that proved enthralling on every level but the athletic.…

For the first time since 1884, sisters had played each other in a Grand Slam final, and for the first time, two ghetto-raised African-Americans have risen to the pinnacle of prominence in a traditionally wealthy and white game. "Tennis has come to a different level now—these girls have raised the bar," said Jeanne

Moutoussamy-Ashe, the widow of Arthur Ashe, after the match in the stadium named for her husband. "I feel tonight the way I'll feel at my daughter's high school and college graduations. Arthur would have liked to have been here for them, because we're all beneficiaries. They've done a wonderful job."

Then, too, there's the Williams family, which, usually because of the sisters' unpredictable father, Richard, has served as a lightning rod for admiration and controversy. There has been much talk about the family's insularity and cockiness, but it was largely overlooked that at its moment of greatest triumph, the Williams clan was breaking apart. Over the last year Venus (above, left) has successfully defended her Wimbledon and U.S. Open titles and solidified her place as the game's top player, while Serena (above, right), who beat No. 8 Justine Henin, No. 3 Lindsay Davenport and Hingis over the last two weeks, seems to have regained the form that brought her the 1999 U.S. Open championship. The daughters achieved all this despite the fact that Oracene and

Richard have been separated for more than a year. Oracene intends to get a divorce, and she's mulling over the best way to push it through.

"Not yet," she said last Saturday night when asked if she had filed for divorce. "Everything has to be done properly. Whenever I feel it's the right time, I will."

Snapping pictures, and declaring his intention to draw cartoons and write a book, Richard unrolled his usual crazy-uncle routine at the Open. Before leaving the grounds and heading home to Florida in the hours leading up to the women's final, he refused to talk about the reason for the separation, but allegations of spousal abuse appear to be part of it. On Feb. 7, 1999, Oracene went to a hospital near the Williamses' home in Palm Beach Gardens, Fla., for treatment of three broken ribs. After telling investigators she had injured herself on a door handle, Oracene told a deputy from the sheriff's office, "I know you know what happened, but I am fearful for my daughters' careers."

When asked about the incident by SI

last January, Williams family lawyer Keven Davis said Richard had been out of town at the time Oracene sustained the broken ribs. When SI asked Oracene in May whether Richard had assaulted her, she said, "It happened. I can't deny that. I would like to deny that, but I can't because it's the truth."

At this year's Open, Oracene and Richard rarely came in contact with each other. The two have agreed to work together on decisions regarding their daughters' careers but, said Oracene last Saturday, "that's it. It's so important for the girls, you have to have that cohesiveness—and they have to believe that. Otherwise they can be torn apart. I would not allow that."

Neither Serena nor Venus would comment on her parents' split, but Oracene said it has affected them "even if they act like it doesn't. They've been able to cope with it, but I know it hurts them. They won't say anything, but I know. They've been able to deal with it, and now they're going on."

On Saturday night the Williams sisters

went on just fine. As in their five previous meetings (Venus had won four), the play was uninspired. There have been not-so-veiled suggestions that Richard had predetermined the outcome of their matches, but after Venus again dominated Serena, the reason for their lackluster meetings appeared obvious. First, neither has faced a player with the speed and power of the other. Second, Serena is intimidated by Venus, as if the idea of supplanting her sister's place in the family pecking order is unthinkable.

When they addressed the crowd after the final, Venus spoke so emotionally of how much she loved Serena and wanted to look out for her that Serena started crying. "She always goes extra—sometimes too much—worrying about Serena," Serena said. "But she's got to realize: I didn't win this time. Enjoy it, because it might be my time next time."

—S.L. Price
excerpted from SI, Sept. 17, 2001

Andy Roddick

It's amazing the number of things 18-year-old Andy Roddick did wrong in his debut at Roland Garros. He didn't practice on the unfamiliar Court Philippe Chatrier before his first match there, against former French Open champ Michael Chang in the second round. He ignored advice to consume bananas and other mineral-rich foods to prevent the cramps that would nearly cripple him in the fifth set of that match. When playing Lleyton Hewitt in the third round, Roddick didn't ask for a three-minute injury break after he apparently strained his left hamstring. Instead he played four more points, then retired.

None of it mattered. No player made a bigger splash during the 2001 French Open. Asked how he felt after Chang's backhand flew wide to give Roddick a 5–7, 6–3, 6–4, 6–7, 7–5 victory, Roddick said, "I almost wanted to cry, but I wanted to scream and yell at the same time."

Plenty of fans felt the same way after that thriller. There was Roddick blasting 129 mph serves and then whirling like a scarecrow on a stick as his body buckled in pain. At 4–4 in the fifth set, Roddick's coach gestured from the stands for him to quit. Roddick shook his head.

As that match showed, there is much to love about Roddick's game. He already has one of the best serves on the tour, a cracking forehand and high energy. He works the crowd effortlessly. The day after the Chang match, players criticized Roddick for having torn off his shirt following his win. After the Hewitt match, many of his peers wondered how injured Roddick was, given that he'd gone to a dance club that same night.

In fact, soon after retiring in the Hewitt match, Roddick had an ultrasound that confirmed he had strained his hamstring.…Regardless, Roddick said he plans to play at Wimbledon.

He has the skills to do well there, but Paris also highlighted his weaknesses: a shaky backhand, a willfulness that can override wisdom and a fragile body. Roddick had arthroscopic knee surgery last year to repair minor ligament damage. As Andre Agassi said on Saturday, "He really needs to take care of himself."

—S.L. Price
excerpted from SI, June 11, 2001

Roddick won three singles titles in 2001, and reached the third round of Wimbledon and the quarterfinals of the U.S. Open —Ed.

THE NUMBERS

2001 Grand Slam Results

AUSTRALIAN OPEN
Men's Singles

WINNER	OPPONENT	SCORE
QUARTERFINALS		
Andre Agassi (6)	Todd Martin	7–5, 6–3, 6–4
Sebastien Grosjean (16)	Carlos Moya	6–1, 6–4, 6–2
Arnaud Clement (15)	Yevgeny Kafelnikov (5)	6–4, 5–7, 7–6 (7–3),7–6 (7–3)
Patrick Rafter (12)	Dominik Hrbaty (14)	6–2, 6–7 (4–7), 7–5, 6–0
SEMIFINALS		
Andre Agassi	Patrick Rafter	7–5, 2–6, 6–7 (5–7), 6–2, 6–3
Arnaud Clement	Sebastien Grosjean	5–7, 2–6, 7–6 (7–4), 7–5, 6–2
FINAL		
Andre Agassi	Arnaud Clement	6–4, 6–2, 6–2

Women's Singles

WINNER	OPPONENT	SCORE
QUARTERFINALS		
Martina Hingis (1)	Serena Williams (6)	6–2, 3–6, 8–6
Venus Williams (3)	Amanda Coetzer (10)	2–6, 6–1, 8–6
Jennifer Capriati (12)	Monica Seles (4)	5–7, 6–4, 6–3
Lindsay Davenport (2)	Anna Kournikova (8)	6–3, 4–6, 9–7
SEMIFINALS		
Martina Hingis	Venus Williams	6–1, 6–1
Jennifer Capriati	Lindsay Davenport	6–3, 6–4
FINAL		
Jennifer Capriati	Martina Hingis	6–4, 6–3

Note: Seedings in parentheses.

FRENCH OPEN
Men's Singles

WINNER	OPPONENT	SCORE
QUARTERFINALS		
Alex Corretja (13)	Roger Federer	7–5, 6–4, 7–5
Sebastien Grosjean (10)	Andre Agassi (3)	1–6, 6–1, 6–1, 6–3,
Gustavo Kuerten (1)	Yevgeny Kafelnikov (7)	6–1, 3–6, 7–6 (7–3), 6–4
Juan Carlos Ferrero (4)	Lleyton Hewitt (6)	6–4, 6–2, 6–1
SEMIFINALS		
Alex Corretja	Sebastien Grosjean	7–6 (7–2), 6–4, 6–4
Gustavo Kuerten	Juan Carlos Ferrero	6–4, 6–4, 6–3
FINAL		
Gustavo Kuerten	Alex Corretja	6–7 (3–7), 7–5, 6–2, 6–0

Women's Singles

WINNER	OPPONENT	SCORE
QUARTERFINALS		
Martina Hingis (1)	Chanda Rubin	6–1, 6–3
Mary Pierce (6)	Monica Seles (3)	6–4, 3–6, 6–4
Arantxa Sánchez Vicario (8)	Venus Williams (4)	6–0, 1–6, 6–2
Conchita Martinez (5)	Marta Marrero	7–6 (7–5), 6–1
SEMIFINALS		
Mary Pierce	Martina Hingis	6–4, 5–7, 6–2
Conchita Martinez	Arantxa Sánchez Vicario	6–1, 6–2
FINAL		
Mary Pierce	Conchita Martinez	6–2, 7–5

Note: Seedings in parentheses.

WIMBLEDON
Men's Singles

WINNER	OPPONENT	SCORE
QUARTERFINALS		
Patrick Rafter (3)	Thomas Enqvist (10)	6–1, 6–3, 7–6 (7–5)
Goran Ivanisevic	Marat Safin (4)	7–6 (7–2), 7–5, 3–6, 7–6 (7–3)
Andre Agassi (2)	Nicolas Escude (24)	6–7 (3), 6–3, 6–4, 6–2
Tim Henman (6)	Roger Federer (15)	7–5, 7–6 (8–6), 2–6, 7–6 (8–6)
SEMIFINALS		
Patrick Rafter	Andre Agassi	2–6, 6–3, 3–6, 6–2,8–6
Goran Ivanisevic	Tim Henman	7–5, 6–7(6–8), 0–6, 7–6 (7–5), 6–3
FINAL		
Goran Ivanisevic	Patrick Rafter	6–3, 3–6, 6–3, 2–6, 9–7

Women's Singles

WINNER	OPPONENT	SCORE
QUARTERFINALS		
Jennifer Capriati (4)	Serena Williams (5)	6–7 (4–7), 7–5, 6–3
Justine Henin (8)	Conchita Martinez (19)	6–1, 6–0
Venus Williams (2)	Nathalie Tauziat (9)	7–5, 6–1
Lindsay Davenport (3)	Kim Clijsters (7)	6–1, 6–2
SEMIFINALS		
Justine Henin	Jennifer Capriati	2–6, 6–4, 6–2
Venus Williams	Lindsay Davenport	6–2, 6–7 (1–7), 6–1
FINAL		
Venus Williams	Justine Henin	6–1, 3–6, 6–0

Note: Seedings in parentheses.

U.S. OPEN
Men's Singles

WINNER	OPPONENT	SCORE
QUARTERFINALS		
Yevgeny Kafelnikov (7)	Gustavo Kuerten (1)	6–4, 6–0, 6–3,
Lleyton Hewitt (4)	Andy Roddick (18)	6–7 (5–7), 6–3, 6–4, 3–6, 6–4
Marat Safin (3)	Mariano Zabaleta	6–4, 6–4, 6–2
Pete Sampras (10)	Andre Agassi (2)	6–7 (7–9), 7–6 (7–2), 7–6 (7–2), 7–6 (7–5)
SEMIFINALS		
Lleyton Hewitt	Yevgeny Kafelnikov	6–1, 6–2, 6–1
Pete Sampras	Marat Safin	6–3, 7–6 (7–5), 6–3
FINAL		
Lleyton Hewitt (4)	Pete Sampras (10)	7–6 (7–4), 6–1, 6–1

Women's Singles

WINNER	OPPONENT	SCORE
QUARTERFINALS		
Venus Williams (4)	Kim Clijsters (5)	6–3, 6–1
Jennifer Capriati (2)	Amelie Mauresmo (8)	6–3, 6–4
Martina Hingis (1)	Daja Bedanova	6–2, 6–0
Serena Williams (10)	Lindsay Davenport (3)	6–3, 6–7 (5–7), 7–5
SEMIFINALS		
Serena Williams	Martina Hingis	6–3, 6–2
Venus Williams	Jennifer Capriati	6–4, 6–2
FINAL		
Venus Williams	Serena Williams	6–2, 6–4

Note: Seedings in parentheses.

Major Tournament Results

MEN'S TOUR

DATE	TOURNAMENT	SITE	WINNER	FINALIST	SCORE
Jan 1–7	Qatar Open	Doha, Qatar	Marcelo Rios	Bohdan Ulihrach	6–3, 2–6, 6–3
Jan 15–28	Australian Open	Melbourne	Andre Agassi	Arnaud Clement	6–4, 6–2, 6–2
Feb 12–18	Marseille Open	Marseille, France	Yevgeny Kafelnikov	Sebastien Grosjean	7–6 (7–5), 6–2
Feb 19–25	ABN/Amro Tournament	Rotterdam, The Netherlands	Nicolas Escude	Roger Federer	7–5, 3–6, 7–6 (7–5)
Feb 19–25	Kroger St. Jude	Memphis	Mark Philippoussis	Davide Sanguinetti	6–3, 6–7 (5–7), 6–3
Feb 26–Mar 3	Dubai Open	Dubai, UAE	Juan Carlos Ferrero	Marat Safin	6–2, 3–1, retired

Major Tournament Results *(Cont.)*

MEN'S TOUR

DATE	TOURNAMENT	SITE	WINNER	FINALIST	SCORE
Mar 12–18	Champions Cup	Indian Wells, CA	Andre Agassi	Pete Sampras	7–6 (7–5), 7–5, 6–1
Mar 21–Apr 1	Ericsson Open	Miami	Andre Agassi	Jan-Michael Gambill	7–6 (7–4), 6–1, 6–0
Apr 9–15	Estoril Open	Estoril, Portugal	Juan Carlos Ferrero	Felix Mantilla	7–6 (7–3), 4–6, 6–3
Apr 16–22	Monte Carlo Open	Monte Carlo	Gustavo Kuerten	Hicham Arazi	6–3, 6–2, 6–4
Apr 23–29	Open Seat Godo	Barcelona	Juan Carlos Ferrero	Carlos Moya	4–6, 7–5, 6–3, 3–6, 7–5
Apr 23–29	Verizon Tennis Challenge	Atlanta	Andy Roddick	Xavier Malisse	6–2, 6–4
Apr 30–May 6	BMW Open	Munich	Jiri Novak	Anthony Dupuis	6–4, 7–5
May 7–13	Italian Open	Rome	Juan Carlos Ferrero	Gustavo Kuerten	3–6, 6–1, 2–6, 6–4, 6–2
May14–20	German Open	Hamburg	Albert Portas	Juan Carlos Ferrero	4–6, 6–2, 0–6, 7–6, (7–5), 7–5
May 28–Jun 10	French Open	Paris	Gustavo Kuerten	Alex Corretja	6–7 (3–7), 7–5, 6–2, 6–0
June 11–17	Gerry Weber Open	Halle, Germany	Thomas Johansson	Frabice Santoro	6–3, 6–7 (5–7), 6–2
June 18–24	Heineken Trophy	S-Hertogenbosch, The Neth.	Lleyton Hewitt	Guillermo Canas	6–3, 6–4
June 25–July 9	Wimbledon	Wimbledon	Goran Ivanisevic	Patrick Rafter	6–3, 3–6, 6–3, 2–6, 9–7
July 10–15	Gstaad Open	Gstaad, Switzerland	Jiri Novak	Juan Carlos Ferrero	6–1, 6–7 (5–7), 7–5
July 16–22	Mercedes Cup	Stuttgart, Germany	Gustavo Kuerten	Guillermo Canas	6–3, 6–2, 6–4
July 23–29	Generali Open	Kitzbuhel, Austria	Nicolas Lapentti	Albert Costa	1–6, 6–4, 7–5, 7–5
Jul 30–Aug 5	Canadian Open	Montreal	Andrei Pavel	Patrick Rafter	7–6 (7–3), 2–6, 6–3
Aug 6–12	Tennis Masters Series	Cincinnati	Gustavo Kuerten	Patrick Rafter	6–1, 6–3
Aug 13–19	RCA Championships	Indianapolis	Patrick Rafter	Gustavo Kuerten	4–2, retired
Aug 13–19	Legg Mason Classic	Washington, D.C.	Andy Roddick	Sjeng Schalken	6–2, 6–3
Aug 27–Sept 9	U.S. Open	New York City	Lleyton Hewitt	Pete Sampras	7–6 (7–4), 6–1, 6–1
Sept 10–16	President's Cup	Tashkent, Uzbekistan	Marat Safin	Yevgeny Kafelnikov	6–2, 6–2
Sept 17–23	Heineken Open	Shanghai	Rainer Schuettler	Michel Kratochvil	6–3, 6–4
Sept 24–30	Salem Open	Hong Kong	Marcelo Rios	Rainer Schuettler	7–6 (7–3), 6–2
Oct 1–7	Kremlin Cup	Moscow	Yevgeny Kafelnikov	Nicolas Kiefer	6–4, 7–5
Oct 8–14	CA Tennis Trophy	Vienna	Tommy Haas	Guillermo Canas	6–2, 7–6 (8–6), 6–4
Oct 15–21	Tennis Masters Series	Stuttgart, Germany	Tommy Haas	Max Mirnyi	6–2, 6–2, 6–2
Oct 22–28	Swiss Indoors	Basel, Switzerland	Tim Henman	Roger Federer	6–3, 6–4, 6–2
Oct 22–28	St. Petersburg Open	St. Petersburg, Russia	Marat Safin	Rainer Schuettler	3–6, 6–3, 6–3
Oct 22–28	Stockholm Open	Stockholm	Sjeng Schalken	Jarkko Nieminen	3–6, 6–3, 6–3, 4–6, 6–3
Oct 29–Nov 4	Tennis Masters Series	Paris	Sebastien Grosjean	Yevgeny Kafelnikov	7–6 (7–3), 6–1, 6–7 (5–7), 6–4
Nov 12–18	Tennis Masters Cup	Sydney	Lleyton Hewitt	Sebastien Grosjean	6–3, 6–3, 6–4

WOMEN'S TOUR

DATE	TOURNAMENT	SITE	WINNER	FINALIST	SCORE
Jan 7–13	Adidas International	Sydney	Martina Hingis	Lindsay Davenport	6–3, 4–6, 7–5
Jan 15–28	Australian Open	Melbourne	Jennfier Capriati	Martina Hingis	6–4, 6–3
Jan 30–Feb 4	Pan Pacific Open	Tokyo	Lindsay Davenport	Martina Hingis	6–7 (4–7), 6–4, 6–2
Feb 5–11	Open Gaz de France	Paris	Amelie Mauresmo	Anke Huber	7–6 (7–2), 6–1
Feb 14–20	Qatar Open	Doha, Qatar	Martina Hingis	Sandrine Testud	6–3, 6–2
Mar 5–18	Tennis Masters Series	Indian Wells, CA	Serena Williams	Kim Clijsters	4–6, 6–4, 6–2
Mar 21–Apr 1	Ericsson Open	Miami	Venus Williams	Jennifer Capriati	4–6, 6–1, 7–6 (7–4)
Apr 9–15	Bausch & Lomb Champs.	Amelia Island, Florida	Amelie Mauresmo	Amanda Coetzer	6–4, 7–5
Apr 16–22	Family Circle Cup	Charleston, SC	Jennifer Capriati	Martina Hingis	6–0, 4–6, 6–4
Apr 30–May 6	Betty Barclay Cup	Hamburg	Venus Williams	Megann Shaughnessy	6–3, 6–0
May 7–13	German Open	Berlin	Amelie Mauresmo	Jennifer Capriati	6–4, 2–6, 6–3
May 14–20	Tennis Masters Series	Rome	Jelena Dokic	Amelie Mauresmo	7–6 (7–3), 6–1
May 21–27	Int'l de Strasbourg	Strasbourg, France	Silvia Farena Elia	Anke Huber	7–5, 0–6, 6–4
May 28–Jun 9	French Open	Paris	Jennifer Capriati	Kim Clijsters	1–6, 6–4, 12–10
June 18–24	Britannic Asset Champs.	Eastbourne, England	Lindsay Davenport	Magui Serna	6–2, 6–0
June 25–July 8	Wimbledon	Wimbledon	Venus Williams	Justine Henin	6–1, 3–6, 6–0
July 23–29	Bank of the West	Stanford	Kim Clijsters	Lindsay Davenport	6–4, 6–7 (5–7), 6–1
July 30–Aug 5	Acura Classic	San Diego	Venus Williams	Monica Seles	6–2, 6–3
Aug 6–12	Estyle.com Classic	Los Angeles	Lindsay Davenport	Monica Seles	6–3, 7–5
Aug 13–19	Rogers AT&T Cup	Toronto	Serena Williams	Jennifer Capriati	6–1, 6–7 (7–9), 6–3
Aug 19–25	Pilot Pen Int'l	New Haven, CT	Venus Williams	Lindsay Davenport	7–6 (8–6), 6–4
Aug 28–Sept 10	U.S. Open	New York City	Venus Williams	Serena Williams	6–2, 6–4
Sept 10–16	Brazil Open	Costa do Sauipe, Brazil	Monica Seles	Jelena Dokic	6–3, 6–3
Sept 10–16	Big Island Championship	Waikoloa, Hawaii	Sandrine Testud	Justine Henin	6–3, 2–0, retired
Sept 17–23	Princess Cup	Tokyo	Jelena Dokic	Arantxa Sánchez-Vicario	6–4, 6–2
Sept 24–30	Sparkassen Cup	Leipzig, Germany	Kim Clijsters	Magdalena Maleeva	6–1, 6–1
Oct 1–7	Japan Open	Tokyo	Monica Seles	Tamarine Tanasugarn	6–3, 6–2
Oct 1–7	Kremlin Cup	Moscow	Jelena Dokic	Elena Dementieva	6–3, 6–3
Oct 8–14	Porsche Tennis Grand Prix	Filderstadt, Germany	Lindsay Davenport	Justine Henin	7–5, 6–4
Oct 8–14	Kiwi Open	Shanghai	Monica Seles	Nicole Pratt	6–2, 6–3
Oct 15–21	Swisscom Challenge	Zurich	Lindsay Davenport	Jelena Dokic	6–3, 6–1
Oct 22–28	Generali Ladies Open	Linz, Austria	Lindsay Davenport	Jelena Dokic	6–4, 6–1
Oct 22–28	Seat Open	Luxembourg	Kim Clijsters	Lisa Raymond	6–2, 6–2
Oct 29–Nov 4	Sanex Championships	Munich	Serena Williams	Lindsay Davenport	walkover
Nov 5–11	Volvo Women's Open	Pattaya City, Thailand	Patty Schnyder	Henrieta Nagyova	6–0, 6–4

Caged Tiger

Trapped by his own impossibly high standards, golf's top player ceded the spotlight to others in 2001

MARK BEECH

Famous for his near misses in majors as well as his icy demeanor, Duval (opposite) warmed up to Royal Lytham and won the 2001 British Open by three strokes.

It's not easy knowing that you're second-best. Just ask David Duval and Phil Mickelson. They are two of the top three golfers in the world, players so talented that in past eras they probably could have counted on winning one or more of golf's Grand Slam events before their careers were over. But unfortunately for them, they compete in the looming shadow of Tiger Woods, the greatest golfer of their, or perhaps any, generation, which makes counting on anything more than a bit presumptuous.

At the beginning of 2001, Duval and Mickelson were trying to escape their ignominious designations as the best players never to have won a major championship. Duval was able to shed that nom de guerre in July, with a convincing victory at the British Open, while Mickelson wore the mantle like a millstone around his neck, coming up just short in the Masters, the U.S. Open and the PGA Championship. Woods, of course, eclipsed everybody despite producing what was, for him, a disappointing season. He won only one major tournament, the Masters at Augusta National in April, but that victory completed a historic sweep that had begun the year before, with victories in the U.S. and British Opens and the PGA Championship.

Because he did not win all four titles in the same calendar year, Woods's sweep wasn't unanimously accepted as a Grand Slam, but that hardly mattered. "I would imagine it was the same way when people were competing against Jack Nicklaus," Duval said after finishing second to Woods in the Masters. "We've got another player who is certainly the best player in the game right now. It's very difficult to win these events. To have your game at the right place at the right time, there's an art to that. It's an accomplishment for him that I don't know what you would compare it to, because I'm not so sure there's something you could compare it with, certainly not in modern golf."

In addition to making him the only player to hold all four major titles at once, Woods's victory at Augusta proved his resourcefulness; it showed that he can win in a variety of ways. Unlike in 1997, when he ran away from the field to win by 12 strokes at Augusta, he bled the 65th Masters to death, bit by bit, picking up a stroke here and another there. Knowing he didn't have his best stuff, Woods didn't press. He watched little-known Chris DiMarco lead the field into the weekend, then turned it on and outlasted Duval and Mickelson on Sunday. Only when Woods holed an 18-footer for a birdie on 18 and a two-stroke victory did he betray how desperately he had wanted to win, covering his eyes with his cap as he leaked tears of triumph. "It was a great putt," he said. "I walked over to the side, and I started thinking, I don't have any more shots to play. I'm done. I just won the Masters."

For Mickelson, 31, his third-place finish at Augusta was the prelude to a tough-luck year. In June, at the U.S. Open at Southern Hills Country Club in Tulsa, Mickelson was two strokes off the lead heading into the final round. But he shot a 75 on Sunday and finished six strokes behind surprise winner Retief Goosen, who defeated Mark Brooks in an 18-hole playoff. At the PGA Championship in Georgia in August, Mickelson had his first major title within reach, only to watch David Toms—who aced No. 15 on Saturday to take the lead—sink a 12-foot birdie putt on the final hole to beat him by a stroke. "I'm confident in the way I have been able to play in these championships," said Mickelson, who had three-putted for bogey on No. 16 to let Toms get away. "But it's frustrating that I haven't been able to break through. I know the off-season will be long. I felt this would be a breakthrough year. I've been playing better than ever. But I wasn't able to beat everyone in the field."

Duval, for his part, produced the kind of year

In her seventh season on the tour, the 26-year-old Webb (above) became the youngest woman to achieve a career Grand Slam when she won the LPGA Championship in Wilmington, Del., in June.

that had been expected of him ever since he shot a 59 at the Bob Hope Desert Classic in 1999. His talent had always gone unquestioned, but he had failed in 26 previous attempts to win a major; one of those losses came at the 1998 Masters, when he blew a three-shot lead to Mark O'Meara over the final three holes. That letdown became a distant memory at the 2001 British Open, though, as Duval swung his way through the mighty course at Royal Lytham and St. Annes, in England, to win his long-overdue first major. Playing with a more relaxed attitude after taking two weeks off to go mountain biking and fishing, he cruised through the final two rounds at 10 under par. "I beat them

all this week," Duval said. "I played really well, and it feels wonderful. I don't know if I can savor it any more than I am now."

As for Woods, though he won the Masters and spent much of the year atop most of the PGA's significant statistical categories (including money won), his failure to win a second major caused many people to see his year as a disappointment—a testament to how preposterously high Woods's performances have raised expectations. The most popular explanations for Tiger's "subpar" year were (in no particular order): that he'd burned out on golf; that he'd sold out to play in too many made-for-TV exhibitions; that he was distracted by his numerous product-endorsement responsibilities; that he was in love with Gabrielle Reece, the model, volleyball player and aspiring golfer; that he was injured; and that he had altered his swing.

Whatever the reason, it probably won't be a problem too much longer. It will be interesting to see if Duval can continue to challenge Woods in 2002 and if Mickelson will be able to challenge him at all.

For the second straight year, two of the four LPGA majors went to Karrie Webb, 26, of Australia. Webb defended her U.S. Women's Open title and added the LPGA Championship prize to her burgeoning trophy case. (She won the Nabisco Championships in 2000.)

Webb's dominance in the majors came as a bit of a surprise this year because of the way Annika Sorenstam, 31, Webb's good friend and chief rival on the LPGA tour, began the season. Sorenstam won four tournaments in a row, a streak capped by the Office Depot title in April. Her most impressive feat during that run came when she fired a second-round 59 at the Standard Register Ping, in Phoenix, the lowest tournament round in the history of women's golf. On the way to that score, she rang up 13 birdies and no bogeys. "I'm absolutely overwhelmed," she said moments after the round. "I can't believe what I just did. Now I see what I can shoot when the putts go in."

But Sorenstam crashed in the U.S. Open, finishing 16th, well behind Webb, who became the first back-to-back Open winner since Sorenstam in 1995 and '96. Webb followed her Open triumph with an emotional victory in the LPGA. Her 71-year-old maternal grandfather, Mick Collinson, had suffered a stroke earlier in the week in Queensland. On the morning of the final round, a shaky Webb learned that he had taken a turn for the worse, and after debating with her family about whether or not to return home, she pressed on to complete a career Grand Slam. "I wanted to win, but I wasn't overly concerned if I didn't," Webb said. "A part of me wanted to play anyway. The fact that my family wanted me to do it is what changed my mind." (Collinson died a few days later.)

Though Webb couldn't prevent Se Ri Pak from winning the Women's British Open in August, her impact on the women's game can hardly be overestimated. Webb forces her competitors to raise their games, just as Woods does on the PGA Tour. And as is also the case with Woods, no matter how high her peers lift their level of play, Webb's game usually goes a little higher.

What was an off year for Woods (above) would have been a career year for most of his rivals: the 25-year-old superstar won five tournaments, including the Masters, and led the tour in scoring and earnings.

PHOTO GALLERY

Spain's Sergio Garcia (left) must have felt like kicking himself after he fell out of contention at the U.S. Open with a final-round score of 77. The 21-year-old would rebound the following week to win the Buick Classic in Harrison, N.Y., by three shots over Scott Hoch.

Annika Sorenstam (above) took a celebratory bath after winning the Nabisco Championship in March. The undisputed star of the LPGA during the spring, Sorenstam won four straight tournaments and became the first woman to break 60 for a round, shooting a 59 at the Standard Register Ping in March.

Tiger Woods (left, teeing off) had his string of victories in four straight majors snapped at Southern Hills, where he shot an opening-round 74 to curtail his chances of repeating as U.S. Open champion. He shot back-to-back 69s during the weekend but still finished seven strokes behind the winner, Retief Goosen of South Africa.

PROFILES

David Toms

David Toms (right), a down-the-middle golfer with a plain manner and the drab clothes of the modern professional, had just made a hole in one. It was a 227-yard shot, over a pond, that landed on the green and bounced three times before smacking the flagstick and disappearing into 15th hole at the Atlanta Athletic Club. This was in mid-August 2001, in the third round of the PGA Championship. Suddenly Toms, at age 34, had a one-stroke lead in the year's last major—a one-stroke lead over the anti-Toms, the flamboyant Phil Mickelson, with his alligator-skin shoes and his Hugo Boss duds and his outsized talent.

For a moment Toms looked as though he didn't know what to do. His playing partner, Shingo Katayama of Japan, with the toy rodeo hat and the infectious enthusiasm, was smiling more than Toms was at the ace. Then Toms, a lifelong Louisianan, started whooping as if he were at one of his beloved LSU football games. The crowd whooped it up too, as it does whenever a hole in one is made, but it wasn't the kind of pandemonium that would have erupted if Mickelson had hit the shot. Mickelson was at the next hole. "I heard the noise," he said after the round. "It didn't sound to me like a hole in one." He wasn't being mean, only truthful. Had Mickelson made that ace, he would have put on his "aw, just lucky again," Cheshire-cat grin, and his fans would have been delirious.…

Mickelson has won 19 Tour events. He is the best player never to have won a major, and, as gracefully as he wears that sash, he was ready to bury it.

Toms is a more anonymous sort. He had won five times on the Tour before last week but has no million-dollar endorsement deals.…

The two men came to Atlanta with a bit of shared history, although Mickelson may not have known it. When he was at Arizona State and Toms at LSU, they

played in the same NCAA tournament in 1989. (Mickelson, a freshman, won it; Toms, a senior, finished eighth.) Toms was a nice college player, even made All-America in the 1988–89 season. Mickelson was a legend, a prodigy who holed impossible shots. He was a four-time first-team All-America. In January 1991, when Mickelson was a college junior, he won a Tour event, the Tucson Open. At that moment Toms, who turned pro in '89, was packing his bags for the Asian tour, going wherever he needed to go to learn the professional game.

On Sunday afternoon at the PGA they were paired in the final group, the only two golfers in the field to have broken 200 for the first three rounds. (Toms had shot 66, 65, 65—14 under par on the par-70 course, which measures 7,213 yards. Mickelson had shot 66, 66, 66.)

Toms, even though he was outdriven by Mickelson by 50 yards on some holes, was still leading by two. Then came the 15th. The flashy one chipped in for a birdie, while Toms found a bunker off the tee and made a bogey. Mickelson had a share of the lead again....

He did not seize the moment. He rattled his next tee shot into the trees, leaving himself 180 yards to the green. His approach shot finished 45 feet below the hole.... Mickelson bogeyed to fall to 14 under. Toms, steady as a drumbeat, made par to remain at 15 under.

Both golfers made par on 17, setting up a showdown on the 18th.... Mickelson plays heroic shots, in the tradition of Arnold Palmer. Often he pulls them off. That's why he's popular.

Toms plays modest shots, rooted in realism. With a downhill lie, a third of the ball submerged in grass and 209 yards to the hole, he blocked out the voices in the crowd urging him to go for broke with his magical five-wood. Instead he hit a pitching wedge to 88 yards, then hit a full lob wedge 10 feet from the hole.

Off the tee Mickelson had drilled a three-wood long and in the fairway. He then smashed his approach shot to 25 feet, left his birdie putt three inches short and tapped in. He had done all he could. Now it was his opponent's turn. Toms read the putt with a clear mind. His stroke was perfect, and the putt dropped for a closing 69 and a four-round total of 265. Nobody has taken fewer strokes in a major.

It was 10 minutes before a disconsolate Mickelson reached his wife, Amy, who is seven months pregnant. They kissed. "I'm all right," the golfer said wearily. He looked like a man whose dog had just been run over.

A few feet away Sonya Toms had moments earlier made a call on her cell phone, changing an airline reservation. "We definitely cannot make the 8 o'clock flight," she said gleefully.

—Michael Bamberger
excerpted from SI, August 27, 2001

Se Ri Pak

Local knowledge is to golf what having the combination is to safecracking: a big edge. Se Ri Pak reaffirmed that last week when she won her third major championship, the 2001 Women's British Open, on a course so foreign to her that she almost expected to see water run uphill and doves fly out of the cups. "I don't have any idea how to play this kind of golf," she said on Sunday after coming from four strokes back in the final round at Sunningdale Golf Club to win by two over fellow Korean Mi Hyun Kim. "But he knew."

He was Colin Cann, Pak's caddie. Cann lives just up the road in breakfasty-sounding Egham, and he's probably the guy you want on your bag when you play for big bucks in Surrey. "It's a very different style of golf from what you have in America," Cann said after the tournament. "Look at how this course changed every day. First it was bone-hard, then soft and wet, the wind kept moving around...."

That's England for you. Three years ago, in her only previous appearance at the British Open, Pak slogged around Royal Lytham and St. Annes in wind, rain and bewilderment. "I played so bad," she recalled on Sunday night. "I said to myself, I can't come back, because it was so hard." It was startling, then, to see Pak light up Sunningdale's 6,277-yard Old Course with a final-round six-under-par 66. "Colin said English golf is fun," Pak would say later—and yeah, the gnarly heather and goofy bounces are a treat when you're winning $221,650 and the champion's crystal bowl. The hardest part was the waiting. Pak spent a nervous 50 minutes behind the 18th green, under the famous Sunningdale oak tree, while 10 other players dragged themselves up the final fairway. Meanwhile, Pak's mother, Jeong Sook Kim, patted Cann on the back and said, "Good job!"

Good timing, too. This year the British became one of the four major titles of women's golf, replacing the defunct du Maurier Classic, and winning it left Pak only one title (the Nabisco Championship) short of a career Grand Slam.

Did the Open feel like a major? Yes and no. At a major the players act as if winning is more important than life itself. They show up a week early to study the greens with a transit and level, or cut out activities that don't directly contribute to victory, such as dining out or reading bedtime stories to their children. By that standard this Open seemed minor. Free-spirited Laura Davies, needing only two points to qualify for the LPGA Hall of Fame, hosted a 12-team soccer tournament in the yard of her Surrey mansion, complete with painted lines, regulation goals and a food-and-drink van. More shocking was the late arrival of Annika Sorenstam and Karrie Webb. The tour's two best players deplaned blinking on Tuesday night, hung over from their Battle at Bighorn exhibition involving Tiger Woods and David Duval. "It was not the ideal way to prepare for a major," conceded LPGA commissioner Ty Votaw, but "it showed an enormous commitment on their part to expose the LPGA to millions of viewers."

Votaw's opinion was not shared by David Davies of *The Guardian*, who considered Webb's first-round 74 at Sunningdale insufficient punishment for having agreed to play under floodlights in front

Davies, who shot 76 and finished 25th.

The troubles of the star players swung the spotlight to Scotland's Catriona Matthew, who's having a breakthrough year in the U.S. "Cat" holed out from the 18th fairway for eagle on Thursday and clawed into the lead Friday with the help of a 216-yard hole in one on 15. On Sunday, alas, she was catatonic, shooting 73 and slipping into a four-way tie for third. Tied with her was Laura Diaz, who birdied the first six holes that day to secure low-American honors.

The 23-year-old Pak (left), meanwhile, began her final round as if she were playing a pro-am. "My caddie and I said, 'Nothing to lose today,'" she said. "I didn't have any chance, so we had fun out there." It was a far different Pak, in other words, from the stressed-out young woman who failed to win in 2000 after winning four times in each of her first two full LPGA seasons. "The first two years [were] so busy, I don't know what happened. I was looking very tight. But now I play, and it's fun."

The real fun started when Pak got to 14 and saw her name on the leader board with that of Kim, her 24-year-old compatriot. The 5' 1" Kim, who has a swing so big that the clubhead almost touches the ground on her backswing, looks as if she should be selling Girl Scout cookies, but she is a birdie machine and has three LPGA wins. Pak, though, had the local knowledge. When Cann told her to land the ball 20 yards short of a green, she did so, and more often than not the ball bounced, hopped and rolled into birdie range. "He knew the course," Pak said.

That was enough, because Pak knew herself. The cool Korean birdied 17 and 18 for a total of 277, 11 under par. "Love my job," said Cann, hugging Pak under the tree.

Love that British golf, said Pak, hugging the crystal bowl. "I wasn't doing well this week, but right now I'm the last person talking in the media center. Got a trophy." She grinned. "That is a huge difference."

Correction, Se Ri. That is a major difference.

—John Garrity
excerpted from SI, August 13, 2001

of yelling yahoos. "For Webb to put such a hollow occasion ahead of trying to win her third successive major championship is simply baffling," Davies wrote.

To be fair, Webb had more than Bighorn to blame for her lack of form. Her grandfather, to whom she was very close, died in Australia a month ago, leaving her unsettled emotionally. Webb's swing was also out of sync at Sunningdale, and her disposition wasn't much better. She threw her putter on one hole, pounded her driver on the ground on another. Asked how many putts she had taken on Thursday, Webb snapped, "You can count them." (Headline in *The Daily Telegraph*: WEBB HER OWN WORST ENEMY.)

Even the infrastructure seemed to conspire against Webb. Sunningdale's spacious practice range was being used for tournament parking, so the players had only a warmup range with limited tee space. "This isn't a driving range where I can set up a camera and look at my swing," Webb said after rebounding with a 67 on Friday, "so I have to count on feel. My swing hasn't felt right in a while."

By Saturday, though, it was apparent that method of attack, not mode of preparation, would determine the outcome. Sunningdale is a heathland course with many of the properties of a links course, including hard, fast fairways and capricious weather. It opens with two easy par 5s but closes with three long par 4s. "The finish is a tremendous test," says Cann. "Birdies are rare."

Webb bookended rounds of 67 and 68 with a pair of 74s and finished 15th. Sorenstam struggled after a first-round 70 and ended up 32nd. Laura Davies, who was in contention for three rounds, bogeyed the first hole on Sunday when her ball hit a rake—misplaced by "some cretin," she said—and bounced into the sand. "The heart went out of me," said

Annika Sorenstam

Lori Kane, acting as Annika Sorenstam's unofficial press agent, wanted to know what it takes to get some attention for women's golf. "I know that here in America everyone is going crazy over March Madness," Kane said on the eve of the 2001 Nabisco Championship, the first major event of the LPGA season. "But I don't care. If you shoot 59, that is just a great score." Kane leaned forward: "I tell you, when those guys on ESPN talk about the important sports, they neglect us."

Sorenstam's recent accomplishments did not go unnoticed among golf fans: two second-place finishes followed by two consecutive wins—the more recent of which featured a second-round 59, the lowest tournament round in the history of women's golf, plus LPGA records for low 36-hole, 54-hole and 72-hole totals. Anyway, Kane's *J'accuse* was so shopworn that it sounded like something recorded on vinyl by, say, Aretha Franklin. So it was up to Sorenstam herself to demonstrate what it takes to get more attention. She did that very nicely at the Nabisco, winning her third straight tournament, her third major and the 26th title of her 7½-year pro career. Then, as if defying *SportsCenter* to ignore her, Sorenstam (right, with husband David Esch) made the traditional dive into the water by the 18th green, winning a record number of style points with a headfirst leap....

Not that style means that much to Sorenstam. Consistency, of the metronomic variety, is her game. Consistency, as in 69 under par for the year....Sorenstam does 750 sit-ups a day to strengthen her abs. She enters miles of personal performance data in her laptop. She practiced her putting all winter....

With the greens firm and birdies hard to come by at the Nabisco, the field clumped up like a crowd on a mountain ledge. The fun was in waiting for someone to fall off....

As is often the case, the contenders had to play around the craters and shell holes of past battles among themselves. Pat Hurst had to be thinking of the week

before, at Moon Valley Country Club, when even after matching her career-best with a 64 in the second round, she trailed Sorenstam by nine shots. Sorenstam had to remember that the first playoff loss of her career was to Rachel Teske (then known by her maiden name, Hetherington) in 1998. Karrie Webb, meanwhile, was never far off the lead. The LPGA Player of the Year each of the past two years tied for second with a final-round 69, and on the back nine missed a birdie putt to tie Sorenstam for the lead.

In previous years she might have buckled...but Sorenstam followed her game plan with ruthless self-discipline. Her only missteps were a bogey on the 3rd hole, and a bogey on the 12th, where she three-putted from 30 feet. Otherwise, it was fairways and greens, fairways and greens, a Sorenstam soliloquy with a foreseeable curtain line....

After sinking an 11-foot birdie putt on number 13, Sorenstam stood at six under. That's when her pursuers, bunched two shots back, began to realize the futility of their efforts....

So there, in the end, was Ms. 59, commanding everyone's attention by rolling in a 15-foot birdie putt on the final hole—an unnecessary but crowd-pleasing flourish. Her sister, Charlotta, three years older and an LPGA player herself, ran onto the green and squirted Annika with champagne. Then, either because voices in the gallery were yelling, "Water!" or because Esch and Charlotta were stalking her with the champion's bathrobe held open, Annika dived into the drink. "I'm so happy," she burbled, dripping pond water.... If she didn't look like the hottest golfer on the planet, Sorenstam had at least played like it.

As the sun dropped behind the San Jacinto mountains, someone asked Sorenstam why it had taken her five years to win her third major, even as she won 21 LPGA events in between. "I struggled," she said, "because I wanted it so badly." Now she is winning for the same reason, and it matters not a jot whether we, they, the Turks, the Eskimos, or the guys at ESPN give her her due. For Sorenstam, it's just nice to be No. 1 again.

—John Garrity
excerpted from SI, April 2, 2001

THE NUMBERS

Men's Majors

THE MASTERS
Augusta National GC (par 72; 6,985 yds);
Augusta, GA, April 5–8

PLAYER	SCORE	($) EARNINGS
Tiger Woods	70-66-68-68—272	1,008,000
David Duval	71-66-70-67—274	604,800
Phil Mickelson	67-69-69-70—275	380,800
Mark Calcavecchia	72-66-68-72—278	246,400
Toshi Izawa	71-66-74-67—278	246,400
Ernie Els	71-68-68-72—279	181,300
Jim Furyk	69-71-70-69—279	181,300
Bernhard Langer	73-69-68-69—279	181,300
Kirk Triplett	68-70-70-71—279	181,300
Angel Cabrera	66-71-70-73—280	128,800
Chris DiMarco	65-69-72-74—280	128,800
Brad Faxon	73-68-68-71—280	128,800
Miguel Angel Jiménez	68-72-71-69—280	128,800
Steve Stricker	66-71-72-71—280	128,800
Paul Azinger	70-71-71-69—281	95,200
Rocco Mediate	72-70-66-73—281	95,200
José María Olazábal	70-68-71-72—281	95,200
Tom Lehman	75-68-71-68—282	81,200
Vijay Singh	69-71-72-69—282	81,200
John Huston	67-75-72-69—283	65,240
Jeff Maggert	72-70-70-71—283	65,240
Mark O'Meara	69-74-72-68—283	65,240
Jesper Parnevik	71-71-72-69—283	65,240

U.S. OPEN
Southern Hills CC (par 70; 6,973 yds);
Tulsa, June 14–17

PLAYER	SCORE	($) EARNINGS
Retief Goosen†	66-70-69-71—276	900,000
Mark Brooks	72-64-70-70—276	530,000
Stewark Cink	69-69-67-72—277	325,310
Rocco Mediate	71-68-67-72—278	226,777
Tom Kite	73-72-72-64—281	172,912

U.S. OPEN *(Cont.)*

PLAYER	SCORE	($) EARNINGS
Paul Azinger	74-67-69-71—281	172,912
Vijay Singh	74-70-74-64—282	125,172
Angel Cabrera	70-71-72-69—282	125,172
Davis Love III	72-69-71-70—282	125,172
Kirk Triplett	72-69-71-70—282	125,172
Phil Mickelson	70-69-68-75—282	125,172
Tiger Woods	74-71-69-69—283	91,733
Matt Gogel	70-69-74-70—283	91,733
Michael Allen	77-68-67-71—283	91,733
Sergio Garcia	70-68-68-77—283	91,733
Scott Hoch	73-73-69-69—284	75,337
Chris DiMarco	69-73-70-72—284	75,337
David Duval	70-69-71-74—284	75,337
Chris Perry	72-71-73-69—285	63,425
Corey Pavin	70-75-68-72—285	63,425
Mike Weir	67-76-68-74—285	63,425

† Won 18-hole playoff, 70 to 72.

BRITISH OPEN
Royal Lytham & St. Annes GC (par 71; 6,905 yds);
Lytham, England, July 19–22

PLAYER	SCORE	($) EARNINGS
David Duval	69-73-65-67—274	858,000
Niclas Fasth	69-69-72-67—277	514,800
Ernie Els	71-71-67-69—278	202,584
Darren Clarke	70-69-69-70—278	202,584
Miguel Angel Jiménez	69-72-67-70—278	202,584
Billy Mayfair	69-72-67-70—278	202,584
Ian Woosnam	72-68-67-71—278	202,584
Bernhard Langer	71-69-67-71—278	202,584
Mikko Ilonen	68-75-70-66—279	91,163
Kevin Sutherland	75-69-68-67—279	91,163
Sergio Garcia	70-72-67-70—279	91,163
Jesper Parnevik	69-68-71-71—279	91,163

BRITISH OPEN *(Cont.)*

PLAYER	SCORE	($) EARNINGS
Vijay Singh	70-70-71-69—280	57,290
Loren Roberts	70-70-70-70—280	57,290
Billy Andrade	69-70-70-71—280	57,290
Retief Goosen	74-68-67-71—280	57,290
Colin Montgomerie	65-70-73-72—280	57,290
Raphael Jacquelin	71-68-69-72—280	57,290
Alex Cejka	69-69-69-73—280	57,290

PGA CHAMPIONSHIP
Atlanta AC (par 70; 7,213 yds);
Duluth, GA, August 16–19

PLAYER	SCORE	($) EARNINGS
David Toms	66-65-65-69—265	936,000
Phil Mickelson	66-66-66-68—266	562,000
Steve Lowery	67-67-66-68—268	354,000
Mark Calcavecchia	71-68-66-65—270	222,500
Shingo Katayama	67-64-69-70—270	222,500
Billy Andrade	68-70-68-66—272	175,000
Scott Hoch	68-70-69-67—274	152,333
Scott Verplank	69-68-70-67—274	152,333
Jim Furyk	70-64-71-69—274	152,333
Kirk Triplett	68-70-71-66—275	122,000
Justin Leonard	70-69-67-69—275	122,000
David Duval	66-68-67-74—275	122,000
Steve Flesch	73-67-70-66—276	94,666
Jesper Parnevik	70-68-70-68—276	94,666
Ernie Els	67-67-70-72—276	94,666
Jose Coceres	69-68-73-67—277	70,666
Robert Allenby	69-67-73-68—277	70,666
Dudley Hart	66-68-73-70—277	70,666
Mike Weir	69-72-66-70—277	70,666
Chris DiMarco	68-67-71-71—277	70,666
Stuart Appleby	66-70-68-73—277	70,666

Men's Tour Results

2001 PGA TOUR EVENTS

TOURNAMENT	FINAL ROUND	WINNER	SCORE/ UNDER PAR	($) EARNINGS
Mercedes Championships	Jan 14	Jim Furyk	274/–18	630,000
Tucson Open	Jan 15	Garrett Willis	273/–15	540,000
Sony Open	Jan 21	Brad Faxon	260/–20	720,000
Phoenix Open	Jan 28	Mark Calcavecchia	256/–28	720,000
Pebble Beach National Pro-Am	Feb 4	Davis Love III	272/–16	720,000
Buick Invitational	Feb 11	Phil Mickelson*	269/–19	630,000
Bob Hope Classic	Feb 18	Joe Durant	324/–36	630,000
Nissan Open	Feb 25	Robert Allenby*	276/–8	612,000
Genuity Championship	Mar 4	Joe Durant	270/–18	810,000
Honda Classic	Mar 11	Jesper Parnevik	270/–18	576,000
Bay Hill Invitational	Mar 18	Tiger Woods	273/–15	630,000
The Players Championship	Mar 26	Tiger Woods	274/–14	1,080,000
BellSouth Classic	Apr 1	Scott McCarron	280/–8	594,000
The Masters	Apr 8	Tiger Woods	272/–16	1,008,000
Worldcom Classic	Apr 15	Jose Coceres*	273/–11	630,000
Houston Open	Apr 22	Hal Sutton	278/–10	612,000
Greater Greensboro Classic	Apr 29	Scott Hoch	272/–16	630,000
Compaq Classic	May 6	David Toms	266/–22	720,000
Byron Nelson Classic	May 13	Robert Damron*	263/–17	810,000
The Colonial	May 20	Sergio Garcia	267/–13	720,000
Kemper Open	May 27	Frank Lickliter	268/–16	630,000
The Memorial	June 3	Tiger Woods	271/–17	558,000
St. Jude Classic	June 10	Bob Estes	267/–17	630,000

2001 PGA TOUR EVENTS *(Cont.)*

TOURNAMENT	FINAL ROUND	WINNER	SCORE/ UNDER PAR	($) EARNINGS
U.S. Open	June 18	Retief Goosen*	270/–4	900,000
Buick Classic	June 25	Sergio Garcia	268/–16	630,000
Greater Hartford Open	July 1	Phil Mickelson	264/–16	558,000
Western Open	July 8	Scott Hoch	267/–21	648,000
Greater Milwaukee Open	July 15	Shigeki Maruyama*	266/–18	558,000
British Open	July 22	David Duval	274/–10	858,300
B.C. Open	July 22	Jeff Sluman*	266/–22	360,000
John Deere Classic	July 29	David Gossett	265/–19	504,000
The International	Aug 5	Tom Pernice Jr.	+34‡	720,000
Buick Open	Aug 12	Kenny Perry	263/–25	558,000
PGA Championship	Aug 19	David Toms	265/–15	936,000
NEC Invitational	Aug 26	Tiger Woods*	268/–12	1,000,000
Reno-Tahoe Open	Aug 26	John Cook	271/–17	540,000
Air Canada Championship	Sept 2	Joel Edwards	265/–19	612,000
Canadian Open	Sept 9	Scott Verplank	266/–14	684,000
Pennsylvania Classic	Sept 23	Robert Allenby	269/–19	594,000
Texas Open	Sept 30	Justin Leonard	266/–18	540,000
Michelob Championship	Oct 7	David Toms	269/–15	630,000
Invensys Classic	Oct 14	Bob Estes	329/–30	810,000
National Car Rental Golf Classic	Oct 21	José Coceres	265/–23	612,000
Buick Challenge	Oct 28	Chris DiMarco	267/–21	612,000
The Tour Championship	Nov 4	Mike Weir*	270/–14	900,000

* Won playoff. †Won on the second extra hole of match play. # Tournament shortened by rain. ‡ Revised Stableford scoring.

Women's Majors

NABISCO CHAMPIONSHIP
Mission Hills CC (par 72; 6,478 yds);
Rancho Mirage, CA, March 22–25

PLAYER	SCORE	($) EARNINGS
Annika Sorenstam	72-70-70-69—281	225,000
Akiko Fukushima	74-68-70-72—284	87,557
Janice Moodie	72-72-70-70—284	87,557
Dottie Pepper	71-71-71-71—284	87,557
Rachel Teske	72-73-66-73—284	87,557
Karrie Webb	73-72-70-69—284	87,557
Brandie Burton	74-69-72-70—285	41,891
Sophie Gustafson	72-74-70-69—285	41,891
Laura Diaz	71-74-69-72—286	33,589
Pat Hurst	70-68-74-74—286	33,589
Tina Barrett	71-73-70-73—287	25,957
Laura Davies	71-73-75-68—287	25,957
Dorothy Delasin	73-70-74-70—287	25,957
Se Ri Pak	73-69-73-72—287	25,957
Juli Inkster	70-75-68-75—288	20,736
Mi Hyun Kim	74-71-70-73—288	20,736
Carin Koch	70-69-75-74—288	20,736
Jeong Jang	74-71-71-73—289	18,220
Liselotte Neumann	70-74-74-71—289	18,220
Michele Redman	71-72-71-75—289	18,220

LPGA CHAMPIONSHIP
DuPont CC (par 71; 6,386 yds);
Wilmington, DE, June 21–24

PLAYER	SCORE	($) EARNINGS
Karrie Webb	67-64-70-69—270	225,000
Laura Diaz	67-71-66-68—272	139,639
Wendy Ward	65-69-71-69—274	90,577
Maria Hjorth	71-67-66-70—274	90,577
Annika Sorenstam	68-69-71-67—275	64,157
Becky Iverson	66-73-67-70—276	48,684
Laura Davies	67-68-70-71—276	48,684
Mi Hyun Kim	70-70-68-69—277	39,250

LPGA CHAMPIONSHIP (Cont.)

PLAYER	SCORE	($) EARNINGS
Helen Alfredsson	68-66-74-70—278	35,476
Maggie Will	68-74-67-70—279	30,245
Michele Redman	69-66-73-71—279	30,245
Rosie Jones	71-69-71-69—280	25,013
Lorie Kane	69-71-71-69—280	25,013
Liselotte Neumann	69-72-68-71—280	25,013
Wendy Doolan	70-71-72-68—281	21,239
Juli Inkster	71-71-69-70—281	21,239
Dottie Pepper	71-72-71-68—282	16,819
Kelly Robbins	69-74-71-68—282	16,819
Carin Koch	69-73-71-69—282	16,819
Meg Mallon	71-74-67-70—282	16,819
Leta Lindley	71-71-70-70—282	16,819
Pat Hurst	72-68-72-70—282	16,819
Terry-Jo Myers	70-71-69-72—282	16,819
Rachel Teske	68-72-70-72—282	16,819
Mhairi McKay	68-72-70-72—282	16,819

U.S. WOMEN'S OPEN
Pine Needles GC (par 70; 6,256 yds);
Southern Pines, NC, May 31–June 3

PLAYER	SCORE	($) EARNINGS
Karrie Webb	70-65-69-69—273	520,000
Se Ri Pak	69-70-70-72—281	310,000
Dottie Pepper	74-69-70-69—282	202,580
Cristie Kerr	69-73-71-70—283	118,697
Sherri Turner	72-70-71-70—283	118,697
Catriona Matthew	72-68-70-73—283	118,697
Lorie Kane	75-68-72-69—284	80,726
Kristi Albers	71-69-74-70—284	80,726
Kelli Kuehne	70-71-72-71—284	80,726
Wendy Doolan	71-70-70-73—284	80,726
Sophie Gustafson	74-66-74-71—285	66,581
Kelly Robbins	72-68-76-70—286	57,088
A.J. Eathorne	67-71-75-73—286	57,088

U.S. WOMEN'S OPEN (Cont.)

PLAYER	SCORE	($) EARNINGS
Juli Inkster	68-72-71-75—286	57,088
Yuri Fudoh	73-68-70-75—286	57,088
Emilee Klein	72-69-75-71—287	46,885
Michele Redman	70-72-73-72—287	46,885
Annika Sorenstam	70-72-73-72—287	46,885
Maria Hjorth	70-71-77-70—288	37,327
Marisa Baena	71-72-75-70—288	37,327
Jill McGill	68-76-72-72—288	37,327
Wendy Ward	70-71-74-73—288	37,327
Dorothy Delasin	75-70-70-73—288	37,327

WOMEN'S BRITISH OPEN
Sunningdale GC; (par 72; 6,277 yds);
Berkshire, England, August 2–5

PLAYER	SCORE	($) EARNINGS
Se Ri Pak	71-70-70-66—277	221,650
Mi Hyun Kim	72-65-71-71—279	143,000
Laura Diaz	74-70-69-67—280	74,092
Iben Tinning	71-69-72-68—280	74,092
Janice Moodie	67-70-71-72—280	74,092
Catriona Matthew	70-65-72-73—280	74,092
Kathryn Marshall	75-71-68-67—281	36,608
Marina Arruti	71-73-70-67—281	36,608
Kristal Parker	72-71-71-67—281	36,608
Kelli Kuehne	71-70-71-69—281	36,608
Kasumi Fujii	71-71-69-70—281	36,608
Raquel Carriedo	73-70-70-69—282	25,382
Tracy Hanson	72-69-70-71—282	25,382
Rosie Jones	70-69-71-72—282	25,382
Pearl Sinn	74-70-72-67—283	20,592
Brandie Burton	72-71-73-67—283	20,592
Jill McGill	70-70-72-71—283	20,592
Karrie Webb	74-67-68-74—283	20,592
Becky Morgan	73-68-71-72—284	17,982
Trish Johnson	70-67-72-75—284	17,982

Women's Tour Results

2001 LPGA TOUR EVENTS

TOURNAMENT	FINAL ROUND	WINNER	SCORE/ UNDER PAR	($) EARNINGS
YourLife Vitamins LPGA Classic	Jan 14	Se Ri Pak	203/–13	150,000
Naples LPGA Memorial	Jan 21	Sophie Gustafson	272/–16	150,000
LPGA Office Depot	Jan 28	Grace Park	280/–6	123,750
Takefuji Classic	Feb 10	Lori Kane	205/–11	127,500
Hawaiian Ladies Open	Feb 17	Catriona Matthew	210/–6	112,500
Welch's/Circle K Championship	Mar 11	Annika Sorenstam	265/–23	112,500
Standard Register PING	Mar 18	Annika Sorenstam	261/–27	150,000
Nabisco Championship	Mar 25	Annika Sorenstam	281/–7	225,000
The Office Depot	Apr 14	Annika Sorenstam*	210/–6	120,000
Longs Drugs Challenge	Apr 22	Se Ri Pak	208/–8	120,000
Kathy Ireland Championship	Apr 29	Rosie Jones*	268/–12	135,000
Chick-fil-A Championship	May 6	Annika Sorenstam*	203/–13	180,000
Electrolux Championship	May 13	Juli Inkster	274/–14	120,000
Champions Classic#	May 20	Wendy Doolan*	132/–12	112,500
Corning Classic	May 27	Carin Koch	270/–18	135,000
U.S. Women's Open	June 3	Karrie Webb	273/–7	520,000
Rochester International	June 10	Laura Davies	279/–9	150,000
Evian Masters	June 16	Rachel Teske	273/–15	315,000
LPGA Championship	June 24	Karrie Webb	270/–14	225,000

2001 LPGA TOUR EVENTS (Cont.)

TOURNAMENT	FINAL ROUND	WINNER	SCORE/ UNDER PAR	($) EARNINGS
ShopRite Classic	July 1	Betsy King	201/–12	180,000
Jamie Farr Classic	July 8	Se Ri Pak	269/–15	150,000
Michelob Light Classic	July 15	Emilee Klein	205/–11	120,000
Sybase Big Apple Classic	July 22	Rosie Jones	272/–12	142,500
Giant Eagle LPGA Classic	July 29	Dorothy Delasin	203/–13	150,000
Women's British Open	Aug 5	Se Ri Pak	277/–11	221,650
New Albany Golf Classic	Aug 12	Wendy Ward	195/–21	150,000
Canadian Women's Open	Aug 19	Annika Sorenstam	272/–16	180,000
Betsy King Classic	Aug 26	H. Daly-Donofrio	273/–15	120,000
State Farm Rail Classic	Sept 2	Kate Golden	267/–21	150,000
Williams Championship	Sept 9	Gloria Park	201/–9	150,000
Asahi Ryokuken International Championship	Sept 23	Tina Fischer	206/–10	180,000
AFLAC Champions	Sept 30	Se Ri Pak	272/–16	122,000
Samsung World Championship	Oct 7	Dorothy Delasin	277/–11	157,000
Mizuno Classic	Nov 4	Annika Sorenstam	203/–13	162,000
Tyco/ADT Championship	Nov 18	Karrie Webb	279/–9	215,000

* Won sudden-death playoff. #Shortened due to rain.

PGA Tour Final 2001 Money Leaders

NAME	EVENTS	BEST FINISH	SCORING AVERAGE*	EARNINGS ($)
Tiger Woods	19	1 (5)	68.81	5,687,777
Phil Mickelson	23	1 (2)	69.21	4,403,883
David Toms	28	1 (3)	69.97	3,791,595
Vijay Singh	26	2 (2)	69.21	3,440,829
Davis Love III	20	1 (1)	69.06	3,169,463
Sergio Garcia	18	1 (2)	69.13	2,898,635
Scott Hoch	24	1 (2)	69.85	2,875,319
David Duval	20	1 (1)	69.73	2,801,760
Bob Estes	26	1 (2)	69.73	2,795,477
Scott Verplank	26	1 (1)	69.88	2,783,401

*Adjusted for average score of field in each tournament entered.

LPGA Tour Final 2001 Money Leaders

NAME	EVENTS	BEST FINISH	SCORING AVERAGE	EARNINGS ($)
Annika Sorenstam	26	1 (8)	69.42	2,105,868
Se Ri Pak	21	1 (5)	69.69	1,623,009
Karrie Webb	22	1 (3)	70.16	1,535,404
Lorie Kane	27	1 (1)	70.59	947,489
Maria Hjorth	29	2 (2)	71.46	848,195
Rosie Jones	23	1 (2)	70.51	785,010
Dottie Pepper	23	2 (2)	70.63	776,482
Mi Hyun Kim	29	2 (3)	70.49	762,363
Laura Diaz	27	2 (4)	70.88	751,466
Catriona Matthew	29	1 (1)	71.41	747,970

Pair of Aces

Led by pitchers Curt Schilling and Randy Johnson, Arizona dethroned the mighty Yankees

MARK BECHTEL

The sight of New York second baseman Alfonso Soriano circling the bases after golfing a home run to left field in the top of the eighth inning of Game 7 of the World Series seemed like the perfect conclusion to the 2001 baseball season. Sure, the Yankees' opponents, the fledgling Arizona Diamondbacks, had two more cracks at New York pitching, but since Soriano's homer gave the Yankees a 2–1 lead, those two cracks would come against Mariano Rivera, arguably the greatest big-game relief pitcher baseball has ever seen. So having Soriano win the series with a home run would have been fitting, since the entire season—and especially the World Series—was defined by dramatic homers. But it didn't happen: The Diamondbacks rallied for two runs in the bottom of the ninth off the normally unhittable Rivera and snatched the title from the Yankees, spoiling the script for New York fans and giving their faithful cause for uproarious celebration in Phoenix.

But Yankee fans, and baseball fans of every stripe, had unforgettable moments to savor in 2001, a spectacular season in which the sport said goodbye to several legends, a few legendary records, and more than a few home run balls.

When Mark McGwire set the single-season home run record in 1998, he established a standard that appeared ready to stand the test of time. Unlike Roger Maris, who eclipsed Babe Ruth's record by a single homer in 1961, Big Mac annihilated Maris's record of 61, cracking 70 home runs—an increase of nearly 15 percent. Given that Ruth's record had stood for 34 years, and Maris's for 37 years, it didn't seem unreasonable to expect a long life for McGwire's record.

But 2001 was a year like no other when it came to long balls. Arizona's Luis Gonzalez, who had never hit more than 31 homers in a season, slugged 13 in April and went into the All-Star break with 35 home runs and a .355 average. San Francisco's Barry Bonds belted homers in six consecutive games in April and had 39 at the break. And Sammy Sosa, who topped 60 homers in both 1998 and '99, overcame a slow start with a brilliant August in which he produced two three-homer games at Wrigley. Slammin' Sammy finished with 64 taters to become the only player in baseball history to top 60 homers in three seasons, but as the season wound down, it was clear that only Bonds had a realistic shot at McGwire's record. (Injuries limited Big Mac to 29 homers in 97 games.)

From July 26 to the end of the season, Bonds never went four games without hitting at least one home run, and he did so despite walking a major league record 177 times. After July 22, he never went consecutive games without walking at least once. Following Bonds's 69th homer on Sept. 29, Houston, which was contending for a playoff spot, walked him eight times in 14 plate appearances. The Astros were determined not to let Bonds beat them. Even when they were trailing 8–1 in the sixth inning of the third game of the series, they walked the Giants' slugger. He finally got a decent pitch to hit from Astros rookie Wilfredo Rodriguez in the ninth inning on Oct. 4—and promptly drilled the pitch 454 feet into the seats at Enron Field for Number 70. "I threw him fastballs," Rodriguez said matter-of-factly. "That's what I do."

The next night, Dodgers ace Chan Ho Park did that, too, grooving one in the first inning that Bonds hit into the right-centerfield stands of Pacific Bell Park to break McGwire's record. There had been some discussion of whether or not the Dodgers—who were out of contention for the playoffs but who are fierce rivals of the Giants—would pitch to Bonds. Happily, fair play prevailed, and Bonds got a fighting chance at the record, and then some: Two innings later he hit a hanging curveball over the rightfield fence for Number 72. He added another one two days later to finish the season with 73 home runs, a total that most base-

Johnson (opposite) scattered six hits in seven innings as Arizona won Game 6 in a rout, 15–2. He came on in relief to win Game 7 as well, and shared the MVP award with Schilling, permanently laying to rest the memories of his past playoff failures.

Pumped Up: The newly buff, 37-year-old Bonds (above, batting) broke three records during his MVP season: He belted 73 homers to top McGwire's three-year-old record of 70; he produced a slugging percentage of .863 to top Babe Ruth's record of .847, set in 1920; and he drew 177 walks, besting Ruth's 78-year-old record of 170.

ball fans would have considered inconceivable as recently as five years ago.

Marvelous though it was, Bonds's quest lacked much of the attendant interest and goodwill that McGwire and Sosa generated in the memorable autumn of 1998. That was partly because of Bonds's reputation for surlinesss, and partly because the record, under threat again after only three years, may have lost some of its luster. When it was all over, Bonds took the tone of a man who understood that his record—perhaps no record— was safe in this day and age. "I don't know if it is going to exist next year," he said. "These young guys are big kids and they are strong kids, and with the new stadiums being converted to a little smaller than in the past, you guys are going to see a lot of wonderful things happen in the game of baseball in the future."

A wonderful thing happened during the All-Star Game at Seattle's Safeco Field, and it also involved the Dodgers' righthander Park. He served up a fat fastball to Cal Ripken in the third inning, and the 40-year-old Orioles third baseman, who had announced that he would retire after the season, knocked it out of the park. Ripken was in the midst of his worst year statistically, but he was still able to provide a fair amount of drama with his

Midsummer Night's Dream of a clout. It wasn't the first time Ripken had homered to add poignancy to an already memorable scene—he hit one out in 1995 on the night he broke Lou Gehrig's record for consecutive games played—and after the game he was asked how he always seemed to come through with the storybook hit. "Gosh, I wish I could explain that," he said. "When you have the chance, just one opportunity in front of a big base-ball crowd, and feel the moment, the electricity, the magic—that's everything."

Joining Ripken in the ranks of future Hall of Famers to hang up their cleats in 2001 were McGwire and San Diego outfielder Tony Gwynn, who saw his playing time severely curtailed by injuries for the second straight year. Gwynn's retirement ended a remarkable career in which he hit better than .300 19 straight times. His career average was .338, and he struck out just 434 times, the second-fewest of any member of the 3,000-hit club, behind Paul Waner. Gwynn played his final game on Oct. 7, the day after Ripken's finale. In the top of the sixth inning, the Qualcomm Stadium scoreboard showed a taped message from Ripken. "We are certainly two of the lucky ones. We both got to play our whole career with the same team," Ripken said. "I hope today is a real happy day for you."

Gwynn's teammate, veteran leadoff man Rickey Henderson, added to the festive atmosphere in San Diego that day. Having broken Ty Cobb's 73-year-old record for career runs three days earlier, Henderson hit a bloop double down the rightfield line in the first inning off Colorado's John Thomson for his 3,000th career hit. He is the 25th player to reach the milestone, and when he took the field in the top of the second, Padres manager Bruce Bochy took him out so that the crowd of 60,103 could properly salute him.

While Ripken and the 42-year-old Henderson and the 41-year-old Gwynn shared the spotlight in the final days of the season, not all of the headlines made in 2001 came courtesy of the game's older set. Cardinals rookie Albert Pujols, who played all of three minor league games above A ball before coming to the majors, set an NL rookie record with 130 RBIs. In the American League, the most dominant newcomer was hardly a novice. Ichiro Suzuki, who won seven consecutive batting titles in Japan, joined the Seattle Mariners and immediately boosted their lineup. Batting first, he set major league records for hits by a rookie and singles in a season, and he scored 127 runs. He was mobbed by the Japanese media from the time he arrived at spring training, and within a couple of weeks he became something of a sensation with the natives in his adopted homeland. The team released a statement declaring, "It is Ichiro's preference to be identified by his first name only. He is the only current Major League Baseball player to have his first name on his jersey." And just like that, Ichiro Suzuki became Ichiro, joining Cher and Madonna in the ranks of the mononymous. "He's a legitimate hitter, no question," said Yankees manager Joe Torre. "I don't think you can pitch him one way. You can go in and out, up and down, and he makes the adjustment. You can get ahead in the count, and Suzuki still seems relaxed. He doesn't seem to have any weaknesses."

Ichiro's presence more than made up for the loss of shortstop Alex Rodriguez, who bolted Seattle for Texas before the season, when the Rangers offered him $25.2 million a season for 10 years. While Rodriguez had a superb season in his first year in Texas, belting 52 homers and driving in 135 runs, the investment failed to pay dividends as the pitching-poor Rangers struggled to a 73–89 record. The Mariners, meanwhile, went 116–46, tying the major league record for wins in a season set by the 1906 Cubs. It was quite an accomplishment for the M's, who in the past three years waved goodbye to Randy Johnson, Ken Griffey Jr. and Rodriguez. In 2001 they made do, to say the least, with pitching, defense and station-to-station baseball.

Indeed, 2001 was a good year for several teams lacking in superstars. The Twins, whose payroll was less than a quarter of the Yankees', came shooting out of the gate with a 14–3 start and showed no signs of letting up. They led the Indians in the AL Central by five games in mid-July before the Tribe finally rallied to overtake them in August. But Minnesota still finished the season at 85–77, a 16-game improvement over its 2000 record. And in the NL East, the Phillies, who tied for the worst record in baseball last year, nearly ended the Braves' decade-long stranglehold on the division title. Yet when the season ended, the eight playoff spots were filled by the usual suspects. Five playoff teams were making repeat appearances from 2000, and the three newcomers—Arizona, Houston and Cleveland—had all made the playoffs in 1999.

But none of the AL contenders had the experience to stay with New York in the postseason. While the Mariners had the single-season wins record and the A's had arguably the best young rotation in baseball, neither team had an answer for the Yankees' mystique. The A's took the first two games of their AL Division Series in New York, but in Oakland the series turned on an amazing play by New York shortstop Derek Jeter, the kind

Seattle manager Lou Piniella said that he would run naked through Times Square if Suzuki (above, 51), a seven-time batting champ in Japan, won the AL batting title. Suzuki delivered, with a .350 average, and was named AL MVP to boot, but Piniella, thankfully, has yet to make good on his vow.

the bunt and Cummings was tagged out at the plate. But Womack saved Brenly an offseason of second-guessing when he stroked a series-winning RBI single four pitches later.

The Diamondbacks then blew through the Braves in five games, setting up one of the most memorable World Series ever played. Behind superb performances from Schilling and Randy Johnson, the D-Backs won the first two games in Phoenix, limiting the Yankees to a combined six hits. New York bounced back to win Game 3 at home, prompting Brenly to send Schilling to the mound on three days' rest for Game 4. Under a full moon on Halloween he once again pitched brilliantly, but Brenly pulled him after seven innings—and just 88 pitches—to bring in Byung-Hyun Kim, who hadn't pitched in 10 days. Kim got through the eighth without trouble, but allowed a one-out single to Paul O'Neill in the ninth. One out later, Tino Martinez homered to center, sending the Bronx into bedlam and the game into extra innings, where Jeter won it with a solo homer in the 10th.

Astonishingly, the Yankees did it again the next night. Despite throwing 61 pitches in Game 4, Kim started the ninth inning of Game 5, with his team again leading by two runs. Posada led off with a double, and after Kim retired the next two Yankee batters, Scott Brosius homered down the line.

With momentum and by all indications, fate, on their side, the Yankees flew to the desert for Games 6 and 7. But the Diamondbacks rebounded with a historic win of their own in Game 6, pounding out a World Series–record 22 hits in a 15–2 win, and setting the stage for a decisive seventh game between 20-game winners Schilling and Roger Clemens. Both pitchers rose to the occasion, and after Soriano's homer it became a battle of the bullpens: Rivera, who has made postseason saves with machinelike efficiency, and a tired but effective Johnson, who started Game 6 and now hoped to finish Game 7. Rivera struck out the side in the eighth, but in the ninth the legendary Yankees closer fell apart: He gave up a single, made a throwing error and surrendered a double to allow Arizona to tie the game. Then he hit Craig Counsell with a pitch to load the bases. With the infield drawn in, Luis Gonzalez lifted a single over Jeter's head, and Jay Bell dashed home with the World Series–winning run. "Win or lose," said Arizona first baseman Mark Grace, "I'm proud to have played in one of the greatest World Series in the history of this great game.... Someone has to tell me we just beat the New York Yankees and Mariano Rivera, because I still don't believe it."

After 21 seasons, 3,001 games—a record 2,632 of them consecutive—and 3,184 hits, Ripken (above) said goodbye to the fans in Baltimore. He retired as one of seven players in baseball history with more than 400 homers—he finished with 431—and 3,000 hits. As the venerable Ripken made a graceful exit, the upstart Diamondbacks (opposite) made a noisy entrance, winning the Fall Classic in their third year of existence, faster than any other expansion team.

of play that separates champions from also-rans. In the seventh inning with the Yanks up 1–0, Terrance Long hit a fly ball over rightfielder Shane Spencer's head. Jeremy Giambi, who was on first, came chugging around third as Spencer's throw sailed off-line and over two cutoff men. Jeter raced across the infield and, in one motion, retrieved the errant throw, spun and backhanded to catcher Jorge Posada, who tagged Giambi, the would-be tying run. "I couldn't believe it," said A's outfielder Johnny Damon. "I thought, What in the heck is he doing there? Then I was amazed that the shovel pass he made was perfect. Jeter made a play that saved their season."

Indeed he did, as the Yanks came back to win the series in five games and then beat the Mariners in five in the best-of-seven LCS. In the National League, the Diamondbacks also won a thriller in the Division Series. The decisive fifth game was tied 1–1 in the bottom of the ninth when Arizona manager Bob Brenly called for a suicide squeeze with Midre Cummings at third, Greg Colbrunn at first and Tony Womack batting. The play backfired when Tony Womack missed

PHOTO GALLERY

Cleveland's Omar Vizquel (above) laid down a bunt during the Indians' 6–5 extra-inning loss to Cincinnati in July. The Indians' fared better than their downstate counterparts, however, winning the AL Central with a 91–71 record while the Reds finished a dismal 66–96, second-to-last in the NL Central. Cleveland and Vizquel lost to Seattle in a tense, five-game AL Division series.

Toronto's Tony Batista (right) tagged out John Valentin of the Red Sox as he tried to go from first to third on Carl Everett's single in May at Fenway. The play symbolized Boston's season—seemingly every Boston season—as the Sox raised fans' hopes only to be counted out in August.

At age 39, the Yankees' Roger Clemens (above) produced one of the best seasons of his illustrious 18-year career. He went 20–3, struck out 213 batters and won a record sixth Cy Young Award. No other pitcher has more than four.

Finishing a game that had been suspended the previous evening because of a problem with the lighting at Qualcomm Stadium, Arizona lefthander Randy Johnson (right) set a record for strikeouts by a reliever, fanning 16 batters in the Diamondbacks' 3–0 victory over San Diego.

Uncork the Champagne: Diamondbacks left-fielder Luis Gonzalez (left, batting) lifted a single to leftfield off New York closer Mariano Rivera in the bottom of the ninth to send Jay Bell home with the World Series—winning run and touch off a wild celebration in the infield of Arizona's Bank One Ballpark. Gonzalez's hit gave the D-backs a 3–2 victory in Game 7 and dethroned the three-time defending champion Yankees.

Barry Bonds

Veteran Los Angeles Dodgers reliever Mike Trombley, who knows a thing or two about big hits, was sitting in the visiting clubhouse at Pacific Bell Park in San Francisco on Oct. 5, 2001, sipping a cup of coffee while watching a Jerry Springer highlight video. Six years earlier, while pitching for the Minnesota Twins, Trombley allowed Eddie Murray's 3,000th hit. Three years earlier, he gave up the 36th of Mark McGwire's record-setting 70 home runs that season. How embarrassing would it

be, he was asked, to surrender Barry Bonds's record-breaking 71st homer? Trombley stopped drinking and turned away from the video high jinks. "Embarrassing?" he said. "You must be kidding me. You're pitching against a team in a major league pennant race in a packed stadium against one of the greatest hitters who's ever played the game. There's nothing embarrassing about it. It's special."

Although Chan Ho Park, the

sullen Los Angeles righthander who a couple of hours later would give up not only Bonds's record-breaking 71st home run but his 72nd as well, might have disagreed with Trombley, it was hard to argue the point. Bonds (above), capping perhaps the greatest offensive season in baseball history, had done something special—and breaking the home run record was only a part of it.

In the final weeks of the season he'd been asked to (in no particular order):

• help provide entertainment for a nation in dire need of diversion;

• lead the San Francisco Giants in a come-from-behind drive for a playoff berth;

• smile and expound for a vast press corps that he had usually shunned;

• watch ball four after ball four after ball four after. . . ;

• play while mourning the death of friend and former bodyguard Franklin Bradley, who died on Sept. 27 from complications during abdominal surgery;

• worry about his impending free agency;

• catch and pass McGwire.

It wasn't easy. In the Giants' three-game set against the Houston Astros last week, Bonds, who entered the series with 69 homers, was walked eight times in 14 plate appearances. The ultimate disgrace came in the third game when, with his team trailing 8–1, Astros manager Larry Dierker ordered that Bonds be intentionally walked. The move enraged San Francisco's players, many of whom, despite their dislike of Bonds, wanted to see him break the single-season home run mark. "In that situation," said Jeff Kent, the Giants' second baseman, "you throw your best stuff and try to get Barry out. You don't intentionally walk him."

At last, in the ninth inning of that game, with San Francisco leading 9–2 on the way to a 10–2 win, Houston rookie lefthander Wilfredo Rodriguez challenged Bonds, who swung and missed at the first offering, a 95-mph fastball. As he had done all season Bonds didn't waste many swings this night. After missing high with another fastball, Rodriguez threw Bonds a 93-mph meatball, and Bonds pounced. As the ball exploded off his bat, he tossed away his piece of black timber, lifted both arms and set off on a Barry Trot (read: slow and cocky) around the bases. He'd dedicated the 70th to Bradley, and it was clear how much coming through for his friend meant to him. Said Bonds, "To be able to say I wanted to do something in my heart and [actually do] it was really, really meaningful."

Oddly, the emotion of number 70 never returned, even as Bonds, supported by a sold-out Pac Bell crowd, surpassed McGwire the following night. When he approached the plate for his first at bat, in the bottom of the first, the Giants—in need of a win to stay alive in the National League playoff hunt—were already trailing the Dodgers 5–0. There was a buzz, but not a buzz. The crowd was loud, but not loud. Bonds's dinger, a 442-foot shot off Park that landed in the rightfield arcade (and in the paws of Jerry Rose, a season-ticket holder from Knights Landing, Calif.), cut the deficit to 5–1. When Bonds hit his second, a 407-foot launch to centerfield, the Giants were behind 8–4; he closed the gap to three runs. The game, which L.A. won 11–10, lasted a *Gone with the Wind*–like 4 hours, 27 minutes. Two records were set this night. One (most homers in a season) was celebrated. The other (longest nine-inning game in major league history) was painfully endured.

Following both homers Bonds rounded the bases with little outward glee. When he crossed home plate after number 71, he pointed upward (in Bradley's honor) and picked up his 11-year-old son, Nikolai, a San Francisco batboy. Bonds's teammates gathered around, patted him on the head and quickly dispersed. There was one semi-noisy, extended curtain call. Bonds hugged several family members seated behind home plate. Then—nothing. "Now batting, number 21, Jeff Kent..."

"When you lose a big game, it takes some of the immediate luster away," said Kent. "Barry will be able to appreciate this one day. We all will. It's historic, a great achievement. But being eliminated from the playoffs—that bruises the fun."

Three years ago, when McGwire and Sammy Sosa were locked in a race to eclipse Roger Maris's 37-year-old record of 61 homers, the nation found itself immersed in a hardball lovefest. Maris's widow and children embraced McGwire as if he were a long-lost cousin. More often than not fans were happy, eager even, to return the home run balls for nothing more than a handshake, a photo and a couple of tickets.

No more. On Oct. 5 in San Francisco there was no McGwire, no Sosa, no Maris family and no commissioner. Bud Selig was in San Diego to celebrate the Padres' Tony Gwynn (retiring after a brilliant career) and Rickey Henderson (who had just broken Ty Cobb's 73-year-old record of 2,245 career runs and was on the verge of getting his 3,000th hit). Even Barry's father, Bobby, was absent, playing in his charity golf tournament in Bridgeport, Conn. Of 100 rightfield fans SI surveyed before the game, 94 insisted that should they be lucky enough to snag the grand prize, it would go to the highest bidder—be it Bonds, eBay or Todd McFarlane, the eccentric Spawn cartoonist who had purchased McGwire's 70th ball for $3 million. Give the ball away? "Ha!" said J.C. Corzo, a 26-year-old construction worker who held a mitt in his left hand and a $9 standing-room-only ticket stub in his right. "I'm going to buy me 50 acres of land in Kentucky and a couple of ATVs." Alas for J.C., he would head home empty-handed.

To his credit, Bonds insisted that winning—not the record—was his main concern. Thus there he was, after the loss, sitting on a dugout step, staring into nothingness, eyes moist, shoulders slumped. Maybe he was thinking of his lost friend. Maybe of his last game as a Giant—a distinct possibility for a man who would soon become a free agent, commanding $18 to $20 million per year. Maybe he was just sad. Yes, Bonds later admitted, the record was nice and meaningful and something he would treasure. Most of all, however, he wanted to find himself in his first World Series, to have a chance to prove wrong those who consider him a prime-time choker (Exhibit A: his .196 lifetime postseason average).

What the new home run king, who would add a valedictory 73rd in Sunday's meaningless season finale, failed to realize was that he had already proved them wrong. In the heat of a million-watt spotlight, Barry Bonds had come through.

—Jeff Pearlman
SI, Oct. 15, 2001

Moises Alou

Click. Moises Alou (opposite) has just taken a picture. It's 8:30 a.m. on May 31. He's asleep in room 512 of the Hyatt Regency San Diego, comfy and serene and—*brring! Hola?* On the phone is a reporter from *The Gazette* of Montreal. He wants to know what Moises thinks of the firing. *Firing?* "Your dad," says the reporter, "has been fired as manager of the Expos. What do you have to say?"

Click. Moises Alou has just taken a picture. It's of the Florida Marlins' clubhouse immediately following Game 7 of the 1997 World Series. Righthander Livan Hernandez is being presented with the Series MVP trophy. Alou had battered the Cleveland Indians, hitting .321 with three homers and nine RBIs. Hernandez had won two games but finished with a 5.27 ERA. So who was really more valuable?…

Click. Moises Alou has just taken a picture. And another picture. And another. His eyes are Kodak Instamatics, his brain a limitless photo album. *Click.* Alou remembers that he hit his first big league home run, as an Expo, on May 27, 1992…. *Click.* Alou remembers the first time he saw Austria, his wife of 12 years. They were juniors at Centro Especializado de Eseñanza High in the Dominican. *Click.* Alou remembers nearly every name and every date, every friend and every bully…. There are things Alou wants to forget but can't. In Norse mythology the god Odin was blessed and cursed by his quest for information. So it goes with Alou and his memories.

In his 11th major league season and his fourth with Houston, the Astros right-fielder is one of the best—yet most overlooked—righthanded hitters of his generation. As of June 10, 2001, his .305 lifetime average ranked 13th among active players with more than 3,000 plate appearances. His success in pressure situations—a career .358 batting average with the bases loaded, .323 with runners in scoring position—speaks for itself….

"I have succeeded as an offensive player for one main reason: I remember," says Alou, 34. "I remember how a guy pitched me five years ago and how he pitched me two years ago…."

Study Alou's face, and you will learn nothing. Is Alou happy? Is Alou mad? For those answers you might have to ask around the Astros' clubhouse. "I don't think aloof is the right word to describe Mo," says manager Larry Dierker, "but it's close."

In their 3½ years together in Houston, Alou and Dierker have had few lengthy chats. Before games Alou sits silently by his locker, in white briefs and a black T-shirt…. You are told, by more than one person, that Alou is moody and stubborn and tough and, at times, an arrogant pain in the butt. You are also told that Alou is witty, open-minded and intelligent. "Guarded is a good description," says Astros first baseman Jeff Bagwell….

This, too, is a result of his memories. The bad ones—the ones that, for most people, fade over time—remain vivid. Alou's career, while splendid in myriad ways, has also been filled with disappointments: The injuries that have taken away his speed and weakened his throwing arm. The dissolution, for financial reasons, of the two best teams he has played for, the '94 Expos and the '97 Marlins….

Click. One big image, made up of many small ones, leaves the deepest scar. In February 1999, just before he was to report to spring training, Alou tore his left anterior cruciate ligament when he tripped and fell on a treadmill at a gym near his house in Santo Domingo. Despite the prognosis that he'd be out for the season, Alou worked diligently in hope of returning in time to help his team win the pennant. Then in August, at home in Houston 10 days before he was to return, Alou reinjured the knee when, while playing with Percio, the middle of his and Austria's three sons, he fell off a bicycle. A crushed Alou stayed home rather than attend the Division Series against the Braves. It is not the lost season that stings Alou so much as the negative reaction to his absence from the playoffs. Houston G.M. Gerry Hunsicker questioned whether Alou should have been riding that bike. The Houston media ripped him….

Partly as a result, in 2000 Houston nearly traded Alou to the New York Yankees. Armed with a no-trade clause, Alou shot down the deal, which he calls "insulting." Says Bagwell, Alou's closest friend on the team: "It was all b-------. He worked hard to come back. Other guys get hurt and there's sympathy. Mo got hurt, and people questioned his desire. Nobody should question Mo. Look at his impact here."

In Bagwell's eyes, that clout goes beyond batting average and clutch hitting. Alou might not be the most affable man in the clubhouse, but his presence— "an aura of pride and respect," says Dierker—carries weight….

Although Moises and Felipe were united in Montreal for five years beginning in 1992 (Moises was a rookie and Felipe the Expos' manager), theirs was not a close relationship. *Click.* Felipe Alou and Maria Beltre divorced when Moises was two. Although proud to be the son of the major leaguer, Moises would only see his father four or five times a year.

Now, when he is home, Moises rides bikes and climbs trees with his kids, and he spoils them rotten…. "When we had our first child, Moises didn't know how to be a dad, because his father was never around," says Austria. "Now he takes fatherhood like a full-time job. He wants the boys to feel special around him."

Click. Alou also wants to feel special around Felipe. Although they occasionally clashed when Moises was an Expo—"It was sometimes hard," says Moises, "playing for my dad and getting to know him for the first time"—the two are now in touch on a regular basis. After hanging up with the *Gazette* reporter on May 31, Moises dialed his father's cell phone number. The two spoke for 10 minutes, Moises more upset than Felipe. "My dad deserves better than the Expos," he says. "Everyone knows Felipe Alou is one of the greatest managers in the world. He'll be managing somewhere next year, and maybe I'll be playing for him." Alou's poker face breaks into a smile. "Winning a World Series together," he says, "it'd be a beautiful thing."

Click. Some memories are truly worth waiting for.

—Jeff Pearlman
excerpted from SI, June 18, 2001

Bret Boone

Bret Boone had grown tired of those third generation questions by 1994, two years after his debut with the Seattle Mariners. His father had played major league baseball and so had his grandfather. It was remarkable, at least in a human genome kind of way, no question. But what more could you say? If he was only going to be some genealogical quirk, with a family tree more interesting than his batting average, well, there must be somebody else to interview. "Hey, Bret," they would ask, "what about your son? Wouldn't that be something if…" You can see how this might grind away at a guy…. The only attention Boone rated was for his ancestry, and, unless you're a Rockefeller, what's the fun in that?

The problem was, Boone's roots were often more interesting than anything he was doing on the diamond. It actually might be better to talk about old Ray Boone, the patriarch of the clan, who shared the RBI title in 1955 and who trots out Ted Williams stories at family picnics, or to talk about Ray's son, Bob, one of the game's better catchers for 19 years and one of the few guys who could talk to Steve Carlton. Bret, though, was up and mostly down, one season to the next, offensive surges deflated by stretches of strikeouts, his stubbornness at the plate offsetting his steady play around second base. After his first full season, with the Cincinnati Reds in '94, when he batted .320 with 68 RBIs, he was entitled to insist on a third-generation-free zone around his cubicle. However, after successive seasons of .267, .233 and .223 in Cincinnati, his run production declining, there wasn't much to talk about except the novelty of his lineage, especially after his younger brother Aaron joined the Reds in '97….

What a difference 84 RBIs make, huh? That's how many the newly buff Boone had at the All-Star break, leading the Mariners to the best record in baseball. Boone's RBI total projects him well beyond Ray's career-best total of 116 and more in line with Hack Wilson's record of 191. "It's not that I'm not proud of my family," Boone says of the attention he's receiving. "I am. But this is better."

Now enterprising reporters are calling 77-year-old Ray (who scouts for the Boston Red Sox, one of the six teams he played for) and 53-year-old Bob, who's managing the Reds, asking how they feel about the three-gen angle, the full flowering of their seed. If it's starting to bore them, maybe they should have learned to hit to all fields, too.

That's the simple explanation for one of baseball's biggest turnarounds. The righthanded hitting Boone, at 32, with nine seasons of inconsistent play behind him, is finally taking simple instruction, not trying to jerk everything down the leftfield line. An off-season conditioning program that added 20 pounds of muscle to his 5' 10" frame probably put pop in his bat. The motivation of a one-year contract might be helping, too….

Although Boone has always had considerable power for a second baseman, he had never come close to this kind of production. In 1998, in his final year with the Reds before successive one-season stints with the Atlanta Braves and the San Diego Padres, he hit a career-high 24 homers and drove in 95 runs for Cincinnati. That season earned him an All-Star berth, giving the Boones (pardon us, Bret) All-Stars across three generations, a unique distinction. This year, however, in addition to hitting .324, Boone has significantly upped his power numbers. He already has 22 homers….

Why now? At first glance (and with his shirt off), the obvious answer would seem to be his new physique…. Boone was sobered last year at San Diego when (sans muscle) he got off to an excellent start, with 16 home runs and 62 RBIs by the All-Star break, then trailed off after suffering a contusion to his right knee. That injury may have cost him as much as $25 million as potential bidders shied away. The Padres could have picked up his option for $4 million but declined. That part of it Boone understood. "I read in the paper they were going to cut $20 million in payroll," he says. "So, O.K., I'm not gonna be there. Anyway, they would have lowballed me." Boone believes other teams consequently backed away, thinking San Diego's failure to re-sign him

had to do with more than economics.

The training program was a way to take matters into his own hands. A one-year contract (as much Seattle's decision as his; still, the Mariners gave him $3.25 million) and then a stab as a free agent was another way to take responsibility for his career. It is hardly a stretch to recognize the motivation of free agency in Boone's season. "Everybody says it's not about the money," he says, "but this is how we make a living."

There are other factors in Boone's resurgence. He credits his father's off-season tutoring as much as anything. The two have had a long and happy relationship in baseball. As a preteenager growing up in San Diego, Bret tagged along with his father to the "office" whenever Dad's team was in Southern California. "A day at the park," Bret says, "was like Christmas for me…."

This past winter the two got together earlier than usual, about two weeks before Christmas, and worked on smoothing out Bret's swing….

If Boone always got along with his father, he didn't seem to do so well with father figures. He came up cocky, storming through the minors and landing in Seattle, at Piniella's feet, full of himself. That first Seattle stint was difficult, with Boone and Piniella often at odds. "It was no feud," Boone says, "but Lou was hard on me. He wants you to show him you're a big league player."

Piniella simply wanted Boone to hit behind the runner every once in a while, not strike out so much (52 whiffs in 271 at bats in '93)…. "I'm a little wiser now," says Boone. "I've been humbled…."

Humble, though, is not a word often associated with Boone. "He's still got that cockiness," says Piniella, "but this time it's all coming together."

It couldn't have happened at a better time, certainly not for the Mariners, who figured to lurch through the season without Rodriguez. And certainly not for Boone, struggling against the pressure of pedigree all these years, who's finally made a name—for himself.

—Richard Hoffer
excerpted from SI, July 16, 2001

THE NUMBERS

Final Standings

National League

EASTERN DIVISION

Team	Won	Lost	Pct	GB	Home	Away
Atlanta	88	74	.543	—	40–41	48–33
Philadelphia	86	76	.531	2	47–34	39–42
New York	82	80	.506	6	44–37	38–43
Florida	76	86	.469	12	46–34	30–52
Montreal	68	94	.420	20	34–47	34–47

CENTRAL DIVISION

Team	Won	Lost	Pct	GB	Home	Away
Houston	93	69	.574	—	44–37	49–32
†St. Louis	93	69	.574	—	54–28	39–41
Chicago	88	74	.543	5	48–33	40–41
Milwaukee	68	94	.420	25	36–45	32–49
Cincinnati	66	96	.407	27	27–54	39–42
Pittsburgh	62	100	.383	31	38–43	24–47

WESTERN DIVISION

Team	Won	Lost	Pct	GB	Home	Away
Arizona	92	70	.568	—	48–33	44–37
San Francisco	90	72	.556	2	49–32	41–40
Los Angeles	86	76	.531	6	44–37	42–39
San Diego	79	83	.488	13	35–56	44–37
Colorado	73	89	.451	19	41–40	32–49

American League

EASTERN DIVISION

Team	Won	Lost	Pct	GB	Home	Away
New York	95	65	.594	—	51–28	44–37
Boston	82	79	.509	13½	41–40	41–39
Toronto	80	82	.494	16	40–42	40–40
Baltimore	63	98	.391	32½	30–50	33–48
Tampa Bay	62	100	.383	34	37–44	25–56

CENTRAL DIVISION

Team	Won	Lost	Pct	GB	Home	Away
Cleveland	91	71	.562	—	44–36	47–35
Minnesota	85	77	.525	6	47–34	38–43
Chicago	83	79	.512	8	46–35	37–44
Detroit	66	96	.407	25	37–44	29–52
Kansas City	65	97	.401	26	35–46	30–51

WESTERN DIVISION

Team	Won	Lost	Pct	GB	Home	Away
Seattle	116	46	.716	—	57–24	59–22
†Oakland	102	60	.630	14	53–28	49–32
Anaheim	75	87	.463	41	39–42	36–45
Texas	73	89	.451	43	41–41	32–38

†Wild-card team.

2001 Individual Leaders

NATIONAL LEAGUE BATTING

Batting Average
Larry Walker, Col	.350
Todd Helton, Col	.336
Moises Alou, Hou	.331
Lance Berkman, Hou	.331
Chipper Jones, Atl	.330
Albert Pujols, StL	.329
Barry Bonds, SF	.328
Sammy Sosa, Chi	.328
Juan Pierre, Col	.327
Luis Gonzalez, Ariz	.325

Hits
Rich Aurilia, SF	206
Juan Pierre, Col	202
Luis Gonzalez, Ariz	198
Todd Helton, Col	197
Albert Pujols, StL	194
Lance Berkman, Hou	191
Fernando Vina, StL	191
Chipper Jones, StL	189
Sammy Sosa, Chi	189
Shawn Green, LA	184
Vladimir Guerrero, Mtl	184

Doubles
Lance Berkman, Hou	55
Todd Helton, Col	54
Jeff Kent, SF	49
Bobby Abreu, Phil	48
Albert Pujols, StL	47

Triples
Jimmy Rollins, Phil	12
Juan Pierre, Col	11
Juan Uribe, Col	11
Luis Castillo, Fla	10
Neifi Perez, Col	8
Michael Tucker, Chi	8
Fernando Vina, StL	8

Home Runs
Barry Bonds, SF	73
Sammy Sosa, Chi	64
Luis Gonzalez, Ariz	57
Shawn Green, LA	49
Todd Helton, Col	49
Richie Sexson, Mil	45
Phil Nevin, SD	41
Jeff Bagwell, Hou	39
Chipper Jones, Atl	38
Larry Walker, Col	38

Runs Scored
Sammy Sosa, Chi	146
Todd Helton, Col	132
Barry Bonds, SF	129
Luis Gonzalez, Ariz	128
Jeff Bagwell, Hou	126
Cliff Floyd, Fla	123
Shawn Green, LA	121
Bobby Abreu, Phil	118
Craig Biggio, Hou	118
Brian Giles, Pitt	116

Total Bases
Sammy Sosa, Chi	425
Luis Gonzalez, Ariz	419
Barry Bonds, SF	411
Todd Helton, Col	402
Shawn Green, LA	370

Stolen Bases
Juan Pierre, Col	46
Jimmy Rollins, Phil	46
Vladimir Guerrero, Mtl	37
Bobby Abreu, Phil	36
Luis Castillo, Fla	33

Runs Batted In
Sammy Sosa, Chi	160
Todd Helton, Col	146
Luis Gonzalez, Ariz	142
Barry Bonds, SF	137
Jeff Bagwell, Hou	130
Albert Pujols, StL	130
Lance Berkman, Hou	126
Phil Nevin, SD	126
Shawn Green, LA	125
Richie Sexson, Mil	125

Slugging Percentage
Barry Bonds, SF	.863
Sammy Sosa, Chi	.737
Luis Gonzalez, Ariz	.688
Todd Helton, Col	.685
Larry Walker, Col	.662

On-Base Percentage
Barry Bonds, SF	.515
Larry Walker, Col	.449
Sammy Sosa, Chi	.437
Todd Helton, Col	.432
Lance Berkman, Hou	.430

Bases on Balls
Barry Bonds, SF	177
Sammy Sosa, Chi	116
Bobby Abreu, Phil	106
Jeff Bagwell, Hou	106
Luis Gonzalez, Ariz	100

NATIONAL LEAGUE PITCHING

Earned Run Average
Randy Johnson, Ariz	2.49
Curt Schilling, Ariz	2.98
John Burkett, Atl	3.04
Greg Maddux, Atl	3.05
Darryl Kile, StL	3.09
Matt Morris, StL	3.16
Russ Ortiz, SF	3.29
Al Leiter, NY	3.31
Kerry Wood, Chi	3.36
Wade Miller, Hou	3.40

Saves
Robb Nen, SF	45
Armando Benitez, NY	43
Trevor Hoffman, SD	43
Jeff Shaw, LA	43
Jose Mesa, Phil	42
Billy Wagner, Hou	39
Danny Graves, Cin	32
Antonio Alfonseca, Fla	28
Tom Gordon, Chi	27
Mike Williams, Pitt-Hou	22

Wins
Curt Schilling, Ariz	22
Matt Morris, StL	22
Randy Johnson, Ariz	21
Jon Lieber, Chi	20
Russ Ortiz, SF	17
Greg Maddux, Atl	17
Tom Glavine, Atl	16
Wade Miller, Hou	16
Darryl Kile, StL	16

Games Pitched
Steve Kline, StL	89
Graeme Lloyd, Mtl	84
Jeff Fassero, Chi	82
Ray King, Mil	82
Felix Rodriguez, SF	80
David Weathers, Mil-Chi	80

Innings Pitched
Curt Schilling, Ariz	256⅔
Randy Johnson, Ariz	249⅔
Chan Ho Park, LA	234
Greg Maddux, Atl	233
Jon Lieber, Chi	232⅓

Strikeouts
Randy Johnson, Ariz	372
Curt Schilling, Ariz	293
Chan Ho Park, LA	218
Kerry Wood, Chi	217
Javier Vazquez, Mtl	208
John Burkett, Atl	187
Matt Morris, StL	185
Wade Miller, Hou	183
Robert Person, Phil	183
Darryl Kile, StL	179

Complete Games
Curt Schilling, Ariz	6
Jon Lieber, Chi	5
Javier Vazquez, Mtl	5
Pedro Astacio, Col-Hou	4
Todd Ritchie, Pitt	4
Randy Wolf, Phil	4

Shutouts
Greg Maddux, Atl	3
Javier Vazquez, Mtl	3
Four tied with two.	

2001 Individual Leaders *(Cont.)*

AMERICAN LEAGUE BATTING

Batting Average

Ichiro Suzuki, Sea	.350
Jason Giambi, Oak	.342
Roberto Alomar, Clev	.336
Bret Boone, Sea	.331
Frank Catalanotto, Tex	.330
Juan Gonzalez, Clev	.325
Alex Rodriguez, Tex	.318
Shannon Stewart, Tor	.316
Derek Jeter, NY	.311
Jeff Conine, Balt	.311

Hits

Ichiro Suzuki, Sea	242
Bret Boone, Sea	206
Shannon Stewart, Tor	202
Alex Rodriguez, Tex	201
Garrett Anderson, Ana	194
Roberto Alomar, Clev	193
Derek Jeter, NY	191
Carlos Beltran, KC	189
Magglio Ordonez, Chi	181
Jason Giambi, Oak	178
Terrence Long, Oak	178

Doubles

Jason Giambi, Oak	47
Mike Sweeney, KC	46
Shannon Stewart, Tor	44
Eric Chavez, Oak	43
Ray Durham, Chi	42

Triples

Cristian Guzman, Minn	14
Roberto Alomar, Clev	12
Carlos Beltran, KC	12
Roger Cedeno, Det	11
Ray Durham, Chi	10

Home Runs

Alex Rodriguez, Tex	52
Jim Thome, Clev	49
Rafael Palmeiro, Tex	47
Troy Glaus, Ana	41
Manny Ramirez, Bos	41
Carlos Delgado, Tor	39
Jason Giambi, Oak	38
Bret Boone, Sea	37
Juan Gonzalez, Clev	35
Jose Cruz Jr., Tor	34
Tino Martinez, NY	34

Runs Scored

Alex Rodriguez, Tex	133
Ichiro Suzuki, Sea	127
Bret Boone, Sea	118
Roberto Alomar, Clev	113
Derek Jeter, NY	110
Jason Giambi, Oak	109
Johnny Damon, Oak	108
Miguel Tejada, Oak	107
Carlos Beltran, KC	106
Ray Durham, Chi	104

Total Bases

Alex Rodriguez, Tex	393
Bret Boone, Sea	360
Jason Giambi, Oak	343
Rafael Palmeiro, Tex	338
Jim Thome, Clev	328

Stolen Bases

Ichiro Suzuki, Sea	56
Roger Cedeno, Det	55
Alfonso Soriano, NY	43
Mark McLemore, Sea	39
Chuck Knoblauch, NY	38

Runs Batted In

Bret Boone, Sea	141
Juan Gonzalez, Clev	140
Alex Rodriguez, Tex	135
Manny Ramirez, Bos	125
Jim Thome, Clev	124
Garret Anderson, Ana	123
Rafael Palmeiro, Tex	123
Jason Giambi, Oak	120
Edgar Martinez, Sea	116
Eric Chavez, Oak	114

Slugging Percentage

Jason Giambi, Oak	.660
Jim Thome, Clev	.624
Alex Rodriguez, Tex	.622
Manny Ramirez, Bos	.609
Juan Gonzalez, Clev	.590

On-Base Percentage

Jason Giambi, Oak	.477
Edgar Martinez, Sea	.423
Jim Thome, Clev	.416
Roberto Alomar, Clev	.415
Carlos Delgado, Tor	.408

Bases on Balls

Jason Giambi, Oak	129
Carlos Delgado, Tor	111
Jim Thome, Clev	111
Troy Glaus, Ana	107
Rafael Palmeiro, Tex	101

AMERICAN LEAGUE PITCHING

Earned Run Average

Freddy Garcia, Sea	3.05
Mike Mussina, NY	3.15
Joe Mays, Minn	3.16
Mark Buehrle, Chi	3.29
Tim Hudson, Oak	3.37
Jamie Moyer, Sea	3.43
Mark Mulder, Oak	3.45
Barry Zito, Oak	3.49
Roger Clemens, NY	3.51
Cory Lidle, Oak	3.59

Saves

Mariano Rivera, NY	50
Kazuhiro Sasaki, Sea	45
Keith Foulke, Chi	42
Troy Percival, Ana	39
Billy Koch, Tor	36
Jason Isringhausen, Oak	34
Bob Wickman, Clev	32
LaTroy Hawkins, Minn	28
Roberto Hernandez, KC	28
Jeff Zimmerman, Tex	28

Shutouts

Mark Mulder, Oak	4
Freddy Garcia, Sea	3
Mike Mussina, NY	3
Six tied with two.	

Games Pitched

Paul Quantrill, Tor	80
Mike Stanton, NY	76
Jason Grimsley, KC	73
Keith Foulke, Chi	72
Pedro Borbon, Tor	71
Arthur Rhodes, Sea	71
Mariano Rivera, NY	71

Wins

Mark Mulder, Oak	21
Roger Clemens, NY	20
Jamie Moyer, Sea	20
Freddy Garcia, Sea	18
Tim Hudson, Oak	18
Paul Abbott, Sea	17
C.C. Sabathia, Clev	17
Barry Zito, Oak	17
Mike Mussina, NY	17
Joe Mays, Minn	17

Innings Pitched

Freddy Garcia, Sea	238⅔
Tim Hudson, Oak	235
Joe Mays, Minn	233⅔
Steve Sparks, Det	232
Mark Mulder, Oak	229⅓
Jeff Weaver, Det	229⅓

Strikeouts

Hideo Nomo, Bos	220
Mike Mussina, NY	214
Roger Clemens, NY	213
Barry Zito, Oak	205
Bartolo Colon, Clev	201
Tim Hudson, Oak	181
C.C. Sabathia, Clev	171
Andy Pettitte, NY	164
Freddy Garcia, Sea	163
Pedro Martinez, Bos	163

Complete Games

Steve Sparks, Det	8
Mark Mulder, Oak	6
Brad Radke, Minn	6
Jeff Weaver, Det	5
Four tied with four.	

2001 Playoffs

NATIONAL LEAGUE DIVISIONAL PLAYOFFS

Oct 9	Atlanta 7 at Houston 4	Oct 9	St. Louis 0 at Arizona 1	
Oct 10	Atlanta 1 at Houston 0	Oct 10	St. Louis 4 at Arizona 1	
Oct 12	Houston 2 at Atlanta 6	Oct 12	Arizona 5 at St. Louis 3	
	(Atlanta won series 3–0)	Oct 13	Arizona 1 at St. Louis 4	
		Oct 14	St. Louis 1 at Arizona 2	
			(Arizona won series 3–2)	

AMERICAN LEAGUE DIVISIONAL PLAYOFFS

Oct 9	Cleveland 5 at Seattle 0	Oct 10	Oakland 5 at New York 3
Oct 11	Cleveland 1 at Seattle 5	Oct 11	Oakland 2 at New York 0
Oct 13	Seattle 2 at Cleveland 17	Oct 13	New York 1 at Oakland 0
Oct 14	Seattle 6 at Cleveland 2	Oct 14	New York 9 at Oakland 2
Oct 15	Cleveland 1 at Seattle 3	Oct 15	Oakland 3 at New York 5
(Seattle won series 3–2)		**(New York won series 3–2)**	

NATIONAL LEAGUE CHAMPIONSHIP SERIES

Oct 16	Atlanta 0 at Arizona 2	Oct 20	Arizona 11 at Atlanta 4
Oct 17	Atlanta 8 at Arizona 1	Oct 21	Arizona 3 at Atlanta 2
Oct 19	Arizona 5 at Atlanta 1	**(Arizona won series 4–1)**	

AMERICAN LEAGUE CHAMPIONSHIP SERIES

Oct 17	New York 4 at Seattle 2	Oct 21	Seattle 1 at New York 3
Oct 18	New York 3 at Seattle 2	Oct 22	Seattle 3 at New York 12
Oct 20	Seattle 14 at New York 3	**(New York won series 4–1)**	

2001 World Series

Game 1   R H E
New York 1 0 0 0 0 0 0 0 1 3 2
Arizona   1 0 4 4 0 0 0 0 x 9 10 0
W—Schilling. **L**—Mussina. **E**—New York: Justice, Brosius. **LOB**—New York 5, Arizona 6. **2B**—New York: Williams, Brosius; Arizona: Miller, Gonzalez, Grace. **HR**—Arizona: Counsell, Gonzalez. **Sac**—Arizona: Counsell. **SF**—Arizona: Williams. **T**—2:44. **A**—49,646.

Game 2   R H E
New York 0 0 0 0 0 0 0 0 0 0 3 0
Arizona   0 1 0 0 0 3 0 x 4 5 0
W—Johnson. **L**—Pettitte. **LOB**—New York 3, Arizona 1. **2B**—Arizona: Bautista. **HR**—Arizona: Williams. **GIDP**—New York: Sojo; Arizona: Miller. **T**—2:35. **A**—49,646.

Game 3   R H E
Arizona   0 0 0 1 0 0 0 0 1 1 3 3
New York 0 1 0 0 0 1 0 0 x 2 7 1
W—Clemens. **L**—Anderson. **SV**—Rivera. **E**—Arizona: Womack, Miller, Grace; New York: Soriano. **LOB**—Arizona 5, New York 8. **HR**—New York: Posada. **SF**—Arizona: Williams. **GIDP**—New York: O'Neill. **SB**—Arizona: Sanders; New York: O'Neill. **CS**—Arizona: Finley. **T**—3:26. **A**—55,820.

Game 4   R H E
Arizona   0 0 0 1 0 0 0 2 0 0 3 6 0
New York 0 0 1 0 0 0 0 2 1 4 7 0
W—Rivera. **L**—Kim. **LOB**—Arizona 7, New York 4. **2B**—Arizona: Womack, Durazo; New York: Brosius. **HR**—Arizona: Grace; New York: Spencer, Martinez, Jeter. **Sac**—Arizona: Counsell 3. **GIDP**—Arizona: Sanders, Womack; New York: Posada. **T**—3:31. **A**—55,863.

Game 5   R H E
Arizona   0 0 0 0 2 0 0 0 0 0 0 0 2 8 0
New York 0 0 0 0 0 0 0 2 0 0 1 3 9 1
W—Hitchcock. **L**—Lopez. **E**—New York: Posada. **LOB**—Arizona 9, New York 8. **HR**—Arizona: Finley, Barajas; New York: Brosius. **Sac**—Arizona: Williams; New York: Brosius. **GIDP**—Arizona: Grace; New York: Posada, O'Neill. **SB**—Arizona: Womack. **CS**—New York: Soriano. **T**—4:15. **A**—56,018.

Game 6   R H E
New York 0 0 0 0 0 2 0 0 0 2 7 1
Arizona   1 3 8 3 0 0 0 x 15 22 0
W—Johnson. **L**—Pettitte. **E**—New York: Soriano. **LOB**—New York 7, Arizona 10. **2B**—New York: Greene; Arizona: Womack, Sanders, Williams 2, Gonzalez, Miller. **GIDP**—New York: Greene; Arizona: Gonzalez. **T**—3:33. **A**—49,707.

Game 7   R H E
New York 0 0 0 0 0 0 1 1 0 2 6 3
Arizona   0 0 0 0 0 0 0 2 3 3 11 0
W—Johnson. **L**—Rivera. **E**—New York: Soriano, Clemens, Rivera. **LOB**—New York 3, Arizona 11. **2B**—New York: O'Neill; Arizona: Womack, Bautista. **HR**—New York: Soriano. **Sac**—Arizona: Miller. **CS**—Arizona: Womack. **T**—3:20. **A**—49,589.

Season of Sadness

In a year of unprecedented national calamity, the racing world came to grips with disasters of its own

MARK BECHTEL

At almost the precise instant that Michael Waltrip, one of auto racing's most personable and least successful drivers, crossed the finish line at the Daytona 500 to win his first race in 462 career starts, Dale Earnhardt, one of the sport's most popular and most successful drivers, crashed into the wall between Turns 3 and 4. A moment of long-delayed joy was instantly snuffed out by tragedy: The impact of the crash killed Earnhardt, the seven-time Winston Cup champion, and left NASCAR without its heart and soul. "Dale was the Michael Jordan of our sport," said H.A. (Humpy) Wheeler, president of Lowe's Motor Speedway near Charlotte. "To think he is not around anymore is incomprehensible. This is a terrible, terrible loss, and for me it ranks right up there with the death of JFK."

Earnhardt was chasing his 77th career win when he died. Number 76 came in a restrictor-plate race in October 2000, the Winston 500 in Talladega, Ala. That race drew raves from spectators for its 49 lead changes, which included Earnhardt's moving from 18th to first during the last five laps. Some drivers, on the other hand, were less effusive in their praise. Said Jeff Gordon, "It was a little too exciting at times for me."

The excitement came thanks to a rules change that NASCAR had made in the wake of three numbingly dull restrictor-plate races earlier in the 2000 season, including a Daytona 500 that had only nine lead changes. The sanctioning body decided to slow the cars down aerodynamically and switch to a less restrictive plate, which would give drivers the power to pass more easily. Not only did the Talladega race feature a breathtaking game of hot potato with the lead, but it also finished without the big wreck that drivers have come to expect at superspeedways.

Pleased with the Talladega experiment, NASCAR stuck with the new rules for the 2001 Daytona 500, which left some drivers skittish.

"The cars are so stable now that you feel like you are Superman, that you can do anything you want with them," Stacey Compton said two days before the race. "Some awfully talented drivers are out here, and we have a tendency to put the cars in some places they don't belong and [still expect to] come out of it. Sometimes you do, sometimes you don't."

Defending Daytona 500 champ Dale Jarrett was also cautious. "Things wouldn't have worked in Talladega if everyone hadn't used his head," he said before the 2001 Daytona. With 27 laps remaining on that fateful Sunday, Jarrett found out firsthand what happens when someone doesn't use his head. Robby Gordon got a little overanxious and tapped Ward Burton from behind, spinning Burton into Tony Stewart, who was sent tumbling through the air, spinning once and flipping twice. Stewart's airborne vehicle tore the hood off teammate Bobby Labonte's car. Nineteen cars—including Jarrett's—were involved in the wreck, and the race was red-flagged for 16 minutes. "You can't do it when you've got idiots out there," said Burton of the move to the less-restrictive plates. Earnhardt, who was just ahead of the crash, stayed out of trouble, and with five laps left he was riding in third place, behind two cars he owned—Waltrip's and Dale Earnhardt Jr.'s.

It had the makings of an interesting showdown. Only one man had gotten his first win faster than Junior, who won in 2000 at Texas in his 12th Winston Cup start, and no driver had gone longer without his first career victory than the 37-year-old Waltrip. Earnhardt seemed content to lay back and run interference for his two employees. "I was monitoring him on the radio," said rival owner Jack Roush. "He was telling the guys in front of him where to go on the track. You can draw your own conclusions what he was doing. Both of those cars up there were his."

As Waltrip outlegged Junior to the finish

Earnhardt's collision into the wall (opposite) during the race's dramatic final lap silenced the Daytona 500 crowd. "Dale's crash was the worst kind of crash," said TV commentator Darrell Waltrip. "It's like the car was shot out of a cannon."

line, Rusty Wallace came up behind Earnhardt Sr.'s car, which wiggled slightly when Wallace closed in. The black Chevrolet marked No. 3 veered left toward the lower portion of the track, took an abrupt right, got hit on the passenger side by Ken Schrader and then barreled into the wall.

The investigation into Earnhardt's death lasted months, and when NASCAR finally issued a report in August, it didn't point the finger at any individual entity. As the investigation wore on, NASCAR did its best to move forward. The week after the crash—in the first of several

results that piqued the interest of garage conspiracy theorists—Steve Park, driving a car owned by Earnhardt, won at Rockingham. Two weeks later storybook ending number two took place as Kevin Harvick, who was tapped by Richard Childress to replace Earnhardt Sr., won in Atlanta, edging Jeff Gordon at the finish line by a matter of inches. When the circuit returned to Daytona in July for the Pepsi 400, Earnhardt Jr. won in dramatic fashion—a little too dramatic for some. Drivers Jimmy Spencer and Johnny Benson both intimated that NASCAR had fixed the outcome of the race, a notion some other dri-

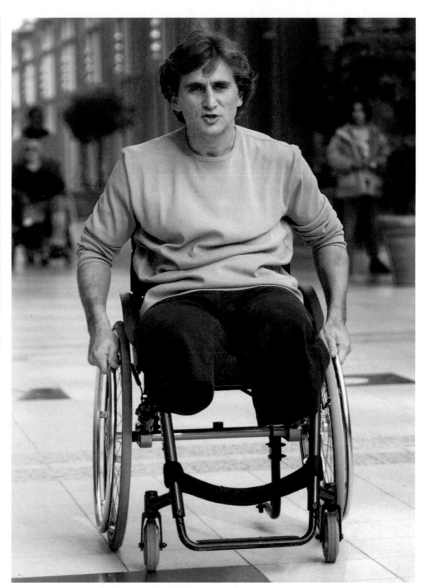

vers had a tough time swallowing. "This," said Labonte, "is not the WWF." Junior was far from pleased that his exploits were being questioned. "It's a shame," he said. "It was a great moment in NASCAR history, and it got kicked in the [groin]."

While Park, Harvick and Junior provided the most memorable wins, the driver who provided the most wins, period, was Jeff Gordon. Gordon struggled through a subpar year in 2000 with his new crew chief, Robbie Loomis. They won only three times and finished ninth in the season points race. But in their second year together

Gordon and Loomis began to click, and Gordon was back on top. The pair's biggest win of the season came at the Brickyard 400 in August, the day after Gordon's 30th birthday. "I try to live in the moment and enjoy as much of my life as I can," he said. "I'm just trying to get through age 30. . . . Hopefully [it] means I'm coming into my prime."

The era of "the Kid" may be over. Unfortunately for Gordon's fellow drivers, though, the dawning era of "the Man" didn't look to be any more enjoyable for them. Heading into the season's final weeks, he had all but wrapped up his fourth Winston Cup title.

Like every other sport, the auto racing world had difficult decisions to make in the wake of the terrorist attacks on the World Trade Center and the Pentagon. NASCAR postponed its races the following weekend, but CART and F/1 elected to run. The Formula One race in Italy

One month after losing both of his legs in a horrific accident during the American Memorial 500 in Germany, two-time CART champion Alex Zanardi (above) met the press in Berlin. Zanardi said his first priority was to learn how to walk with artificial legs, but he held out hope to someday race again.

Jeff Gordon (opposite, 24) took the checkered flag at Watkins Glen in August, a victory that set a career record for road wins (7). Gordon reestablished himself as NASCAR's most talented driver in 2001. He seized his fourth Winston Cup championship, winning six races and making 19 top five finishes.

should have been a joyous occasion for Michael Schumacher and his Ferrari Formula One team. They had already clinched both the drivers' title and the constructors' title, and the return to Ferrari's home country should have been one long party. Instead, the Ferraris ran with black nose cones, and a somber mood prevailed. "Everyone is emotionally down," Schumacher said. "It's a weekend where a lot of things are not right, and you should question whether we should race here."

As for CART's decision to go on with the German 500, CEO Joseph Heitzler said that "we will be racing with a great deal of sadness and compassion." He also announced that CART would change the name of the race to the American Memorial but otherwise proceed as planned. Heitzler and CART hoped that by carrying on in the face of tragedy they might make a small step toward healing. Sadly, the decision only resulted in more heartache as a terrifying crash left one of the sport's most popular drivers, Alex Zanardi, in critical but stable condition with both of his legs amputated close to the knee.

A 34-year-old from Italy, Zanardi was leading the race with 12 laps to go when he made a quick pit stop to refuel. As he was leaving the pits he lost control and slid across the patch of grass that separates the pit road exit from the track. He ended up facing sideways and directly in the path of Alex Tagliani, who was going nearly 200 miles an hour when he T-boned Zanardi's car, scattering debris all over the track.

Zanardi had returned to CART in 2001 after a disastrous campaign with Frank Williams in F/1. After the 1999 season Williams bought out the remainder of Zanardi's contract, and the racer returned to his home in Monaco, where he spent 2000 mostly being a husband to his wife, Daniela, a father to his son, Niccolo, and the captain of his 58-foot boat, *Hakuna Matata*, a Swahili phrase made familiar by *The Lion King* that translates to "no worries for the rest of your days." But a worry-free existence meant no racing, and eventually Zanardi's desire to drive brought him back to the United States. Morris Nunn, who had been an engineer with Zanardi's CART team before forming his own team in 2000, hired him for the 2001 season, but the two were unable to duplicate their previous success. Zanardi's best finish in 2001 was fourth, and he hadn't led a single lap all year until that Saturday in Germany—a day on which a very dark week in a dark year became a little darker still.

PHOTO GALLERY

Spiderman: After winning the 85th Indianapolis 500 in May, 26-year-old Helio Castroneves of Brazil lived up to his superhero nickname, scaling the steel-mesh net near the finish line to celebrate his victory with cheering Brickyard fans.

Michael Schumacher of Germany (right) went airborne after a collision during a practice session for the season-opening Australian Grand Prix in March. Thankfully, neither driver was injured in the accident, and Schumacher bounced back to win the race the next day. He won the following week in Malaysia as well, and took nine races during the F/I season.

With a sixth-place finish at the NAPA 500 on Nov. 18 at Atlanta Motor Speedway, Jeff Gordon (above) clinched the 2001 Winston Cup championship. The title was the fourth of Gordon's career, placing him in elite company: Only Richard Petty and Dale Earnhardt, who both won seven Winston Cup titles, have won more.

Twelve days after the terrorist attacks on New York City and Washington, D.C., Dale Earnhardt Jr. (left, 8) paid tribute to the victims by flying the American flag outside the window of his Chevrolet during his victory lap following the Cal Ripken Jr. 400 in Dover, Delaware. The win was Earnhardt Jr.'s second of the NASCAR season.

PROFILES

Dale Earnhardt Jr.

Life was so simple and sweet back on that breezy afternoon in Mooresville, N.C., last August. Dale Earnhardt Jr. (right), seven months into his first season on the Winston Cup tour, hopped into his 1971 cherry-red Corvette convertible and went roaring into the Carolina country-side, not a care in the world. With one hand on the wheel and the other hanging out of the car, Junior whizzed down Highway 136 and through the rolling foothills of the Blue Ridge. That's when he shared a secret with his passenger. "The key to all the success I've had," he said, "is my dad. It's that simple. He's taught me how to drive, how to live with integrity and how to be a man."

In the wake of his father's death, those lessons must now serve as beacons for Junior as he walks into a future that has suddenly become clouded. It had long been thought that Junior would eventually be handed the keys to the Earnhardt kingdom, but no one believed it would happen when he was just 26 years old. In racing years, he's still just a pup. In an interview last fall, Dale Sr. sat in the back of his hauler at Rockingham, stroked his bristled mustache and considered for a few moments what the distant horizons had in store for his son. He spoke about Dale Earnhardt Inc. as well as his racing team, founded in 1996, which currently has three drivers. "In the grand scheme of things, I'd like Junior to take over DEI and run the entire operation," Earnhardt said. "I'd like my other kids to also be involved if they want, but really Dale Jr. has shown the most interest."

Is Junior capable of ascending to the Earnhardt throne at such a tender age? There are several reasons to believe he is uniquely prepared to step in behind his father. There is much substance to Junior's style. A popular image of Dale Jr. is that of a wild party boy who drives cars simply to pass the time. Not true. While Junior certainly has done a few things to cultivate such a reputation,

you're more likely to find him at home surfing the Internet than out boozing with the boys. He is also an aspiring writer who can sculpt sentences in fresh ways to express his ideas. Last season, for example, Junior decided to put some thoughts about his father down on paper. Late one night in the computer room at his house in Mooresville, he spent 45 minutes transforming memories of his youth into prose.

"This man [Dale. Sr.] could lead the world's finest army," Junior wrote in the essay that was eventually posted on NASCAR's official website. "He has wis-

dom that knows no bounds. No fire could burn his character, no stone could break it. Every step he takes has purpose. Every walk has reason."

The coming weeks and months will certainly be the most difficult of Junior's young life. But just as happened with Dale Sr. when his own father died, at age 45, Junior's growth will be accelerated as a result of this tragedy. He'll be able to do this, his friends say, because of the depth of his character. "Junior is obviously going through a really tough time right now," says driver Matt Kenseth, a longtime friend. "But he'll get through this. He'll persevere. He's a tough guy."

The strengths of Senior are evident in Junior. Dale Sr. was a terror on the track, a driver who had as much courage as anyone in a generation. But that wasn't the only attribute that propelled his success. He was also fiercely loyal and profoundly talented. Look closely, and you can see these same characteristics in his son.

"I've always felt most at home with people who have known me all my life," Junior said late last season. "These are the people I want around me in the good times and the bad." It's no coincidence that Junior's crew chief is Tony Eury Jr., his best friend and cousin. Eury will be an especially important figure in Junior's life this season, the one Junior will turn to in the darkest times.

On the track Junior, like his father, drives in a fast and furious manner, always pushing his car to its limits. He's still raw, but he's getting better by the race. "He's got a good feel for the car," says Bobby Labonte. "He's not scared of it. He's not afraid to make changes. If they do make a change, he can go out and feel it and say, 'This is what the car is doing.' And they always make it better. Then you throw all that out the window, and he's a great driver on top of that." Success—and Junior will surely enjoy some this season—can only help the healing.

Junior tells the truth, the whole truth and nothing but the truth. It's refreshing to listen to him tell stories. Not only does he give you the hard-core, nonfiction account of all aspects of his life—no matter how embarrassing they may be to him—but he also does so by laughing at himself. He's not afraid to tell you about the girls who have giggled in his face while rebuffing his advances or about the times he's had a little too much fun a little too late at night. His honesty and self-deprecation have made Junior a favorite of the media, and these qualities will serve him well as he deals with the manifold pressures of chasing the ghost of his father.

"I miss my father, and I've cried for him," Junior said five days after Dale Sr.'s death. "I'm trying to maintain a good focus for the future and just remember that he's in a better place, a place that we all want to be."

Also remember that if history has taught us one thing about this family, it is this: Never underestimate an Earnhardt.

—Lars Anderson
SI, Feb. 28, 2001

Michael Schumacher

Last September in Indianapolis, Michael Schumacher (right) was asked which teams he feared heading into next year's Formula One season. Questions about 2002 were only logical because Schumacher had rendered further discussion of the 2001 season moot on Aug. 19, when he won the Grand Prix of Hungary and clinched his fourth world driving title. His victory two weeks later at Belgium was the 52nd of Schumacher's F/1 career, breaking the mark he had shared with Alain Prost. On September 30 he nearly extended that record at the United States Grand Prix at Indy, but he finished second to two-time F/1 champ Mika Hakkinen.

After Schumacher's initial response—"Fear is obviously the wrong word," he said—he turned his attention to teams that might have a shot at challenging Ferrari's hegemony. The first one he named was not McLaren, for whom Hakkinen won the world title in 1998 and '99. (Hakkinen of Finland, who turned 33 on Sept. 28, is taking next year off to spend time with his infant son.) Rather, the first rival to pop into the 32-year-old Schumacher's head was the resurgent Williams team, which has struggled mightily since

1997, when it won its ninth Constructors' Championship.

With experienced technical minds and a pair of talented young drivers— F/1 rookie Juan Montoya and Schumacher's 26-year-old brother, Ralf—Williams is enjoying a renaissance. Ralf Schumacher ended a 3½-year winless drought at San Marino on April 15, and since then he has added two victories. While Ralf has been the more consistent of the Williams drivers, Montoya poses a greater threat to the champ next year. Team boss Frank Williams was so eager to lure Montoya, who had been a test driver for him in

1997, back to England from the U.S. that he let go of Jenson Button, a popular 21-year-old Briton. Technical glitches have prevented Montoya from completing 11 of the 16 events this season, but he has a first, two seconds and a fourth in the five races he has finished. "The overwhelming sentiment on the team is one of deep anxiety," says Williams, "anxiety that we won't keep it going."

A cheeky 26-year-old from Bogota, Montoya claimed the CART championship in 1999, as a rookie, and won the Indy 500 the following year before making the jump to F/1. He had a great

chance for another victory at the Brickyard on Sept. 30. In a move that left his front tires smoking, he blazed past Michael Schumacher on the inside of Turn 1 for the lead on the 34th of 73 laps. Montoya called it "good fun." Alas, hydraulic problems forced him off the track five laps later.

Schumacher described the race as a pretty ho-hum affair—except for Montoya's pass. "I still don't know where he came from," Schumacher said. At least he knows whom to look out for next year.

—Mark Bechtel
SI, Oct. 8, 2001

Jeff Gordon

His wife on his arm, Jeff Gordon walked out of the Palace Hotel in August and into the New York City nightfall. Brooke Gordon had organized a surprise evening out in Manhattan to celebrate her husband's 30th birthday, so excitement awaited. Sparing no expense, the Gordons plunged into the city: First they dined at Daniel, an elegant East Side restaurant known for its decadent desserts. Then they moved into some prime seats for *The Producers*, the most coveted ticket on Broadway. They ended the night back at a plush suite in the Palace, a luxurious Midtown hotel. It was a very grown-up evening for Gordon, one that underscored the fact that he was passing an important mile marker in his life.

"Ever since I've been racing, I've always been the young guy," says Gordon, relaxing in the back of his transporter a few weeks after his birthday celebration. "When I was little, all my friends were older, so I always wanted to be older. But turning 30 and spending that time in New York, that's when it hit me that I'm not really considered young anymore. I've got to be more of a leader and assume more responsibility."

This 2001 edition of Jeff Gordon, Winston Cup champion, is, in fact, largely a result of his blossoming maturity. When he won his first three points titles, in 1995, '97 and '98, Gordon usually kept his mouth shut and let crew

chief Ray Evernham make all the important decisions. Evernham hired the crew, concocted the race strategy and was always the loudest voice in team meetings. So when Evernham suddenly left Hendrick Motorsports in September 1999, it was as if the 24 team had been lobotomized.

It took Gordon almost the full 2000 season—during which he learned many lessons—before he emerged as the bellwether of his racing team, the one everyone turns to in time of crisis, the one who commands everyone's attention every time he steps into a room. This is why Gordon's fourth championship is his most impressive: This one fundamentally belongs to him. . . .

"Jeff has been ready to be a leader for some time," says Evernham, who owns a two-car Dodge team. "Jeff and I first got together when he was 18. My role was to be the mentor, and he was the student. But he doesn't need a mentor anymore. He always was the key to his team's success and now, finally, I think he realizes that."

To appreciate how far Gordon has come, turn the clock back to Sept. 28, 1999—the day that Evernham left Hendrick Motorsports to lead Dodge's reentry into Winston Cup. On that day, Gordon bashers everywhere rejoiced, thinking that the Kid's dominance was over. . . .

Before Evernham left, however, he

frequently told Gordon how much he admired Robbie Loomis, John Andretti's crew chief. This turned out to be Evernham's final gift to Gordon. "Through our conversations I found Robbie to be a low-key guy, and I thought he and Jeff would get along," recalls Evernham. "Jeff didn't need a crew chief to be the leader of the team; he just needed someone who believed in him," recalls Evernham. "And Robbie thought that Jeff was the best driver in the world. . . .

Loomis met with Gordon and quickly agreed to join Hendrick Motorsports. . . . Despite having 14 new faces on the team and the fact that Loomis and team manager Brian Whitesell had to adapt to the new Monte Carlos that were introduced at the start of the 2000 season, the team was optimistic that it could challenge for a championship in its first season. That dream was quickly shattered. Gordon's average finish in the first 14 races was just 15th, and he was out of championship contention by June. The biggest problem, Loomis and Gordon now agree, was communication. As Loomis would listen to Gordon's comments while he was driving the car or talking in the garage after practice, it was as if Gordon was speaking in a different language. . . . "Jeff and Ray had been together for years, so they could communicate without even talking," recalls Loomis. "But Jeff and I didn't have that luxury last year."

For Loomis the low point came at Dover on June 4, 2000. After finishing 32nd in the MBNA Platinum 400, he walked outside the track to his car, which was parked in an outer lot. Before he made it there, though, he was stopped by a fan who yelled, "You're ruining Jeff Gordon's career, Loomis! You suck!" Loomis kept his eyes on the ground, his mouth shut and continued walking through the dusk, heading into a future that seemed more gloomy by the day.

Then it happened: Loomis and Gordon (right) started to mesh. In the first 23 races of the 2000 season they had only 11 top 10 finishes, but in the last 11 races they had 10, including a victory at Richmond. The quality of the car didn't suddenly improve, but the quality of the communication did. "Late in the 2000 season, because I had been around Jeff for a while, I started to understand what adjustments needed to be made just by how forcefully Jeff would say something over the radio," says Loomis. "We finally learned each other's language."...

What makes the 24 team special, of course, is Gordon himself. It seems almost laughable now that his success was once considered by some to be merely a result of Evernham's genius. What makes Gordon so dominant, pure and simple, is his driving ability. "Jeff has the ability to see things on the racetrack in slow motion," says Whitesell. "His eye-to-hand coordination is just unbelievable."

"Jeff can fit more in a millisecond than anybody else," says Evernham. "He has a different sense of time than the rest of us."

"I feel like I'm getting to be a better driver every day," says Gordon. "I'm just starting to come into my prime." Dale Earnhardt won six of his record-tying seven championships after turning 35. If Gordon's best days are indeed yet to come, then he'd better prepare for more special nights in New York. That's where, at the end-of-the-season awards banquet, the champion gives a speech.

—Lars Anderson
excerpted from SI *Presents*,
Dec. 5, 2001

THE NUMBERS

Indy Racing League

2001 RESULTS

DATE	RACE	WINNER (START POS.)	CHASSIS–ENGINE	AVG SPEED (MPH)
Mar 18	Pennzoil 200	Sam Hornish (2)	Dallara-Oldsmobile	125.072
Apr 8	Grand Prix of Miami	Sam Hornish (5)	Dallara-Oldsmobile	148.508
Apr 28	zMAX 500K	Greg Ray (1)	Dallara-Oldsmobile	133.647
May 27	Indianapolis 500	Helio Castroneves (11)	Dallara-Oldsmobile	153.601
June 9	Casino Magic 500K	Scott Sharp (2)	Dallara-Oldsmobile	150.873
June 17	Radisson Indy 200*	Buddy Lazier (13)	Dallara-Oldsmobile	142.987
June 30	SunTrust Indy Challenge	Buddy Lazier (4)	Dallara-Oldsmobile	97.435
July 8	Ameristar Casino 200*	Eddie Cheever (2)	Dallara-Infiniti	148.914
July 21	Harrah's Indy 200*	Buddy Lazier (6)	Dallara-Oldsmobile	144.809
Aug 12	Belterra Casino 300	Buddy Lazier (11)	Dallara-Oldsmobile	174.910
Aug 26	Gateway Indy	Al Unser Jr. (8)	G Force–Oldsmobile	136.379
Sept 2	Delphi 300	Jacques Lazier (1)	Dallara-Oldsmobile	172.146
Oct 6	Chevy 500	Sam Hornish (1)	Dallara-Oldsmobile	168.523

Note: Distances are in miles unless followed by K (kilometers) or * (laps).

2001 CHAMPIONSHIP STANDINGS

DRIVER	STARTS	HIGHEST FINISH	PTS
Sam Hornish	13	1	503
Buddy Lazier	13	1	398
Scott Sharp	13	1	355
Billy Boat	13	2	313
Eliseo Salazar	13	2	308

Championship Auto Racing Teams

2001 RESULTS

DATE	SITE	WINNER (START POS.)	CAR	AVG SPEED (MPH)
Mar 11	Monterrey	Cristiano da Matta (2)	Toyota-Lola	81.548
Apr 8	Long Beach	Helio Castroneves (1)	Honda-Reynard	86.223
May 6	Nazareth	Scott Dixon (23)	Toyota-Reynard	114.840
May 18	Japan	Kenny Brack (6)	Ford-Cosworth–Lola	178.113
June 3	Milwaukee	Kenny Brack (1)	Ford-Cosworth–Lola	122.066
June 17	Detroit	Helio Castroneves (1)	Honda-Reynard	89.008
June 24	Portland	Max Papis (1)	Ford-Cosworth–Lola	74.606
July 1	Cleveland	Dario Franchitti (14)	Honda-Reynard	118.007
July 15	Toronto	Michael Andretti (13)	Honda-Reynard	83.375
July 22	Michigan	Patrick Carpentier (21)	Ford-Cosworth–Reynard	171.498
July 29	Chicago	Kenny Brack (8)	Ford-Cosworth–Lola	132.031
Aug 12	Mid-Ohio	Helio Castroneves (2)	Honda-Reynard	106.627
Aug 19	Elkhart Lake	Bruno Junqueira (10)	Toyota-Lola	90.721
Sept 2	Vancouver	Roberto Moreno (7)	Toyota-Reynard	80.543
Sept 15	Germany	Kenny Brack (2)	Ford-Cosworth–Lola	155.319
Sept 22	England	Gil de Ferran (2)	Honda-Reynard	153.408
Oct 7	Houston	Gil de Ferran (1)	Honda-Reynard	79.521
Oct 14	Laguna Seca	Max Papis (25)	Ford-Cosworth–Lola	84.919
Oct 28	Australia	Cristiano da Matta (3)	Toyota-Lola	97.511
Nov 4	Fontana	Cristiano da Matta (2)	Toyota-Lola	149.073

2001 CHAMPIONSHIP STANDINGS

DRIVER	STARTS	WINS	PTS
Gil de Ferran	20	2	199
Kenny Brack	20	4	163
Michael Andretti	20	1	147
Helio Castroneves	20	3	141
Cristiano da Matta	20	3	140

2001 CHAMPIONSHIP STANDINGS *(Cont.)*

DRIVER	STARTS	WINS	PTS
Max Papis	20	2	107
Dario Franchitti	20	1	105
Scott Dixon	20	1	98
Tony Kanaan	20	0	93
Patrick Carpentier	20	1	91

National Association for Stock Car Auto Racing

2001 WINSTON CUP SERIES RESULTS

DATE	TRACK/DISTANCE	WINNER (START POS.)	CAR	AVG SPEED	WINNINGS ($)
Feb 18	Daytona 500	Michael Waltrip (19)	Chevrolet	161.783	1,331,185
Feb 25	N Carolina 400	Steve Park (2)	Chevrolet	111.817	144,593
Mar 4	Las Vegas 400	Jeff Gordon (24)	Chevrolet	135.546	1,369,600
Mar 11	Atlanta 500	Kevin Harvick (5)	Chevrolet	143.273	158,427
Mar 18	Darlington 400	Dale Jarrett (2)	Ford	126.557	214,612
Mar 25	Bristol 500*	Elliott Sadler (38)	Ford	86.949	124,700
Apr 1	Texas 500	Dale Jarrett (3)	Ford	141.804	444,527
Apr 8	Martinsville 500*	Dale Jarrett (13)	Ford	70.799	170,027
Apr 22	Talladega 500	Bobby Hamilton (14)	Chevrolet	184.003	173,855
Apr 29	California 500	Rusty Wallace (19)	Ford	143.118	195,090
May 5	Richmond 400*	Tony Stewart (7)	Pontiac	95.872	150,175
May 27	Charlotte 600	Jeff Burton (18)	Ford	138.107	258,846
June 3	Dover Downs 400	Jeff Gordon (2)	Chevrolet	120.361	183,907
June 10	Michigan 400	Jeff Gordon (1)	Chevrolet	134.203	240,137
June 17	Pocono 500	Ricky Rudd (1)	Ford	134.389	189,542
June 24	Sears Point 350K	Tony Stewart (3)	Pontiac	75.889	139,875
July 7	Daytona 400	Dale Earnhardt Jr. (13)	Chevrolet	157.601	185,873
July 15	Chicago 400	Kevin Harvick (6)	Chevrolet	121.200	162,500
July 22	New Hampshire 300*	Dale Jarrett (9)	Ford	102.131	238,027
July 29	Pocono 500	Bobby Labonte (11)	Pontiac	134.590	189,427
Aug 5	Indianapolis 400	Jeff Gordon (27)	Chevrolet	130.790	428,452
Aug 12	Watkins Glen 90*	Jeff Gordon (13)	Chevrolet	89.081	173,402
Aug 19	Michigan 400	Sterling Marlin (15)	Dodge	140.513	157,830
Aug 25	Bristol 500*	Tony Stewart (18)	Pontiac	85.106	189,415
Sept 2	Darlington 500	Ward Burton (37)	Dodge	122.773	181,435
Sept 8	Richmond 400*	Ricky Rudd (9)	Ford	95.146	171,992
Sept 23	Dover Downs 400	Dale Earnhardt Jr. (3)	Chevrolet	101.559	168,858
Sept 30	Kansas 400	Jeff Gordon (2)	Chevrolet	110.576	254,377
Oct 7	Lowe's 500	Sterling Marlin (13)	Dodge	139.006	196,360
Oct 15	Martinsville 500	Ricky Craven (6)	Ford	75.750	130,475
Oct 21	Talladega 500	Dale Earnhardt Jr. (6)	Chevrolet	185.240	165,773
Oct 28	Phoenix 500	Jeff Burton (3)	Ford	102.613	213,491
Nov 4	N Carolina 400	Joe Nemechek (13)	Chevrolet	128.941	157,535
Nov 11	Miami 400	Bill Elliott (1)	Dodge	117.449	319,273
Nov 18	Atlanta 500	Bobby Labonte (39)	Pontiac	n/a	233,227
Nov 23	New Hampshire 300	Robby Gordon (31)	Chevrolet	103.594	203,924

Distances are in miles unless followed by K (kilometers) or * (laps).

DRIVER	PTS	STARTS	WINS	TOP 5	TOP 10	DRIVER	PTS	STARTS	WINS	TOP 5	TOP 10
Jeff Gordon	5112	36	6	18	24	Bobby Labonte	4561	36	2	9	20
Tony Stewart	4763	36	3	15	22	Rusty Wallace	4481	36	1	8	14
Sterling Marlin	4741	36	2	12	20	Dale Earnhardt Jr.	4460	36	3	9	15
Ricky Rudd	4706	36	2	14	22	Kevin Harvick	4406	35	2	6	16
Dale Jarrett	4612	36	4	12	19	Jeff Burton	4394	36	2	8	16

Formula One Racing

2001 FORMULA ONE RESULTS

DATE	GRAND PRIX	WINNER	CAR	TIME
Mar 4	Australia	Michael Schumacher	Ferrari	1:38:26.533
Mar 18	Malaysia	Michael Schumacher	Ferrari	1:47:34.801
Apr 1	Brazil	David Coulthard	McLaren-Mercedes	1:39:00.834
Apr 15	San Marino	Ralf Schumacher	BMW-Williams	1:30:44.817
Apr 29	Spain	Michael Schumacher	Ferrari	1:31:03.305
May 13	Austria	David Coulthard	McLaren-Mercedes	1:27:45.927
May 27	Monaco	Michael Schumacher	Ferrari	1:47:22.561
June 10	Canada	Ralf Schumacher	BMW-Williams	1:34:31.522
June 24	Europe	Michael Schumacher	Ferrari	1:29:42.724
July 1	France	Michael Schumacher	Ferrari	1:33:35.636
July 15	Britain	Mika Hakkinen	McLaren-Mercedes	1:25:33.770
July 29	Germany	Ralf Schumacher	BMW-Williams	1:18:17.873
Aug 19	Hungary	Michael Schumacher	Ferrari	1:41:49.675
Sept 2	Belgium	Michael Schumacher	Ferrari	1:08:05.002
Sept 16	Italy	Juan Pablo Montoya	BMW-Williams	1:16:58.493
Sept 30	United States	Mika Hakkinen	McLaren-Mercedes	1:32:42.840
Oct 14	Japan	Michael Schumacher	Ferrari	1:27:33.298

2001 CHAMPIONSHIP STANDINGS

DRIVER	STARTS	HIGHEST FINISH	PTS
Michael Schumacher	17	1	123
David Coulthard	17	1	65
Rubens Barrichello	17	2	56
Ralf Schumacher	17	1	49
Mika Hakkinen	17	1	37
Juan Pablo Montoya	17	1	31
Nick Heidfeld	17	3	13
Jacques Villeneuve	17	3	12
Kimi Raikkonen	17	4	9
Jarno Trulli	17	4	9

Miami Nice

Ditching the trash-talking ways of previous Hurricanes teams, Miami gave the BCS an unbeaten and undisputed champion

B.J. SCHECTER

Let the record show that for the fourth consecutive year the best team won the national championship. There is not a whisper of controversy or a shred of doubt about those results, but there was plenty of carping, passionate debate and outrage-in-waiting leading up to them. The much maligned, four-year-old Bowl Championship Series, which rates teams in an effort to guarantee that the best two play for the national championship, has been rejiggered and retooled each off-season to compensate for its flaws. Much has been said about the near-comic complexity, distortions and injustices of the BCS system, but this much is true: Tennessee (champions of the 1998 season), Florida State (1999), Oklahoma (2000) and Miami (2001) were inarguably, undeniably, the best teams in the country during their respective championship seasons.

That's the good news. The bad news is that the carpers, complainers and passionate debaters had a point, and that the greatest strength of the BCS, especially during the past two seasons, seems to have been good fortune. The system has been vindicated by the right team prevailing at the right time. Miami proved its might this year with an impressive 37–14 stomping of Nebraska in the Rose Bowl. No one could argue with the 13–0 Hurricanes being crowned national champs. Nor could anyone complain about Oklahoma's national title following the 2000 season, when the Sooners capped a perfect season with a 13–2 victory over Florida State in the Orange Bowl.

But what would have happened if Florida State had upset the orange cart with a victory over Oklahoma in 2000, or if Nebraska had pruned Miami this season? A split vote, that's what, and the entire convoluted BCS system would have been undermined. Its sole purpose, after all, is to produce a clear-cut national champion.

But no system, short of one involving playoffs, can guarantee a controversy-free result every year.

It's against all odds that the BCS has a perfect 4–0 record and seemingly only a matter of time before it produces a genuine season-ending controversy.

Before the Rose Bowl, bashers of the system from coast to coast wondered how Nebraska (11–1), which was coming off an embarrassing 62–36 loss to Colorado and didn't even win its own conference, could be a more worthy national title contender than, say, Pac-10 champion Oregon (10–1) or Big 12 champ Colorado (10–2).

But the Hurricanes stormed the Rose Bowl and swept away all debate, proving they were in a class by themselves. Miami raced to a 34–0 half-time lead and held on to win its fifth national title, completing an impressive comeback from NCAA purgatory. When Butch Davis took over the Miami program in 1995, the Hurricanes were a mess. The team was filled with bad seeds who had frequent brushes with the law, and the NCAA had recently stripped the Hurricanes of 31 scholarships for rules violations. It took more than six years, but when Davis left Miami for the NFL's Cleveland Browns after the 2000 season, the Hurricanes were national title contenders again.

And Davis did it the right way, by instilling a no-nonsense approach and winning with class. He booted the thugs off the team, changed Miami's recruiting philosophy and banned the woofing, showboating antics that Miami had become famous for. When Davis left, the players lobbied for soft-spoken offensive coordinator Larry Coker to get the job. "By hiring coach Coker we know we can keep this thing going," said junior quarterback Ken Dorsey during Miami's search for a new coach. "There's no feeling-out process or a new set of rules. He's comfortable with us, we're comfortable with him." After unsuccessfully attempting to hire a bigger name, Miami finally settled on Coker. "When he was named coach there was no doubt we were going to win the national championship," said senior safety Ed Reed.

Rising to the Occasion: With the national championship on the line, Dorsey (opposite) threw for a career-high 362 yards and three touchdowns in the Rose Bowl against Nebraska. The junior quarterback was named Co-MVP of the game.

Heisman candidate Harrington (above, 3) and Oregon believed they deserved a shot at the national title, but denied that, they proved themselves with a convincing 38-16 win over Colorado in the Fiesta Bowl. The Ducks finished the season ranked second in the nation in both the AP and coaches' polls.

lineman Dan Klecko got in the face of Hurricanes tackle Martin Bibla after a running play during which Klecko felt he was held. Fellow Hurricanes offensive lineman Joaquin Gonzalez quickly interceded. "He was ready to fight," says Gonzalez of Klecko. "I put my arm around him and said, 'Dude, you have the most beautiful eyes I've ever seen.' He had no clue what to do."

Miami players were just as resourceful when it came to winning close games. Late in their Nov. 10 meeting with Boston College in Chestnut Hill, the Hurricanes led 12–7 but were giving up chunks of yardage to the Eagles as time wound down. A 21-yard pass from Boston College quarterback Brian St. Pierre to receiver Dedric Dewalt brought BC to the Miami nine-yard line with one minute remaining. On the next play, Hurricanes cornerback Mike Rumph deflected a St. Pierre pass into the arms of defensive tackle Matt Walters, who started rumbling upfield with the ball. As Walters was about to be tackled, safety Ed Reed ripped the ball out of his hands and raced 80 yards for a touchdown, giving Miami an 18–7 victory. Reed figured in the Hurricanes' other tight win—a 26–24 defeat of 13th-ranked Virginia Tech on Dec. 1—making an interception late in the game to preserve the victory.

When they hit their stride, the Hurricanes were all but unstoppable. Led by a quarterback who looked like a displaced member of the tennis team, Miami could be utterly dominating. California native Ken Dorsey, a rail-thin 6' 5", 200-pound junior signal-caller, had long dreamed about playing in the Rose Bowl. Problem was, most of the top-flight programs that caught a glimpse of his gangly frame decided not to take a chance on him. California didn't want him; Michigan passed. Miami rolled the dice on Dorsey and soon found out that the heart of an unusually fiery competitor burned within the lean, soft-spoken exterior.

Dorsey never forgot his only loss in two seasons as a starter—a 34–29 defeat at Washington in 2000—and used it as motivation. It worked. With the Rose Bowl win over Nebraska, Dorsey improved his record as a starter to 26–1. He picked apart the Cornhuskers secondary with precision passing, throwing for a career-high 362 yards and three touchdowns, and was named the game's co-MVP.

On the other side of the ball, Miami's defense blunted Nebraska's normally razor-sharp option offense. Even though he rushed for 114 yards, Eric Crouch, the Cornuskers' Heisman Trophy–winning quarterback, wasn't much of a factor. More often than not, the option play left him, well, limited options. "Even if they did get

Coker didn't change much from the Davis regime, and the Hurricanes didn't miss a beat. Possessed of blazing team speed, Miami bottled up opponents on defense and blew past them on offense. Some wondered whether Coker, in his first head coaching position, would crack under the immense pressure that comes with being Miami's football coach. Those concerns were misplaced, to say the least, as Coker relied on the stoicism instilled in him during his more than 25 years as an assistant and strode the sidelines with quiet confidence in his new, high-profile position. Some of his understated persona even rubbed off on the Hurricanes, who were, dare we say, humble—an adjective that almost certainly has never been applied to them in the past.

To illustrate how far Miami has come since the trash-talking days of the late '80s and early '90s, one need look no further than their game against Temple on Nov. 3. In the first half, Owls defensive

outside," said Miami sophomore linebacker D.J. Williams, "we felt we had the speed to run them down." Williams did just that, stripping Crouch of the football in the first quarter for the first of two turnovers by the Nebraska quarterback. Crouch also threw an interception that was returned for a touchdown in the second quarter.

Among the swarming Miami defense, Williams stood out in the first half, and sophomore linebacker Jonathan Vilma starred in the second. He had eight tackles, including two bone-crushing hits that drew roars from the crowd. Not that Vilma or his teammates were about to gloat. These Hurricanes knew that actions speak louder than words. "We have a lot of quiet, easygoing guys like me who leave it all on the field," said Vilma. "People talk at us and we listen and say, 'That's nice. Now look at the scoreboard.'"

Fans watching the scoreboards during the last two weeks of the college football season had to

wonder if they were hallucinating. After Nebraska was walloped by Colorado, it looked like the Cornhuskers would need a minor miracle to get back into the national championship race. They got a succession of them, as contenders began to fall one by one. First, Oklahoma was upset by Oklahoma State on Nov. 24. It was the Sooners' second loss of the season, effectively ending the defending champs chances of repeating. Then Florida absorbed *its* second loss of the year, a 34–32 loss at home to Tennessee on Dec. 1.

The following weekend, Colorado edged Texas 39–37 in the Big 12 championship game, opening the BCS door for 10–1 Tennessee. On Dec. 8, the day Tennessee faced LSU for the SEC title in Atlanta, Nebraska's Crouch won the Heisman by a narrow margin over Florida quarterback Rex Grossman. Crouch's day got even better, for in Atlanta, Matt Mauck, a little-used backup quarterback from Santa Claus, Ind., gave Crouch and

Running back Clinton Portis (above) sparked Miami's 27-point second quarter in the Rose Bowl, dashing 39 yards for a score at the start of the period to give Miami a 14–0 lead. A junior, Portis finished with 104 yards rushing on 20 carries.

Mauck (above), a 22-year-old freshman backup who spent four years playing minor league baseball, ran for two touchdowns and led LSU on five scoring drives in the SEC championship game against Tennessee. The Tigers' 31–20 victory dashed the Vols' national title hopes.

lous amount of money on publicity, but it accomplished its goal of drawing attention to the team, which had the talent to back up the hype: SPORTS ILLUSTRATED picked Oregon as its preseaon No. 2, and the Ducks lived up to that lofty ranking with six straight wins to start the season.

A 49–42 loss to Stanford on Oct. 20 took Oregon temporarily out of the national championship picture, but the Ducks stayed the course and won the rest of their games to take the Pac-10 title. With a win over Colorado in the Fiesta Bowl, Oregon could put itself in a position to claim a piece of the national title. Harrington didn't miss his opportunity. In front of a national television audience, he produced a Joe Montana–like performance, completing passes from all over the field to seven receivers and leading Oregon to a convincing 38–16 win. "Not only was it the biggest win, but it was on the biggest stage, and we did it in one of the most emphatic manners," said Harrington, who threw for 350 yards and four touchdowns. "We made a statement today, 38 unanswered points, and shot down the hottest team in the country."

One of the hottest teams early in the season was unheralded Fresno State. Unranked in the preseason, Fresno vaulted into the Top 10 with wins over three quality opponents to start the year. The Bulldogs opened the season with a head-turning 24–22 victory at Colorado and then showed the win was no fluke by knocking off Oregon State 44–24 at home the following week. (Oregon State was SI's preseason No. 1.) On Sept. 8, the Bulldogs pulled off their most impressive win, rallying from a 20–10 halftime deficit at Wisconsin to shock the Badgers 32–20. After the victory over Wisconsin, Bulldogs players and coaches played it cool, their relatively muted celebration suggesting that they'd expected to win. Instead of whooping and hollering, Fresno State players held their index fingers to their lips and said, "Shhh! Fresno State football—it's a secret."

It wouldn't be a secret for long. With strong-armed quarterback David Carr, a variety of players ignored by bigger programs and gutsy coach Pat Hill, the Bulldogs threatened to crash the BCS party. (Fresno State plays in the Western Athletic Conference, which doesn't have an automatic bid to one of the four BCS games.) But Fresno's star dropped precipitously with consecutive losses to Boise State and Hawaii in October. Brigham Young, which won its first 12 games, also caused a stir by threatening to take the NCAA to court if it were left out of the BCS, but the Cougars wisely scrapped that idea after they were blown out by Hawaii in their season finale.

In a year that will be forever remembered for

Nebraska an early Christmas present, leading the Tigers to a 31–20 upset of Tennessee.

The series of improbable results nearly short-circuited the BCS computers, not to mention the wiring of Oregon coach Mike Bellotti, whose 10–1 Ducks felt snubbed by the system. Bellotti didn't mince words, "I liken the BCS to a bad disease," he said, "like a cancer." The Ducks would prove that as a motivating force, righteous indignation has few equals. With a chip teetering on its collective shoulder, Oregon traveled to Tempe, Ariz., for a Fiesta Bowl showdown against Colorado.

At the beginning of the season, Oregon had been the darling of the college football nation. Something of a new kid on the block, Oregon embarked on a huge public relations campaign during the summer to promote quarterback Joey Harrington as a Heisman Trophy candidate. Alumni and boosters paid $250,000 to rent a 100-foot billboard in New York City that set Harrington's mug towering over Times Square. Ducks supporters rented smaller billboards all up and down the West Coast. Initially, Oregon took a lot of heat for spending what seemed like a ridicu-

catastrophe, tragedy struck college football before practices officially started. During a routine conditioning drill, Northwestern defensive back Rashidi Wheeler collapsed and died of an acute bronchial asthma attack on Aug. 3. The nation, of course, would endure horrific losses the following month as hijacked planes hit New York City, Washington, D.C., and western Pennsylvania. In addition to raising many security concerns and causing many schools to institute no-fly zones over their stadiums, the Sept. 11 attacks created widespread debate over whether or not games should be played on Sept. 15. While most schools postponed or canceled their games, the SEC, which had the Tennessee-Florida game on its schedule that Saturday, was determined to play. In the end, the SEC games were postponed, under pressure, along with the rest of the nation's schedule.

The bowl season and its aftermath brought a couple of high-profile coaching changes. Notre Dame fired coach Bob Davie, who had gone 35–25 during five seasons in South Bend. The school hired former Georgia Tech coach George O'Leary to replace Davie, but forced him to resign five

days later after a New Hampshire newspaper revealed that O'Leary had lied on his résumé for more than 20 years. Notre Dame quickly papered over this p.r. disaster by hiring former Stanford coach Tyrone Willingham, who had run a spotless program in Palo Alto. Willingham would be the first African-American to lead the most storied college football program in the country, following the likes of Knute Rockne and Ara Parseghian.

Florida coach Steve Spurrier shocked the college football world by unexpectedly resigning after 12 seasons. He later signed a five-year deal to coach the NFL's Washington Redskins. The Gators tried to sign big-name coaches Bob Stoops (Oklahoma) and Mike Shanahan (Denver Broncos) before finally settling on New Orleans Saints defensive coordinator Ron Zook.

In a year when infinitely larger issues occupied our attention, it was almost refreshing to see fans and coaches getting riled up about the BCS at season's end. It was left to Miami to cut through the static with a clear reminder of a perennial college football truth, BCS or no: Win all your games and there are no lingering questions.

Colorado's Bobby Purify (above, 42) set the tone for his team's 62–36 trouncing of Nebraska on Nov. 23, scampering 39 yards for a touchdown 2:43 into the first quarter. Purify ran for 154 yards but was outdone by his teammate Chris Brown, who rushed for 198 yards and a school-record six touchdowns.

PHOTO GALLERY

Badger Ballet: Wisconsin defensive back Joey Boese (above) approximated classical dance's panché arabesque position while picking off a pass intended for Penn State tight end John Gilmore (rear) in the fourth quarter of the Badgers' 18–6 road victory on Sept. 22. Both Penn State and Wisconsin finished the season under .500.

Cardinal Rules: Six-foot-seven Teyo Johnson of Stanford (right) outreached UCLA's Joe Hunter and Marques Anderson to make a one-handed touchdown catch during the Cardinal's 38–28 upset of the Bruins on Oct. 27. The loss was UCLA's first of the year after six wins.

Florida State flanker Atrews Bell (above, with ball) leaped over Virginia Tech defensive back Larry Austin to catch a pass from quarterback Chris Rix in the third quarter of the Seminoles' 30–17 victory in the Gator Bowl on New Year's Day. Both the Hokies and the Seminoles finished the season with 8–4 records.

As the Cornhuskers faithful erupted behind him, Nebraska quarterback Eric Crouch (left) raced to the end zone with a pass from wingback Mike Stuntz to complete a 63-yard trick play against Oklahoma on Oct. 27. The touchdown sealed Nebraska's 20–10 victory and ended the Sooners' 20-game winning streak, the longest in Division I-A at the time.

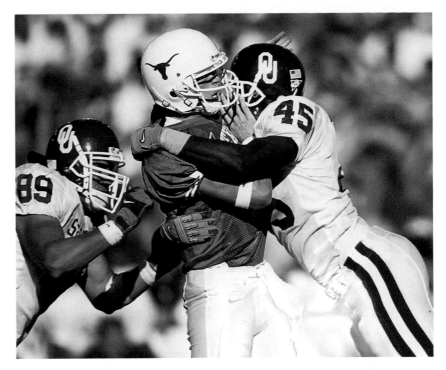

Sooner Sandwich: Oklahoma's Jimmy Wilkerson (above, 45) and Cory Heinecke (89) converged on Texas quarterback Chris Simms in the fourth quarter of the Sooners' 14–3 victory over the Longhorns in a battle of unbeatens at the Cotton Bowl on Oct. 6.

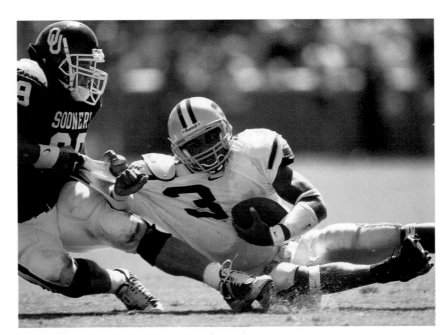

What a Drag: Oklahoma's Cory Heinecke (above, left) pulled Kansas State quarterback Ell Roberson to the turf during the Sooners' 38–37 win on Sept. 29. The game kicked off a four-game losing skid for the Wildcats.

Fresno State's Bernard Berrian (left) blazed 96 yards for a touchdown on the opening kickoff of the second half to jump-start the Bulldogs' 32–20 upset victory over 23rd-ranked Wisconsin on Sept. 8. Berrian, a junior wideout, finished the game with 182 return yards and 102 receiving yards.

PROFILES

Eric Crouch

What's it like being Eric Crouch in Lincoln, Neb.? "Let me put it this way," says Crouch, the Cornhuskers' senior quarterback. "The fans know what doors I come out of and what days I come out of them." . . .

As he left the football complex last Thursday, he was approached by a dozen or so autograph seekers. "It's pretty intense, and that's O.K.," says Crouch. "I understand my role here. I find the joy in it."

Leading the Cornhuskers to an 11–0 record and a No. 1 ranking in the BCS ratings, as Crouch (opposite) has done, is but one facet of that role. Between discharging his football duties and carrying 11 credit hours (including working as a lab instructor overseeing 30 students in an exercise and health-behavior class), Crouch, an exercise-science major, is winning games but losing sleep. "I'm putting in, on average, 16-hour days," he says . . . .

Last month he stopped by a Lincoln hospital to cheer up one patient but ended up visiting everyone on the floor. He's gregarious to a fault—until the conversation turns to his child. Crouch lives with his longtime girlfriend, Nicole Kousgaard, and their two-year-old daughter, Alexi. Raise the subject of Alexi, and the usually chatty Crouch chooses his words carefully. "I'm very proud of Lexi," says Eric, who has dated Kousgaard since they were students at Omaha's Millard North High. "The only downside about what I do is that I have almost no privacy. I have to feel there's something in my life that everyone else doesn't have."

It's a source of pride to his mother, Susan Sanchez, that as a popular grade school kid, Eric often befriended students whom others teased. "I talk to them, become friends with them," he would tell his mother, "and they don't get picked on anymore." Who would have thought that such a good guy would be such a badass on the field? Who could have predicted that this pretty-boy would play the game with such a mean streak?

Not the Creighton Prep fullback whom Crouch knocked out of the game as a high school sophomore in 1994. And not the Iowa safety who met Crouch at the goal line two years ago. "It was at the end of a 40-yard run," says Nebraska left tackle David Volk, "and Eric dropped his shoulder, laid the guy out and went in standing up."

As it turns out, the 6' 1", 192-pound Crouch, who until this season had spent most of his Nebraska career playing hurt and who prides himself on his stoicism, shed some of the most storied tears in Cornhuskers history. It happened in August 1999, when coach Frank Solich gave junior Bobby Newcombe the starting quarterback job. Crouch, then a sophomore, felt he'd outperformed Newcombe in preseason camp, and got in his car and headed home. "He just wanted to come home and be with someone who cared about him," says Sanchez. "Anybody who knows Eric knows he's not a quitter. Everyone's entitled to cry once in a while."

Solich replaced Newcombe with Crouch later in the season, and a career was launched . . . .

Crouch has no peer in the college game at running the option, which is the main reason why he's the leading candidate for the Heisman Trophy. [Crouch won the Heisman.—Ed.] Iowa State coach Dan McCarney says that Crouch is the best offensive player he's ever coached against. Adds Kansas State coach Bill Snyder, "If you get just a little bit out of position, he makes you look like a fourth-grader." . . .

His 95-yard carnival ride of a run against Missouri on Sept. 29—the longest by a Nebraska player—actually went for 103 yards. After having taken the snap at his own five-yard line, Crouch dropped back into the end zone and barely missed being sacked for a safety before zigzagging his way to one of the most remarkable plays of the season . . . .

Last year Crouch suffered from chronic back pain, inflamed bursas in both elbows and a torn labrum in his right shoulder that affected his passing and required off-season surgery.

That operation was performed last January, and Crouch's rehab went smoothly . . . .

[Former Dallas Cowboys scout Gil] Brandt is a Crouch fan and believes there's a place for him in the NFL. It could be at receiver, could be at safety, could be at quarterback. "Every year, you're seeing offenses go a little bit further, become a little bit more creative," says Brandt. "Maybe you bring Crouch in as a third-and-one quarterback to run the option. Maybe you put him in the shotgun on the goal line. He'd scare the heck out of people."

Could Crouch be an every-down quarterback in the league? Maybe. While he has completed an impressive 57.1% of his passes this season, he's also thrown more interceptions (eight) than touchdown passes (seven) . . . .

"Right now," he says, "to worry about only football and get paid for it—I can't even imagine how great that would be."

Crouch offers a brief glimpse into his private life: "On Mondays, I get up at 6:30, get Lexi ready for day care, drop her off at 8:30." Lexi, he confirms, is out of diapers and into pull-ups. Bedtime goes much more smoothly if he's there to arrange her hair. On those nights when he gets home after Lexi is asleep, he goes into her room before he crashes. He just wants to look at her.

"These days," he says, "it seems like I wake up, catch my breath, and it's time to go to bed again. Then, in the middle of the night, I get an elbow in the ribs"—Nicole's signal that it's his turn to minister to their crying child. Crouch goes without complaint. He knows his role and finds the joy in it.

—Austin Murphy
excerpted from SI, Nov. 26, 2001

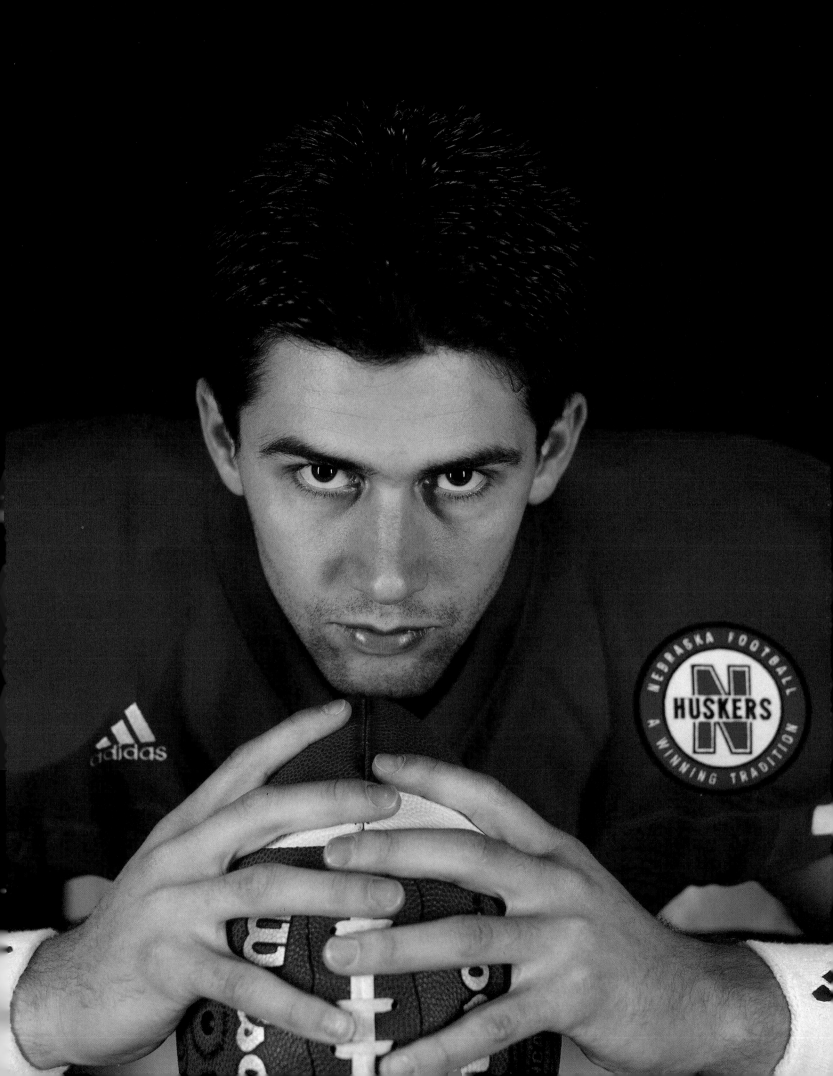

Julius Peppers

Big Head never liked football much. Same as any kid with a Tobacco Road address, Julius Frazier Peppers's dreams were wrapped up in basketball. He would shoot hoops for an hour in the morning before the school bus arrived, and he'd shoot through the evening until his mother, Bessie, came out of the family's trailer home in Bailey, N.C., to fetch him for bed. Basketball was in his genes and in his name, but he didn't think about the origin of things . . . .

He never considered playing varsity football until a spring day in 1995 when Southern Nash Senior High football coach Ray Davis cut a deal with the 15-year-old freshman basketball player who at 6' 5" and 225 pounds was a foot taller than Davis and 45 pounds heavier. "I said, 'Julius, why don't you come out for football in the fall?' " Davis recalls. "I promised him we'd let him carry the ball, and his eyes lit up. The rest is history."

Peppers (left) was the best basketball player and among the best football players ever at Southern Nash, where he received so many recruiting letters that he was given his own mail slot in the school office . . . . In his final football game, when Northeast Guilford High ran a sweep away from Peppers, he chased down the running back, stole the ball from behind and raced 90 yards the other way for a touchdown . . . . Davis still shakes his head in disbelief as he recalls a three-hour football practice on a scorching summer day before Peppers's junior season, after which all the other Firebirds lay sprawled on the grass or huddled around the water spigot. Peppers strolled over to one end zone and began doing backflips the length of the field. No hands. For 100 yards. In full pads and helmet.

He was called Big Head because he had a large hat size, not an inflated ego. "As a kid I never saw myself as unusual," Peppers says. "I always thought that lots of people could do what I did. More and more I realized I was wrong."

He wound up accepting a football scholarship to North Carolina, moving only 53 miles west of Bailey to Chapel Hill, where he could join the basketball team as a walk-on. Recruiters had convinced him that his greatest potential was in football, and he quickly demonstrated the wisdom of that judgment. As a sophomore last season he led the nation with 15 sacks, one short of the school record Lawrence Taylor set in 1980. "He's one of those rare pass rushers who has a dominant effect on a game," Duke coach Carl Franks says. "He's simply a better athlete than any offensive tackle he faces."

Peppers has never wavered from his commitment to football, but neither has he let go of his first love. In November 1999 he joined the North Carolina basketball team, figuring that playing power forward would keep him in shape—and out of spring football practice. Although he wasn't counting on much playing time, Peppers quickly moved up the bench and into the role of sixth man . . . .

While scouts from the NFL and the NBA believe Peppers could excel in either league, he has made up his mind to play football. He's made a full-scale commitment to training. That means working out five days a week for three to four hours a day. "I'll miss basketball," he says, "but I think I'll be a much better football player now that I'm training for it like a normal player." . . .

George Kurney grew up in Sims, three miles east of Bailey, during the 1960s. He shot baskets every day on a dirt court in his yard and dreamed of being Oscar Robertson. By the time Kurney had reached the ninth grade at Rock Ridge High, he could dunk with either hand. Rock Ridge coach James Kent told Kurney that he had the potential to play college ball, but the next season Kurney quit the team. His father, William, had died two years earlier, and his mother, Mildred, had taken a job in the evenings. So if George missed the bus after school to stay for basketball practice, he had to walk the six miles home. Shortly after he dropped basketball, he dropped out of school. He worked odd jobs while becoming a recreation-league hoops mainstay . . . .

In 1979 Kurney was driving to a rec game when he saw Bessie Peppers standing on her porch. A few weeks later he asked her out, and they began a two-year relationship that on Jan. 18, 1980, produced a nine-pound, 14-ounce baby boy . . . .

George all but vanished from Julius's life before he was seven, leaving Bessie to raise their son. Although Kurney now lives in Bailey, a half mile from Bessie, he and Julius speak infrequently. "A lot of people tell me that I could have done what Julius is doing," says Kurney, age 41. "He got his size from me, and he's using it to fulfill the dream that I never experienced. I hope someday he'll decide to share it with me." Julius says he has no plans to invite his father into his life. "He and I talk sometimes, but not like a father and son," Peppers says.

One night after a basketball game at Southern Nash, Kent told Julius how much he reminded him of George Kurney. Julius pointedly informed Kent that Kurney was his father, but that he was his mother's son. Bessie made sure Julius was a well-mannered boy . . . . Even now, after a sack or a dunk, he heads quietly back to the huddle or downcourt as if nothing had happened.

"There are really two Juliuses," Bessie says. "He's normally a quiet, shy, thoughtful kid, but when he puts on a uniform, he can become quite a bully." . . .

NFL scouts say that Peppers has the potential to be the No. 1 pick in the 2002 draft. "I still believe that if I committed to basketball, I could make an impact in the NBA," says Peppers. "But my coaches say that in football I could be another Lawrence Taylor or Jevon Kearse."

Because of his outstanding NCAA tournament play on national television, as opposed to the North Carolina football team's combined 9–13 record in 1999 and 2000, most casual sports fans still think of Peppers as a basketball player. But Peppers is only 12 sacks shy of Greg Ellis's school career record (32.5). "On a learning curve of zero to 10, Julius is still a five," says North Carolina coach John Bunting, who played 11 years at linebacker in the NFL. "That room for growth should be exciting to him and scary to everybody else."

—Tim Crothers
excerpted from SI, Aug. 13, 2001

David Carr

For such a huge victory, it seemed a rather muted celebration. On the other hand, what are we to expect from a team whose motto is, Shut up and hit somebody? After storming from behind to stun No. 23 Wisconsin in Madison last Saturday, a handful of Fresno State Bulldogs unveiled a new shtick. Instead of wagging their index fingers in the air, they held them to their lips like librarians. "Shhh!" they said. "Fresno State football—it's a secret."

Not for long. The Bulldogs' 32–20 win before 78,506 at Camp Randall Stadium marked their third straight upset of an opponent from a major conference. It came 13 days after a dramatic 24–22 victory at Colorado and six days after the Bulldogs had extended their home winning streak to 16 games by knocking off then No. 10 Oregon State 44–24. The surprising start moved Fresno State, unranked in the preseason, to No. 11. Not one of the 10 unbeaten teams ranked above the Bulldogs has such an impressive collection of wins, mainly because none is coached by Pat (Have Playbook, Will Travel) Hill. Now in his fifth season at Fresno, Hill knows that wins over Western Athletic Conference opponents won't bring his program national prominence, so he has made the Bulldogs' nonconference schedule as tough as possible. "We'll go anywhere and play anyone," says the 49-year-old Hill . . . .

If his scheduling philosophy is, No cupcakes, Hill's recruiting credo could be, Lock up the valley. He wants gifted players in the San Joaquin Valley to dream of becoming Bulldogs. It's working. More than half of Hill's starters hail from this fertile plain between the Sierra Nevada and the Pacific. It is an area bounded by Bakersfield to the south and Sacramento to the north and bisected by State Highway 99, where a billboard urges motorists to DEMAND ILLEGAL ALIENS BE DEPORTED. THE JOB YOU SAVE MAY BE YOUR OWN.

The comeback against Wisconsin— Fresno State was down 20–10 at the half—was kick-started by homegrown junior wideout Bernard Berrian . . . . His 96-yard kickoff return for a touchdown to open the second half triggered a

22-point run that carried the Bulldogs to victory. Berrian returned six kicks for 182 yards, caught eight passes for 102 yards and rushed twice for another 16. He comes from Winton (pop. 8,560), a speck on the map approximately 60 miles northwest of Fresno.

Berrian's afternoon notwithstanding, the most valuable recruit Hill has landed at Fresno State was the first one he visited. Some 12 hours and two flights after his final game as a Ravens assistant, Hill knocked on the door of the Carr family in Bakersfield. "He hadn't gotten a lot of sleep, and the airline had damaged his suitcase," recalls Sheryl Carr, whose son David had just completed his senior season as the quarterback at Stockdale High. "He was holding it together with duct tape and bungee cords."

Hill was in over his head at the Carr house, or so it seemed. David (opposite) already had scholarship offers from Washington and UCLA. Many others, including Purdue and Arizona, were very interested. What kind of kid would choose Fresno over any of those programs?

The kind of kid who spent most of his elementary and junior high years living in Fresno (the Carrs moved to Bakersfield when David was 13), hustling over to campus every weekday afternoon in the fall to catch the end of Bulldogs practice. The kind of kid who, along with his father, Rodger, and younger brother Darren, would scale not one but two barbed-wire fences at dusk to sneak onto the field at Bulldog Stadium. "Is the stadium open?" Sheryl would ask as they would leave the house. "Kind of," they'd reply. David would throw to Rodger, who was covered by Darren (now a promising defensive tackle at Bakersfield College).

"I'm gonna walk down that ramp someday," Rodger recalls his 11-year-old son saying as he stood near the walkway the players use to reach the field.

David accepted Fresno State's scholarship offer without visiting another school. "There's no other place that would've felt like home," he says. "I'd watched those guys take water breaks. I'd gotten Trent Dilfer's autograph. Bulldog football was the only college football I knew."

There was another reason that he wanted to stay close to home. Shortly after the end of his senior season, he returned from a three-day church youth camp with his head spinning. Says Rodger, "The first thing he said when he got home was, 'Oh, Dad, I think I found her.' "

David had met a beautiful blonde named Melody Tipton. On the last day of camp he got her phone number, and they went to a movie the next Friday night . . . .

In March 1999 they were married, and just over a year later Melody gave birth to Austin Duke Carr, now 16 months old, who displays his father's natural throwing motion while chucking the television remote all over the family's modest Fresno apartment.

Carr rode the bench for three years behind Billy Volek, now a backup quarterback with the Tennessee Titans. Realizing that he wasn't likely to play much, Carr decided to redshirt as a junior. During the week he ran the scout team, earning raves as "the best quarterback we saw all season" from Kevin Coyle, the defensive coordinator at the time. On game days he sat in the press box alongside offensive coordinator Andy Ludwig, charting coverages, keeping his head in the game and even suggesting plays on occasion. Watching highlights of the games with his family, he would pipe up and say, "I called that play!"

Last season, on the long-awaited day of Carr's first start, the ramp he walked down happened to be at the Horseshoe in Columbus, where Ohio State administered a 43–10 beating to Fresno State in general and to Carr in particular. (He completed 26 of 44 passes for 238 yards, threw four interceptions and, by the tally of the coaching staff, took 34 hard shots.) Watching at home, his wife and mother cried for him.

The Bulldogs finished the season 7–5 despite many injuries. Though he looked like a walking, talking welt at the season's end, the 6' 3", 225-pound Carr was the team's only offensive starter not to miss a game, a testament to his great strength. (He bench-presses 390 pounds, squats 500 and power-cleans 300.) Ludwig, who is also Carr's position coach, is loath to discuss his pupil's NFL prospects, believing that it can only distract from the business at hand. "I will say this," Ludwig

says. "It's hard to imagine a guy being more physically prepared."

Hill is less reticent. "He can throw, he can throw with touch, he can move in the pocket and manufacture a play," he says. "I don't think there's any doubt about his pro prospects."

Hill made this assessment in his office in early September, while several NFL scouts studied film of Carr in an adjacent room. Carr has been told that in a preseason report released by Blesto, an NFL scouting service, he was among the top three quarterbacks listed. To which Dilfer, a Fresno State star who is now the Seattle Seahawks backup, might respond, "Duh!"

"I work out with him," says Dilfer, "and he's making throws right now that only a handful of people in the NFL can make. He's an absolute stud."

Carr completed 22 of his 38 throws against the Badgers, with two touchdown passes and one interception, and he will now, presumably, make his way onto various Heisman Watch lists. For their part, the Bulldogs hope to make their way through the rest of their eight conference and two nonconference games, including a trip to Colorado State—and on to one of the four BCS bowls. However, even if Fresno State goes undefeated, one of the eight major bowl spots isn't a certainty because the BCS guarantees berths to the champions of the six power conferences (ACC, Big East, Big 12, Big Ten, Pac-10 and SEC) but not the WAC.

After Saturday's game, Hill stood among reporters, venting preemptive outrage. "Why should a school from the WAC get shut out," he said, "if we've beaten some of the best teams in the country on the road?"

Hill has come a long way since that morning five years ago when he showed up at Carr's front door. In addition to Hill's ugly suitcase, the family still remembers his vow to David before leaving: "We will play big-time football."

That he's kept that promise is not really a secret.

—Austin Murphy
excerpted from SI, Sept. 17, 2001

Fresno State finished 11–3, losing 44–35 to Michigan State in the Silicon Valley Classic. Carr passed for 531 yards in the defeat.—Ed.

THE NUMBERS

Final Polls

ASSOCIATED PRESS

		RECORD	PTS	HEAD COACH	SI PRESEASON RANK
1.	Miami (FL) (72)	12–0	1800	Larry Coker	3
2.	Oregon	11–1	1726	Mike Belotti	7
3.	Florida	10–2	1611	Steve Spurrier	2
4.	Tennessee	11–2	1581	Phillip Fulmer	9
5.	Texas	11–2	1374	Mack Brown	4
6.	Oklahoma	11–2	1373	Bob Stoops	5
7.	Louisiana St	10–3	1350	Nick Saban	13
8.	Nebraska	11–2	1348	Frank Solich	8
9.	Colorado	10–3	1335	Gary Barnett	27
10.	Washington St	10–2	1074	Mike Price	79
11.	Maryland	10–2	1065	Ralph Friedgen	63
12.	Illinois	10–2	1045	Ron Turner	49
13.	S Carolina	9–3	975	Lou Holtz	19
14.	Syracuse	10–3	856	Paul Pasqualoni	41
15.	Florida St	8–4	686	Bobby Bowden	6
16.	Stanford	9–3	673	Tyrone Willingham	42
17.	Louisville	11–2	621	John L. Smith	34
18.	Virginia Tech	8–4	437	Frank Beamer	10
19.	Washington	8–4	414	Rick Neuheisel	16
20.	Michigan	8–4	325	Lloyd Carr	14
21.	Boston College	8–4	318	Tom O'Brien	46
22.	Georgia	8–4	277	Mark Richt	26
23.	Toledo	10–2	237	Tom Amstutz	55
24.	Georgia Tech	8–5	178	George O'Leary	11
25.	Brigham Young	12–2	144	Gary Crowton	38

Note: As voted by a panel of 72 sportswriters and broadcasters following bowl games (1st-place votes in parentheses).

USA TODAY/ESPN

		PTS	PREV RANK
1.	Miami (FL) (60)	1500	1
2.	Oregon	1434	2
3.	Florida	1351	5
4.	Tennessee	1284	8
5.	Texas	1207	9
6.	Oklahoma	1141	10
7.	Nebraska	1101	4
8.	Louisiana St	1099	12
9.	Colorado	1031	3
10.	Maryland	885	6
11.	Washington St	879	13
12.	Illinois	846	7
13.	S Carolina	837	14
14.	Syracuse	736	18
15.	Florida St	556	24
16.	Louisville	524	22
17.	Stanford	502	11
18.	Virginia Tech	394	16
19.	Washington	369	20
20.	Michigan	363	15
21.	Marshall	223	25
22.	Toledo	188	—
23.	Boston College	174	—
24.	Brigham Young	172	17
25.	Georgia	163	21

Note: As voted by a panel of 60 Division I-A head coaches; 25 points for 1st, 24 for 2nd, etc. (1st-place votes in parentheses).

Bowls

NCAA DIVISION I-A BOWL RESULTS

DATE	BOWL	RESULT	PAYOUT/TEAM ($)	ATTENDANCE
12-18-01	New Orleans	Colorado St 45, N Texas 14	750,000	27,004
12-19-01	GMAC	Marshall 64, E Carolina 61	750,000	40,139
12-20-01	Tangerine	Pittsburgh 34, N Carolina St 19	750,000	28,562
12-25-01	Las Vegas	Utah 10, Southern Cal 6	800,000	30,894
12-27-01	Seattle	Georgia Tech 24, Stanford 14	750,000	30,144
12-27-01	Independence	Alabama 14, Iowa St 13	1 million	45,627
12-28-01	Galleryfurniture.com	Texas A&M 28, Texas Christian 9	750,000	53,480
12-28-01	Music City	Boston College 20, Georgia 16	750,000	46,125
12-28-01	Holiday	Texas 47, Washington 43	2 million	60,548
12-29-01	Motor City	Toledo 23, Cincinnati 16	750,000	44,164
12-29-01	Alamo	Iowa 16, Texas Tech 13	1.2 million	65,232
12-29-01	Insight.com	Syracuse 26, Kansas St 3	750,000	40,028
12-31-01	Sun	Washington St 33, Purdue 27	1 million	47,812
12-31-01	Humanitarian	Clemson 49, Louisiana Tech 24	750,000	23,472
12-31-01	Silicon Valley Classic	Michigan St 44, Fresno St 35	750,000	30,456
12-31-01	Liberty	Louisville 28, Brigham Young 10	1.3 million	58,968
12-31-01	Peach	N Carolina 16, Auburn 10	1.8 million	71,827
1-1-02	Cotton	Oklahoma 10, Arkansas 3	2 million	72,955
1-1-02	Outback	S Carolina 31, Ohio St 28	2.2 million	66,249
1-1-02	Gator	Florida St 30, Virginia Tech 17	1.4 million	72,202
1-1-02	Florida Citrus	Tennessee 45, Michigan 17	4.25 million	59,693
1-1-02	Fiesta	Oregon 38, Colorado 16	11–13 million	74,118
1-1-02	Sugar	Louisiana St 47, Illinois 34	11–13 million	77,688
1-2-02	Orange	Florida 56, Maryland 23	11–13 million	73,640
1-3-02	Rose	Miami 37, Nebraska 14	11–13 million	93,781

Awards

HEISMAN MEMORIAL TROPHY

PLAYER, SCHOOL	CLASS	POS	1ST	2ND	3RD	TOTAL
Eric Crouch, Nebraska	Sr	QB	162	98	88	770
Rex Grossman, Florida	So	QB	137	105	87	708
Ken Dorsey, Miami (FL)	Jr	QB	109	122	67	638
Joey Harrington, Oregon	Sr	QB	54	68	66	364
David Carr, Fresno St	Sr	QB	34	60	58	280
Antwaan Randle El, Indiana	Sr	QB	46	39	51	267
Roy Williams, Oklahoma	Jr	S	13	36	35	146
Bryant McKinnie, Miami (FL)	Sr	OT	26	12	14	116
Dwight Freeney, Syracuse	Sr	DE	2	6	24	42
Julius Peppers, N Carolina	Jr	DE	2	10	15	41

Note: Former Heisman winners and the media vote, with ballots allowing for three names (three points for 1st, two for 2nd, one for 3rd).

OFFENSIVE PLAYERS OF THE YEAR

Maxwell Award (Player)	Ken Dorsey, Miami (FL), QB
Associated Press Player of the Year	Rex Grossman, Florida, QB
Walter Camp Player of the Year	Eric Crouch, Nebraska, QB

OTHER AWARDS

Davey O'Brien Award (QB)	Eric Crouch, Nebraska, QB
Doak Walker Award (RB)	Luke Staley, Brigham Young, RB
Biletnikoff Award (WR)	Josh Reed, Louisiana St, WR
Vince Lombardi/Rotary Award (Lineman)	Julius Peppers, N Carolina, DE
Outland Trophy (Interior lineman)	Bryant McKinnie, Miami (FL), OL
Butkus Award (Linebacker)	Rocky Calmus, Oklahoma, LB
Jim Thorpe Award (Defensive back)	Roy Williams, Oklahoma, S

COACHES' AWARDS

Walter Camp Award	Ralph Friedgen, Maryland
Eddie Robinson Award (Div I-AA)	Pete Lembo, Lehigh
Bobby Dodd Award	Ralph Friedgen, Maryland

AFCA Coaches of the Year

Division I-A	(tie) Larry Coker, Miami (FL); Ralph Friedgen, Maryland
Division I-AA	Bobby Johnson, Furman
Division II	Dale Lennon, N Dakota
Division III	Larry Kehres, Mt. Union

Awards *(Cont.)*

FOOTBALL WRITERS ASSOCIATION OF AMERICA ALL-AMERICA TEAM
Offense

Antwaan Randle El, Indiana, Sr	Quarterback
Travis Stephens, Tennessee, Sr	Running Back
Luke Staley, Brigham Young, Jr	Running Back
Daniel Graham, Colorado, Sr	Tight End
Toniu Fonoti, Nebraska, Jr	Offensive Lineman
Bryant McKinnie, Miami (FL), Sr	Offensive Lineman
LeCharles Bentley, Ohio St, Sr	Center
Mike Pearson, Florida, Jr	Offensive Lineman
Joaquin Gonzalez, Miami (FL), Sr	Offensive Lineman
Josh Reed, Louisiana St, Jr	Wide Receiver
Jabar Gaffney, Florida, So	Wide Receiver
Seth Marler, Tulane, Jr	Place Kicker
Luke Powell, Stanford, Jr	Kick Returner

FOOTBALL WRITERS ASSOCIATION OF AMERICA ALL-AMERICA TEAM *(Cont.)*
Defense

Rocky Calmus, Oklahoma, Sr	Linebacker
E.J. Henderson, Maryland, Jr	Linebacker
Robert Thomas, UCLA, Sr	Linebacker
John Henderson, Tennessee, Sr	Defensive Lineman
Dwight Freeney, Syracuse, Sr	Defensive Lineman
Julius Peppers, N Carolina, Jr	Defensive Lineman
Alex Brown, Florida, Sr	Defensive Lineman
Roy Williams, Oklahoma, Jr	Defensive Back
Edward Reed, Miami (FL), Sr	Defensive Back
Quentin Jammer, Texas, Sr	Defensive Back
Troy Polamalu, Southern Cal, Jr	Defensive Back
David Zastudil, Ohio, Sr	Punter

2001 NCAA Individual Leaders (Division I-A)

Scoring

Scoring	CLASS	GP	TD	XP	FG	PTS	PTS/GAME
Luke Staley, Brigham Young	Jr	11	28	0	0	170	15.45
Dwone Hicks, Middle Tennessee St	Jr	11	24	0	0	148	13.45
Chester Taylor, Toledo	Jr	11	23	0	0	138	12.55
Todd Sievers, Miami (FL)	Jr	11	0	56	21	119	10.82
Levron Williams, Indiana	Sr	11	19	0	0	114	10.36
Jeff Chandler, Florida	Sr	10	0	46	19	103	10.30
William Green, Boston College	Jr	10	17	0	0	102	10.20
Leonard Henry, E Carolina	Sr	11	18	0	0	108	9.82
Ricky Williams, Texas Tech	Sr	11	18	0	0	108	9.82
Eric Crouch, Nebraska	Sr	12	19	0	0	116	9.67

Rushing

Rushing	CLASS	GP	CAR	YDS	AVG	TD	YDS/GAME
Chance Kretschmer, Nevada	Fr	11	302	1732	5.74	15	157.45
William Green, Boston College	Jr	10	265	1559	5.88	15	155.90
Luke Staley, Brigham Young	Jr	11	196	1582	8.07	24	143.82
Larry Ned, San Diego St	Sr	11	311	1549	4.98	15	140.82
Anthony Davis, Wisconsin	Fr	11	291	1466	5.04	11	133.27
Leonard Henry, E Carolina	Sr	11	184	1432	7.78	16	130.18
Chester Taylor, Toledo	Jr	11	268	1430	5.34	20	130.00
Levron Williams, Indiana	Sr	11	212	1401	6.61	17	127.36
Dameon Hunter, Utah	Sr	11	257	1396	5.43	9	126.91
Marcus Merriweather, Ball St	Sr	10	268	1244	4.64	12	124.40

Field Goals

Field Goals	CLASS	GP	FGA	FG	PCT	FG/GAME
Todd Sievers, Miami (FL)	Jr	11	26	21	.808	1.91
Jeff Chandler, Florida	Sr	10	22	19	.864	1.90
Steve Azar, Northern Illinois	So	11	26	20	.769	1.82
Jarvis Wallum, Wyoming	Jr	11	23	20	.870	1.82
Travis Dorsch, Purdue	Sr	11	25	20	.800	1.82
Asen Asparuhov, Fresno St	Jr	13	30	23	.767	1.77
Tim Duncan, Oklahoma	Sr	12	28	20	.714	1.67
Jeremy Flores, Colorado	Sr	11	24	18	.750	1.64
Josh Scobee, Louisiana Tech	So	11	22	18	.818	1.64
Luke Manget, Georgia Tech	Jr	12	28	19	.679	1.58
Justin Ayat, Hawaii	Fr	12	29	19	.655	1.58

Receptions per Game

Receptions per Game	CLASS	GP	NO.	YDS	TD	R/GAME
Kevin Curtis, Utah St	Jr	11	100	1531	10	9.09
Ricky Williams, Texas Tech	Sr	11	92	617	4	8.36
Josh Reed, Louisiana St	Jr	12	94	1740	7	7.83
Darius Watts, Marshall	So	12	91	1417	18	7.58
Don Shoals, Tulsa	Sr	10	75	908	4	7.50

Receiving Yards per Game

Receiving Yards per Game	CLASS	GP	NO.	YDS	TD	YDS/GAME
Josh Reed, Louisiana St	Jr	12	94	1740	7	145.00
Ashley Lelie, Hawaii	Jr	12	84	1713	19	142.75
Kevin Curtis, Utah St	Jr	11	100	1531	10	139.18
Lee Evans, Wisconsin	Jr	12	75	1545	9	128.75
Edell Shepherd, San Jose St	Sr	12	83	1500	14	125.00

Passing Efficiency

Passing Efficiency	CLASS	GP	ATT	COMP	PCT COMP	YDS	YDS/ATT	TD	INT	RATING PTS
Rex Grossman, Florida	So	11	395	259	65.57	3896	9.86	34	12	170.8
David Carr, Fresno St	Sr	13	476	308	64.71	4299	9.03	42	7	166.7
Wes Counts, Middle Tennessee St	Sr	11	259	188	72.59	2327	8.98	17	4	166.6
Ryan Dinwiddie, Boise St	So	11	322	201	62.42	3043	9.45	29	11	164.7
Byron Leftwich, Marshall	Jr	12	470	315	67.02	4132	8.79	38	7	164.6
Jeff Smoker, Michigan St	So	10	230	144	62.61	2203	9.58	18	7	162.8
Brandon Doman, Brigham Young	Sr	13	408	261	63.97	3542	8.68	33	8	159.7
Chris Rix, Florida St	Fr	11	286	165	57.69	2734	9.56	24	13	156.6
Jeff Krohn, Arizona St	So	10	213	115	53.99	1942	9.12	19	7	153.4
Nick Rolovich, Hawaii	Sr	10	405	233	57.53	3361	8.30	34	9	150.5

Note: Minimum 15 attempts per game.

DIVISION I-A TEAM SINGLE-GAME HIGHS
Rushing and Passing

Rushing and passing plays: 76—Marquel Blackwell, S Florida, Sept 8 (vs Pittsburgh).
Rushing and passing yards: 657—Brian Lindgren, Idaho, Oct 6 (vs Middle Tennessee St).
Rushing plays: 47—Larry Ned, San Diego St, Nov 17 (vs Wyoming).
Net rushing yards: 327—Chance Kretschmer, Nevada, Nov 24 (vs Texas–El Paso).
Passes attempted: 71—Brian Lindgren, Idaho, Oct 6 (vs Middle Tennessee St).
Passes completed: 49—Brian Lindgren, Idaho, Oct 6 (vs Middle Tennessee St).
Passing yards: 637—Brian Lindgren, Idaho, Oct 6 (vs Middle Tennessee St).

DIVISION I-A TEAM SINGLE-GAME HIGHS *(Cont.)*
Receiving and Returns

Passes caught: 19—Josh Reed, Louisiana St, Nov 3 (vs Alabama).
Receiving yards: 326—Nate Burleson, Nevada, Nov 10 (vs San Jose St).
Punt return yards: 186—Keenan Howry, Oregon, Oct 20 (vs Stanford).
Kickoff return yards: 249—Chad Owens, Hawaii, Dec 8 (vs Brigham Young).

Brady's Bunch

Led by unheralded second-year quarterback Tom Brady, the feisty New England Patriots scored a stunning Super Bowl upset

HANK HERSCH

No one knew what to expect of Tom Brady. A fourth-string quarterback in 2000, he took over in the second game of the 2001 season, after New England Patriots starter Drew Bledsoe went down with a chest injury. Though he had been a lowly sixth-round draft choice in 2000, the 24-year-old Brady had a swagger about him that belied his boyish looks, which included a dime-sized dimple in his chin. He stood 6' 4" and weighed 220 pounds, and when he started dishing out advice on route adjustments during training camp as if he were a seasoned veteran, Patriots wide receiver David Patten recalls thinking, If he's this confident as a backup, I can only imagine how he'd be running the show.

No one knew what to expect from Tom Brady. The St. Louis Rams had tied New England at 17–all, and with 1:21 remaining in Super Bowl XXXVI, Brady had the ball on his own 17-yard line with no timeouts left. Analyst John Madden told the millions watching on television that the Patriots should simply run out the clock and try to win in overtime—too much ground to cover, too little time to do it in, too much risk involved. Coach Bill Belichick thought about doing that, too. Then he thought about Brady. "With a quarterback like Tom, going for a win is not that dangerous," Belichick said, "because he's not going to make a mistake."

Brady, a second-year man out of Michigan, proved that Belichick's belief in him was well-founded. He completed five passes and took New England 53 yards in 74 seconds to put the Patriots in position to win the game with a 48-yard field goal. Out trotted Adam Vinatieri to split the uprights as time expired. Despite being outgained by 160 yards, the Patriots had won, 20–17, and seized the first Super Bowl in franchise history. Along with Vinatieri, they had the cooler-than-dry-ice Brady to thank. For his preternatural poise on the final drive, Brady was

named MVP of the game. "You're looking at a team that had some guts," Rams defensive end Chidi Ahanotu said. "Brady never flinched, and they've got one hell of a gutsy coach."

The Patriots' ascendancy from AFC East doormat to conference champion may have been the most stunning turnaround of 2001, but it was by no means the only one. But then, such volatility hardly seemed surprising in light of the season's start: The terrorist attacks of Sept. 11 that leveled the World Trade Center occurred two days after the Sunday openers. Commissioner Paul Tagliabue weighed conflicting opinions from the league's owners on whether to let the Week 2 games proceed, some arguing that postponing the games would signal a victory for the terrorists, others that it would give the nation needed time to grieve.

On Sept. 13, the player reps voted 17–11 to call them off. "It's one thing to see it on TV," said New York Giants cornerback Jason Sehorn. "It's another thing, every day, to look from our practice field and see the towers gone. And it's another thing to even consider playing while they're still pulling people out of the rubble." The following day Tagliabue announced that he would reschedule the games for the end of the season. Three minutes after releasing his decision, the NFL's offices in midtown Manhattan were evacuated because of a bomb threat at a building across the street.

Although at first it seemed that the postponement might force the league to cancel the wild-card round of the playoffs, the National Auto Dealers Association, who had planned a convention in New Orleans for the first weekend of February, consented to give up that date so that the Super Bowl could move back a week and still take place in the Superdome.

One team that quickly made it clear that it would be booking no postseason dates was the

Carolina Panthers. After a Week 1 win over the Minnesota Vikings, they lost a league-record 15 straight, drawing a franchise-low 21,070 fans for their season finale at Ericsson Stadium. After that ignominious end George Seifert, whose .755 winning percentage over eight years with the San Francisco 49ers had been the highest in NFL history, became one of the six coaches who lost their jobs in 2001. (One of those men, former Tampa Bay coach Tony Dungy, quickly found a new head coaching position with the Indianapolis Colts.)

Before the season began, a similar fate seemed likely for Dick Jauron of the Chicago Bears, who received tepid support from the team's new general manager, Jerry Angelo. But then the Bears did something they hadn't done in Jauron's two previous seasons: They found ways to win. In back-to-back victories over the San Francisco 49ers and the Cleveland Browns, the Bears overcame two-touchdown deficits in the fourth quarter, then won in overtime on interception returns by free safety Mike Brown.

Those two improbable wins should have been sign enough that Chicago was for real, but still,

Brady (above) completed 16 of 27 passes for 145 yards and one touchdown, but it was his poise down the stretch, not his overall statistics, that won him the Super Bowl MVP trophy as New England beat St. Louis in a thriller.

Dungy (above), one of six NFL head coaches who were dismissed at the end of the season, quickly found a new home in Indianapolis. The Colts, who fired Jim Mora at season's end, signed the former Tampa Bay coach to a five-year contract.

Defensive Rookie of the Year, Kendrell Bell, and a rejuvenated Kordell Stewart at quarterback. After leading Pittsburgh to the AFC title game in 1997, his first season as a starter, Stewart had gone through a pair of offensive coordinators, endured a humiliating switch to wide receiver, seen his career passing rating plummet to an abysmal 68.4 and developed bitter feelings toward head coach Bill Cowher.

At a team meeting before the 1999 season Stewart even felt compelled to deny rumors that he was gay, launching into graphic descriptions of his favorite heterosexual acts. "At one point," Stewart recalls, "I said, 'You'd better not leave your girlfriends around me, because I'm out to prove a point.' "

After clearing the air with Cowher during an emotional three-hour phone call in the off-season, Stewart regained his form as a game-breaker. In a new home (Heinz Field) with a new offensive coordinator (Mike Mularkey) and using a recharged pair of starting receivers (Hines Ward and Plaxico Burress, each of whom surpassed 1,000 yards), Stewart completed a career-best 60.2% of his passes for 3,109 yards. His run ended in the AFC Championship Game, when visiting New England intercepted him on each of Pittsburgh's last two possessions to preserve a 24–17 victory.

A week earlier Pittsburgh's defense had helped end the reign of the defending Super Bowl champion, Baltimore, completely bottling the Ravens' attack in a 27–10 victory. Before the game, Steelers defensive coordinator Tim Lewis told his troops they would have to stuff the run and force Elvis Grbac to win with his arm. "Good quarterback, good pocket presence," Lewis said, "but when you get to him make sure you brush him. He doesn't like to be hit."

Despite Trent Dilfer's 11–1 record as a starter in 2000, Baltimore coach Brian Billick had opted to let Dilfer walk over the summer and sign Grbac. While Dilfer went 4–0 and had a 92.0 rating for the Seattle Seahawks, Grbac threw 18 interceptions against 15 touchdowns for the Ravens and ranked 28th among quarterbacks. Rattled by the pressure in Pittsburgh Grbac threw a pair of first-half interceptions, and may begin 2002 as a marked man. "You could see it in his eyes—he freaked out," said Steelers safety Lee Flowers. "By the end he was dropping three steps and ducking."

The New York Giants, Super Bowl XXXV's other entry, failed to even make the playoffs, finishing 7–9. Their lone mark of distinction belonged to end Michael Strahan, the Defensive

few fans believed in these new Monsters of the Midway. With middle linebacker Brian Urlacher anchoring the NFL's eighth-ranked defense and Anthony Thomas rushing for 1,183 yards to win the Offensive Rookie of the Year award, Chicago shocked the league by going 13–3. They had won only 11 games during the previous two seasons. Though the Bears lost to the Philadelphia Eagles 33–19 in the second round of the playoffs, Jauron was named Coach of the Year. "He's the type of leader you want to play for," said linebacker Rosevelt Colvin. "In three years here I've only seen him really yell at a guy one time." Said quarterback Jim Miller of his coach, "Like Tom Landry, the guy does not waver. And we've taken on his personality."

Much like the Bears, the Pittsburgh Steelers rocketed to a 13–3 record after a string of mediocre seasons. Crucial to their resurgence was a sack-happy linebacking corps buoyed by the

Player of the Year, who made 22 ½ sacks to break Mark Gastineau's 17-year-old record of 22. In a five-game spurt the 6' 5", 275-pound Strahan racked up 12 ½ sacks, and after dropping Eagles quarterback Donovan McNabb 3 ½ times in Week 16, he entered the final game of the season needing one sack for the record.

He got it in the waning minutes of the Giants' 35–24 loss to Green Bay, when Packers quarterback Brett Favre took the snap from center, rolled out and then fell in the face of Strahan's charge. The play had all the appearances of a gift from Favre to Strahan: The Packer linemen thought it was a running play and thus did not pass-block, allowing Strahan easy passage into the backfield, and Favre ran right at the Giants defensive end before curling up at his feet to give up the record-breaking "sack."

Strahan (above) made 22 ½ sacks for the Giants, but the last one, which broke Mark Gastineau's NFL record, seemed to be prearranged by Green Bay's Favre.

Though he was bottled up by New England in the Super Bowl, Warner (above) was a most deserving regular-season MVP, completing 68.7% of his passes for 4,830 yards and 36 touchdowns.

Observers questioned why Green Bay would be passing in that situation instead of running to milk the clock, and the Green Bay offensive line, when questioned about the play, referred reporters to Favre, who coyly denied giftwrapping the record for his friend. Pundits and fans alike cried foul.

After their divisional playoff game against New England, the Oakland Raiders were crying foul as well—only at an infinitely louder volume. With 1:43 remaining they had held a 13–10 lead over the Patriots on the snow-covered field in

Foxboro Stadium. Oakland cornerback Charles Woodson, a teammate of Brady's at Michigan, blitzed the young Patriots quarterback and knocked the ball loose as Brady appeared to fake a throw and start to tuck the ball in to run. The Raiders recovered the football, and New England's six-game winning streak seemed to be at an end.

That is, until Brady watched the replay—which was being reviewed by referee Walt Coleman—on the stadium's jumbo video screen. "We're getting the ball back!" Brady screamed at

Patriots offensive coordinator Charlie Weis. "What play do you want to run?"

According to Rule 3, Section 21, Article 2 of the NFL rulebook, a passer who has begun to bring the ball forward can't be deemed to have fumbled if he hasn't tucked the ball into his body. Coleman's ruling gave New England new life, and Brady did not squander the second chance. He moved the Patriots 14 more yards to the Oakland 28-yard line. Seven yards behind that snowbound line of scrimmage, as yet more snow swirled in the wind, Vinatieri nailed a game-tying 45-yard field goal. Brady then completed eight more passes in a row to set up Vinatieri's winning 23-yarder in overtime. "We didn't lose this game," said Oakland linebacker William Thomas, "it was taken from us." Paraphrasing Lefty Gomez, Patriots guard Mike Compton said, "Sometimes luck is better than skill."

The Patriots would need both luck and skill, in equally heaping portions it seemed, in the Superdome against St. Louis, whose lethal offense was known as The Greatest Show on Turf. In quarterback Kurt Warner the Rams had the NFL's Most Valuable Player; in running back Marshall Faulk, the league's Offensive Player of the Year. More important, new defensive coordinator Lovie Smith and seven new starters on defense had transformed a unit that ranked last in points allowed in 2000 into the sixth-ranked D in '01. "It's not even close," said coach Mike Martz, comparing his team to the Rams' Supe XXXIV champs. "We've got so much speed on defense that we didn't have two years ago. We're cresting, and I've never been around a team more confident."

After dispatching the Eagles 29–24 in the NFC title game, St. Louis came to New Orleans a two-touchdown favorite. In a 24–17 win over the Patriots in Week 10, Belichick had blitzed Warner repeatedly and without success. This time he emphasized coverage, having cornerbacks Ty Law and Otis Smith press, mixing in zones and hoping to force Warner to hold the ball. The Rams fumbled once and Warner threw two interceptions, one of which Ty Law returned 49 yards for a touchdown.

St. Louis offense didn't find its rhythm until the fourth quarter, by which time New England had built a 17–3 lead. Fatigue began to set in on the Patriots' D. "Tired, man," Law said. "Actually drained. On the ropes." Warner engineered a pair of touchdown drives, capping the second one with a pass to wideout Ricky Proehl, who made a nifty cutback along the sidelines and plunged into the end zone

for a 26-yard score that tied the game with 1:37 to play.

That set the stage for Vinatieri's kick, which instantly became the most famous in the history of the Super Bowl, eclipsing Jim O'Brien's last-second game-winner for the Baltimore Colts against Dallas in Super Bowl V, and Scott Norwood's famous miss for Buffalo in Super Bowl XXV against the Giants. And it was all made possible by a kid who had thrown all of three NFL passes before the 2001 season began. Said Brady, "Only you know what you're capable of."

Vinatieri (above, after his Super Bowl–winning kick) was arguably New England's MVP of the playoffs: He made two crucial field goals in the snow against Oakland in the second round, then sealed the title in New Orleans.

PHOTO GALLERY

Dandy Randy: Vikings receiver Randy Moss (left) stretched his 6′ 4″ frame to the limit to latch on to a pass from quarterback Todd Bouman during the fourth quarter of Minnesota's 21–16 loss to Pittsburgh at Heinz Field on Dec. 22.

Snow Bowl: Oakland linebacker Greg Biekert (above, left) plowed into Patriots tight end Jermaine Wiggins in the third quarter of their AFC Divisional Playoff game in Foxboro, Mass., on Jan. 20. Four inches of snow fell during the game, which New England won 16–13 in overtime.

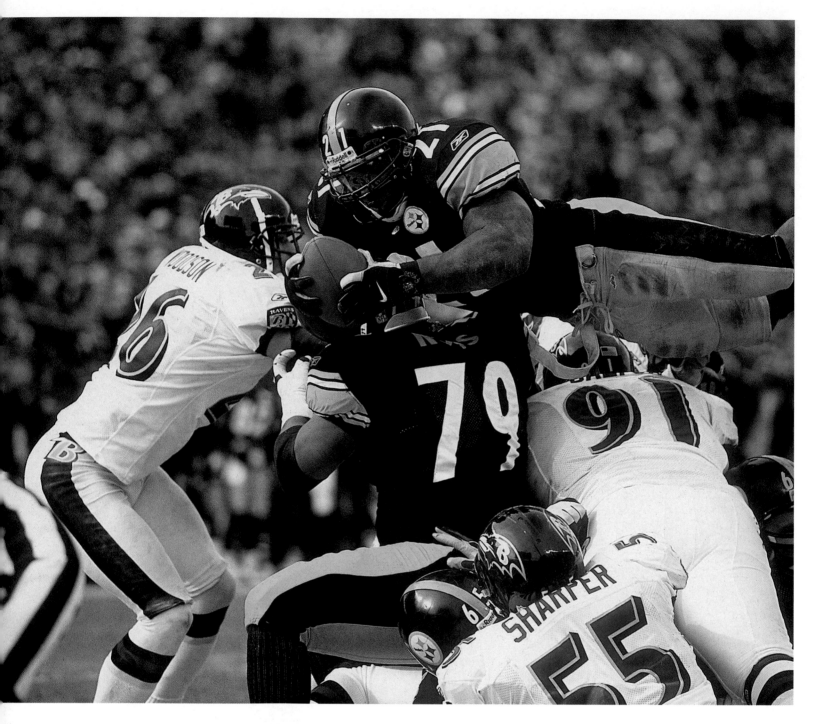

Sixteen–Zeroue: Pittsburgh running back Amos Zeroue (above) plunged over the Baltimore line for his second touchdown of the day, giving the Steelers a 16–0 lead over the Ravens in the second quarter of their Divisional Playoff game on Jan. 20 at Heinz Field. Pittsburgh won the game 27–10.

Packers running back Ahman Green (right) churned up muddy Lambeau Field during the fourth quarter of his team's wild-card matchup with San Francsico on Jan. 13. Green rushed 21 times for 86 yards and scored a touchdown as the Packers won 25–15.

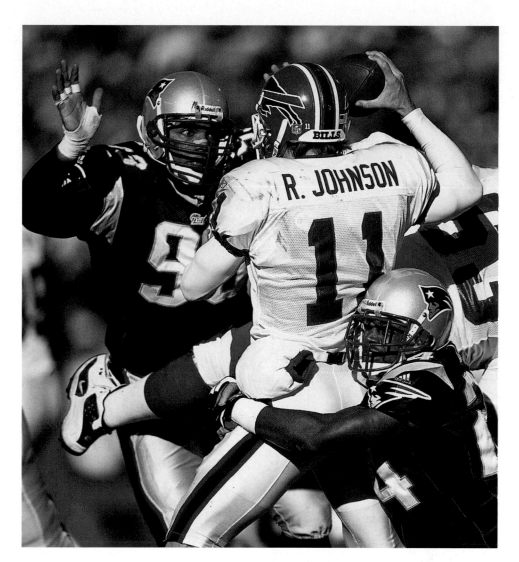

Mastering Johnson: While his teammate cornerback Ty Law (above, 24) went low, New England defensive end Richard Seymour (93) went high to squelch a pass attempt by Buffalo quarterback Rob Johnson during the Patriots' 21–11 home win on Nov. 11.

Loose Gannon: Oakland quarterback Rich Gannon (left) eluded the Kansas City defense and dived into the corner of the end zone for a two-point conversion in the third quarter of the Raiders' 27–24 victory over the Chiefs on Sept. 9 at Arrowhead Stadium.

Marshall Faulk

Marshall Faulk is not a rocket scientist, but sometimes he tries to think like one, and on occasion the St. Louis Rams' luminous running back has been known to contemplate celestial conundrums rather than chill like a typical pro football star. Yet it wasn't long ago that Faulk's idea of the big picture was a close-up image of himself. To appreciate his personal expansion, and how he

emerged from the ashes of his snuffed stardom to become the best player in his sport, you have to go back to a chilly Monday afternoon on the last day of November 1998, when Faulk sat in a small, nondescript office at the Indianapolis Colts' training facility and discovered the largest truth of his professional life. In a meeting room minutes earlier Faulk and his teammates

had watched videotape of their 38–31 loss to the Baltimore Ravens the previous afternoon. Deep into a miserable season, the Colts had been given a chance to salvage some dignity in the city the franchise had abandoned 14 years earlier, and much of the footage played out like a Faulk highlight reel. In the first quarter alone he silenced a bitter Baltimore crowd by scoring on a

34-yard reception and a 68-yard run to stake Indianapolis to a 17–3 lead. With 1:13 left Faulk had a career-best 192 rushing yards and seven catches for 75 more, yet his team now trailed by seven points. On second-and-one from the Ravens' 24, Colts rookie quarterback Peyton Manning threw high to Faulk in the flat. The ball slipped through Faulk's hands, caromed off his helmet and was intercepted. Game over.

Watching the play on tape, Faulk braced himself for a scolding. Not only did he feel he should have caught the pass, but he also knew he had run a poor route, breaking it off four yards past the line of scrimmage rather than the designed six. Sure enough, coach Jim Mora paused the tape to point out Faulk's error, growling, "Marshall, we've got to have you run the f------ route the way you're supposed to." For a moment a feeling of defiance washed over the running back.

Faulk was a player who had been known to snipe back at critical coaches, but following Mora's rebuke, he merely slumped in his seat. The pressure began to build in his head, and he felt a deep sense of embarrassment and remorse. By the time he entered the office of running backs coach Gene Huey, Faulk understood the scope of his mistake. After eight years of carrying himself like a star—the first three as a record-setting runner at San Diego State, the next five in Indianapolis—he felt like the smallest dust particle in the cosmos.

For several minutes Faulk sat in Huey's office and cried like a guest on Oprah. "I was crushed," he recalls. "I mean crushed. I knew that what Coach Mora had said was right, that I had let my teammates down, and I knew I never wanted to experience that feeling again. In the past, I would have responded, 'Look at the stats—what more could I have done?' This time I knew it wasn't about that. My neglect had affected the team's ability to win. It had probably happened before, but this was the first time I felt accountable. It was the first time I really cared."

Huey told Faulk not to despair, that his ability to bounce back from such distress would make him a better player and person. Faulk's resolve would be tested less than three weeks later, when on the night before a game against the Seahawks in Seattle, Mora accused him of arriving late for a team meeting and benched him for the start of the game. The next spring he was traded to the Rams, a franchise that had been the most feeble in the NFL in the '90s and had a reputation as dubious as his. Players, coaches and staffers in St. Louis had heard the whispers—Faulk was a cancer at worst, a moody, me-first prima donna at best—and steeled themselves for the drama that was sure to unfold.

What St. Louis got instead was perhaps the smartest, most talented and least selfish running back in the game. In two seasons with the Rams the 28-year-old Faulk has won a Super Bowl ring, the NFL MVP award and the respect of his teammates. In '99 he became only the second player in league history to gain 1,000 yards rushing and 1,000 receiving in the same year, joining former San Francisco 49ers running back Roger Craig. Faulk also set an NFL record with 2,429 yards from scrimmage and helped St. Louis live out a worst-to-first fantasy. Last season, despite missing two games with a right knee injury, he scored an NFL-record 26 touchdowns and was voted the league's MVP.

Dick Vermeil, who was the St. Louis coach in '99, believes Faulk belongs in the company of Jim Brown, Walter Payton, O.J. Simpson, Barry Sanders, Eric Dickerson, Red Grange and anyone else whose name comes up when the best runners of all time are discussed. "To talk about the great backs and not include him is a mistake," says Vermeil, who now coaches the Kansas City Chiefs. "I've been around some great players, and he's better—he's an elite player."

Rams coach Mike Martz, who replaced Vermeil after the '99 season, has constructed one of the most explosive offenses in NFL history around Faulk, whom Martz regards as not only a great player but also a "very good friend" and a leader in whom he has "complete trust." That faith extends to the sideline during a game, when Faulk will suggest adjustments, and to the locker room, where Faulk is sensitive to intrasquad issues. "He has brought things to my attention that I wasn't aware of, and he's honest with me," says Martz, who last year had to deal with tension between offensive and defensive players. "His perspective is so mature, and it's amazing how dead-on his opinions have been."

It would be one thing if Faulk had merely transformed himself into an agreeable coach's pet, but Martz's Faulkophilia is the norm in St. Louis. Echoing the words of more than a dozen current or former Rams players interviewed for this story, quarterback Kurt Warner says Faulk is "a guy who's on top of everything in his life, someone I would feel comfortable going into business with or taking advice from. I had heard all the rumors about how he was standoffish or hard to get along with, or worse. All I can say is that he was the complete opposite when he came to the Rams. We're grateful to have him."

Faulk, too, is thankful for his good fortune . . . . Thrust into the spotlight since the day in September 1991, when, as a San Diego State freshman, he *came off the bench* to run for 386 yards, an NCAA record at the time, and score seven touchdowns against Pacific, Faulk was weary of fame by the time the Colts made him the second choice in the '94 draft. He was an instant success in the NFL as well, rushing for 1,282 yards to win the Offensive Rookie of the Year award and make the Pro Bowl. Then his fortunes started to change. Injuries marred his next three seasons and, with his physical gifts diminished, Faulk had to rely on finesse and guile. "I learned how to play the game a different way, to think my way around the field," he says. "Then, once I was healthy, I was reading plays so much quicker than before yet moving at my previous speed, and it felt like I had an unfair advantage." It often looks that way, too.

—Michael Silver
excerpted from SI, Sept. 3, 2001

Faulk ran for 1,382 yards and caught 83 passes for 765 yards during the 2001 season, finishing second to his teammate Kurt Warner in voting for the league MVP award.—Ed.

Tom Brady

Free agent David Patten had it all figured out when he signed with the New England Patriots in early April. He would build a strong relationship with quarterback Drew Bledsoe, and more passes would come his way. Getting in tight with the team leader, Patten figured, was the best way for a new receiver to operate. As Patten schmoozed with Bledsoe through minicamps and training camp and into the preseason, however, he kept noticing Tom Brady, a lanky second-year reserve quarterback who swaggered around the locker room.

Brady would sit in the weight room and instruct teammates on pass route adjustments or the best ways to detect a flaw in a defense. During minicamps he controlled the huddle as if he were running a game-winning drive. "Tom carried himself like this was his team," Patten says. "I thought, If he's this confident as a backup, I can only imagine how he'd be running the show."

Now we know. Since Bledsoe left the lineup after shearing a blood vessel in his chest during a 10–3 loss to the New York Jets on Sept. 23, Brady has become the surprise of the NFL's first half. He owns a 5–2 record as a starter and an 88.9 passer rating that ranked fourth in the AFC after Sunday's 21–11 win over the Buffalo Bills, and a detached attitude suggesting success hasn't turned his head.

Brady, 24, grew up in San Mateo, Calif., where he admired how San Francisco 49ers quarterbacks Joe Montana and Steve Young made the game look easy. Brady operates with a similarly cool approach, a natural feel for the game and of how to maneuver in the spotlight. "People talk about how we've got the ball rolling lately, but you can never buy into the hype," says Brady. "It's easy to believe everything that's being said about me, but I'm mature enough to know I'm not the only reason we're playing well."

An improved running game and a reconstructed offensive line have helped Brady, but he has been the big difference in New England's overcoming an 0–2 start. So meticulous is Brady in his game preparation that he advised Bledsoe, a nine-year veteran and three-time Pro Bowler, on strategy during preseason games. Brady also doesn't rattle when blitzed, makes smart decisions—he set a league record by not throwing an interception until the 163rd attempt of his career—and calls plays with a pronounced authority. "Some guys just say the play," says Pats running back J.R. Redmond. "He makes you think we're about to do something big."

Brady has even been impressive in defeat. "Every time he got to the line against us, he was looking over the defense and calling audibles," said Denver Broncos linebacker John Mobley after a 31–20 victory over New England on Oct. 28. "He was very much in command."

That loss to Denver was a critical juncture for Brady. He played well before throwing four fourth-quarter interceptions, mistakes that could have sent him into a funk. Instead, he rebounded with a 250-yard, three-touchdown performance in a 24–10 win over the Atlanta Falcons the next week. "Inexperienced quarterbacks need to show they can deal with the highs and lows of this league," says New England offensive coordinator Charlie Weis. "The jury is still out until you face adversity, and Tom proved he can deal with it."

Brady is well-versed in dealing with disappointment. Upon arriving at Michigan in 1995 and redshirting, he sat behind Scott Dreisbach and Brian Griese for two seasons before becoming the starter as a junior. Although he set school records for attempts (350) and completions (214) in '98, threw 20 touchdown passes as a senior and finished his career with a 20–5 record as a starter, he wound up sharing time his senior year with Drew Henson, the nation's top recruit, and plummeted to the sixth round of the 2000 draft. "The big question scouts had on him was why [Michigan] would try to play a freshman over him," says Bills general manager Tom Donahoe. "That had everybody concerned."

"When I went in the sixth round, it wasn't anything new," Brady says. "My whole college career had been about competition. Coming in here, I needed to just slug it out." His new Patriots teammates gave him grief about his frail 6' 4", 204-pound frame, with center Damien Woody offering him extra food after practice. Brady's deficient lower-body strength affected his delivery—he usually wound up to throw go-routes and deep outs—and he wasn't especially mobile. The coaches did like his instincts, poise and leadership, so they made him the fourth-string quarterback behind Bledsoe, Michael Bishop and John Friesz.

Often on the inactive list, Brady hit the weight room hard. By season's end the velocity on his throws had improved enough that some receivers complained that he was putting too much zing on the ball. Brady, who now weighs 220 pounds, also badgered Friesz, a 10-year veteran, for insights on the offense. This year, "he's been asking questions in meetings you normally wouldn't attribute to a second-year guy," Bledsoe says. "Instead of wondering who his second receiver on a play was, he wanted to know about reading the defense or where to put the ball when he saw a specific coverage."

"Even at the end of last year I felt like a stronger player," says Brady. "I could make throws that I couldn't make before. I was more elusive. Plus, I didn't feel I had to prove anything to myself anymore." Or to anyone else. Brady moved to No. 2 on the depth chart after winning a training-camp battle with Damon Huard, who had been a backup for the Miami Dolphins last year. (Friesz had been released during the off-season, and Bishop waived during camp.)

Brady has shown enough that opposing defenses are mixing up their coverages more and, as Bledsoe says, "preparing like they're going to face me." That may not be good news for Bledsoe, who received a 10-year, $103 million extension last March but has won only seven of his last 26 starts. Though he remains confident that he'll be the Patriots' starter for years to come, the cost of waiving or trading him in the off-season (a cap hit of $6.8 million) doesn't differ much from the price of keeping him on the roster for 2002 ($6.2 million). New England could be as much as $12 million under next year's cap and is sure to keep that in mind if Brady continues to excel. "Right now Tom is our starting quarterback," says Patriots coach Bill Belichick when asked about a potential quarterback controversy. "Until Drew is cleared to play [Bledsoe hasn't received a projection for his return and remains limited to noncontact drills], it's not even an issue."

Brady also wants it that way. "I'm still only a second-year player," he says. "People can talk about a quarter-back controversy, but one thing I learned in college is that the coach decides who plays, and when he says to go in there, you play your butt off. That's all I've been trying to do."

—Jeffri Chadiha
SI, Nov. 19, 2001

Bledsoe received medical clearance to return to action in late November, but could not unseat Brady as New England's starter. Brady sprained his ankle in the AFC title game and was replaced by Bledsoe, but returned the following week and was named MVP of Super Bowl XXXVI. —Ed.

Donovan McNabb

He paid $600 for the suit, a lot of money for something that would mostly hang in the closet. Still, they booed him.

Anybody else, and you don't start by mentioning what the suit cost, but this is Donovan McNabb, and for the man to have shelled out that much for an outfit tells you how important the day was. It was a huge day: the one in April 1999 when the Philadelphia Eagles drafted him. Next to his wedding day and the days when his children are born, the day a football player is drafted by the NFL is the biggest of his life. That's what the players always say, anyway, explaining why so many of them break down and cry upon hearing their names called.

They show up at Madison Square Garden dressed as if for a coronation. They preen like peacocks. Compared with the others, McNabb got off cheap. The suit was a blue double-breasted, over a blue shirt and a blue-and-orange tie. The shirt and tie cost extra, McNabb points out. "I got an allowance when I was growing up," he says, "and I always tried to hold on to that, tried to make it last. I guess I never got over it." He gets it from his dad, the practical gene. (To a man, McNabb's Eagles teammates call it a tightwad gene.) Donovan inherited other genes from Sam McNabb as well: the work-ethic gene, the pride gene, the humility gene, the gene that makes him want to win at everything he does. Sam and his wife, Wilma, instilled in Donovan an appreciation of the fundamentals, and one of these was the merit of a life lived with an eye out for tomorrow. "Just because you have it, doesn't mean you have to spend it," Sam taught him.

So when Donovan studies a restaurant menu and refuses to order anything marked Market Price, that's Sam's influence. When he buys a house for less than $400,000 in a suburban New Jersey neighborhood although he could afford a mansion on the old, moneyed Main Line of Philadelphia, that's Sam too. When Donovan tries to get a better deal on a leather coat that's already reduced

by half, who else but Sam?

Sam has worked for the power company in Chicago for 25 years, most recently as a quality-control man in the reliability department. Reliable only begins to describe Sam, and Wilma too. They used to build TV shows around couples like this. Wilma was the attractive mother whose counsel her children sought when they wanted to unburden themselves of secrets. She seemed to

spend the better part of her life in the kitchen, despite having a full-time job as a registered nurse. Sam was the all-powerful, all-knowing presence who sat on the edge of his son's bed at night and dispensed pearls of wisdom while Donovan, the little knucklehead, looked on with a dewy-eyed mix of awe and bewilderment.

When Donovan and his big brother, Sean, were growing up, Sam also lectured them about the importance of showing

class and "humbleness," as he called it. He believed that if you were nice to people, they would be nice to you. These were "the traits you carry with you for a lifetime," he told the boys, never imagining a day when his hard-won homilies would be trampled by a bunch of wack jobs from Philadelphia.

NFL commissioner Paul Tagliabue announced that with the second pick, Philadelphia had chosen McNabb, the quarterback from Syracuse. Donovan came to his feet and heard what sounded like an ocean roar. The booing actually had started earlier, when it was announced which players were in the greenroom, and McNabb's name incited catcalls from a boisterous contingent of Eagles fans who wanted the team to take running back Ricky Williams of Texas, the Heisman Trophy winner. As McNabb strode across the stage, the noise intensified to the point that it was almost riotous. He stared, mystified, at the audience. "I was shocked," he says, "but I wasn't as shocked as my parents were. It heated me up. I was ready to put on the pads right there, to show them I was a good pick."

When he came off the stage, he found his mother crying. A moment passed before it occurred to him that her tears were of happiness and excitement, not anger and embarrassment. "Were they booing you?" Sam asked, perplexed. Donovan didn't answer right away. He couldn't answer. He was laughing so hard that his body shook and his stomach hurt. "Yes, they were booing me," he said at last. "They're still booing me."

Other families might have started for the exit, heads bowed. But these were the McNabbs. The McNabbs laughed.

As anniversaries go, this isn't one the quarterback cares to celebrate. During the week leading up to the NFL draft this April, McNabb was so busy preparing for the upcoming season that he had no time for the past. He spent each day working out at the Eagles' new practice facility, the NovaCare Complex, across from Veterans Stadium. He lifted weights, threw passes, did some running, met with coaches and reporters and clowned around with teammates. At night he played basketball. "Donovan's usually the first player to

arrive and the last one to leave," says Andy Reid, the team's coach. "He's always here."

The day after the 2001 draft, Reid bumped into the quarterback at the complex and said, "It's been two years."

"Two years," McNabb repeated. Then he and Reid had a laugh together. McNabb can do that now that he has emerged as one of the league's top young stars. Last season he did more than silence the boo-birds; he made them wish they'd stayed home that day two years ago and yelled at the dog instead of at a 22-year-old in a new suit. The kid the city rejected is now the man Philadelphians hope will never leave. Fans who cursed his selection are forever introducing themselves to him and apologizing, but McNabb harbors no grudge. "I don't think about it anymore," he says. "It's over with. Time to move on."

Philadelphia had the likes of Norm Van Brocklin, Sonny Jurgensen, Ron Jaworski and Randall Cunningham quarterbacking the Eagles, and now it has McNabb, who promises to be better than all of them. "We're two years in, and Donovan hasn't reached his potential yet," says Reid. "That will happen in two more years, when he moves into his prime. As a rule it takes four years for a quarterback to master the position. That's the exciting part, to think about what's ahead of him."

Last year he carried a team with average talent to six road wins and an 11–5 record and into the second round of the playoffs. McNabb accounted for 3,999 total yards, which was roughly 75% of the Eagles' production, and easily led the league in that category. He also became the team's first quarterback since Cunningham in 1994 to pass for more than 3,000 yards in a season. The Eagles' only other offensive star, running back Duce Staley, went down with a foot injury in the fifth game, and Philadelphia's other runners combined for a pathetic 737 yards. To make up for that, McNabb rushed for 629 yards, best among NFL quarterbacks.

"Donovan's a gamer," says Tampa Bay Buccaneers cornerback Ronde Barber. "Last year all you heard was 'Daunte this, Daunte that,' " as in Daunte Culpepper,

the Minnesota Vikings' quarterback. "But Daunte, I think, lives off his receivers, while Donovan doesn't have any [of the Vikings' caliber]. Donovan lives off Donovan."

McNabb was never better than in November, when he led Philly to four straight wins, two of them (against the Dallas Cowboys and the Pittsburgh Steelers) in overtime. McNabb and the Eagles run the West Coast offense, which challenges the quarterback to make quick decisions and react as either a passer or a runner. "You need a good athlete to play quarterback in our system," says offensive coordinator Rod Dowhower. "We send so many receivers out, and you can't block everybody on pass protection, so your quarterback isn't going to have that classic pocket where he can sit back and read the play. He has to move around. The other thing is, opponents will blitz from all directions, and he has to be quick about getting the ball out of his hands. If he can't pass it, he has to be able to run."

McNabb is the prototype for football's new-generation quarterback. At 6' 3" and nearly 230 pounds, he's the ideal size. He's been timed at 4.4 in the 40, though he runs the distance more regularly at 4.5, and he's thick and padded with muscle from a fierce regimen of weight training. In another era he likely would've played tailback, and he would've played it well. . . .

"It's not time to relax yet," he says. "It's not time to take a break and look back on what I've accomplished. My dad told me something when I was younger that I'll never forget. He said there will always be somebody out there who's better than I am, and the only way I'll beat this guy is to outwork him. I believe that. I can't let up because right now someone is out there studying film, lifting weights and running and throwing passes. He wants to be better so that he can help his team win. I can see this guy. I always keep him in mind."

—John Ed Bradley
excerpted from SI, July 30, 2001

McNabb passed for 3,233 yards and 25 touchdowns in 2001 as Philadelphia went 11–5, won the NFC East, and reached the NFC title game.—Ed.

THE NUMBERS

2001 NFL Final Standings

AMERICAN FOOTBALL CONFERENCE

Eastern Division

	W	L	T	PCT	PTS	OP
New England	11	5	0	.688	371	272
†Miami	11	5	0	.688	344	290
†NY Jets	10	6	0	.625	308	295
Indianapolis	6	10	0	.375	413	486
Buffalo	3	13	0	.188	265	420

Central Division

	W	L	T	PCT	PTS	OP
Pittsburgh	13	3	0	.812	352	212
†Baltimore	10	6	0	.625	303	265
Tennessee	7	9	0	.438	336	388
Cleveland	7	9	0	.438	285	319
Cincinnati	6	10	0	.375	226	309
Jacksonville	6	10	0	.375	294	286

Western Division

	W	L	T	PCT	PTS	OP
Oakland	10	6	0	.625	399	327
Seattle	9	7	0	.562	301	324
Denver	8	8	0	.500	340	339
Kansas City	6	10	0	.375	320	344
San Diego	5	11	0	.312	332	321

NATIONAL FOOTBALL CONFERENCE

Eastern Division

	W	L	T	PCT	PTS	OP
Philadelphia	11	5	0	.688	343	208
Washington	8	8	0	.500	256	303
NY Giants	7	9	0	.438	294	321
Arizona	7	9	0	.438	295	343
Dallas	5	11	0	.312	246	338

†Wild-card team.

Central Division

	W	L	T	PCT	PTS	OP
Chicago	13	3	0	.812	338	203
†Green Bay	12	4	0	.750	390	266
†Tampa Bay	9	7	0	.562	324	280
Minnesota	5	11	0	.312	290	390
Detroit	2	14	0	.125	270	424

Western Division

	W	L	T	PCT	PTS	OP
St. Louis	14	2	0	.875	503	273
†San Francisco	12	4	0	.750	409	282
New Orleans	7	9	0	.438	333	409
Atlanta	7	9	0	.438	291	377
Carolina	1	15	0	.062	253	410

2001 NFL Individual Leaders

AMERICAN FOOTBALL CONFERENCE

Scoring

TOUCHDOWNS	TD	RUSH	REC	RET	2PT	PTS
Alexander, Sea	16	14	2	0	0	96
Harrison, Ind	15	0	15	0	0	90
Smith, NE	13	12	1	0	0	78
Dillon, Cin	13	10	3	0	0	78
Smith, Den	11	0	11	0	1	68
Mason, Tenn	10	0	9	1	1	62
Brown, Oak	10	0	9	1	0	60
Martin, NYJ	10	10	0	0	0	60
Holmes, KC	10	8	2	0	0	60
Mack, Jax	10	9	1	0	0	60
Tomlinson, SD	10	10	0	0	0	60
Rhodes, Ind	10	9	0	1	0	60

KICKING	PAT	FG	LG	PTS
Vanderjagt, Ind	41/42	28/34	52	125
Elam, Den	31/31	31/36	50	124
Brown, Pitt	34/37	30/44	55	124
Vinatieri, NE	41/42	24/30	54	113
Janikowski, Oak	42/42	23/28	52	111
Peterson, KC	27/28	27/35	51	108
Hall, NYJ	32/32	24/31	53	104
Stover, Balt	24/24	26/31	49	102
Mare, Mia	39/40	19/21	46	96
Dawson, Cle	29/30	22/25	48	95

Passing

	COMP	ATT	PCT COMP	YDS	AVG GAIN	TD	PCT TD	INT	PCT INT	LG	RATING PTS
Gannon, Oak	361	549	65.8	3828	6.97	27	4.9	9	1.6	49	95.5
McNair, Tenn	264	431	61.3	3350	7.77	21	4.9	12	2.8	t71	90.2
Brady, NE	264	413	63.9	2843	6.88	18	4.4	12	2.9	t91	86.5
Manning, Ind	343	547	62.7	4131	7.55	26	4.8	23	4.2	t86	84.1
Brunell, Jax	289	473	61.1	3309	7.00	19	4.0	13	2.7	44	84.1
Stewart, Pitt	266	442	60.2	3109	7.03	14	3.2	11	2.5	t90	81.7
Fiedler, Mia	273	450	60.7	3290	7.31	20	4.4	19	4.2	t74	80.3
Griese, Den	275	451	61.0	2827	6.27	23	5.1	19	4.2	t65	78.5
Van Pelt, Buff	178	307	58.0	2056	6.70	12	3.9	11	3.6	t80	76.4
Testaverde, NYJ	260	441	59.0	2752	6.24	15	3.4	14	3.2	t40	75.3

Pass Receiving

RECEPTIONS	NO.	YDS	AVG	LG	TD
Smith, Den	113	1343	11.9	t65	11
Smith, Jax	112	1373	12.3	t35	8
Harrison, Ind	109	1524	14.0	68	15
Brown, NE	101	1199	11.9	t60	5
Ward, Pitt	94	1003	10.7	34	4
McCardell, Jax	93	1110	11.9	45	6
Brown, Oak	91	1165	12.8	t46	9
Johnson, Cle	84	1097	13.1	t55	9
Rice, Oak	83	1139	13.7	t40	9
Centers, Buff	80	620	7.8	26	2

Pass Receiving (Cont.)

YARDS	YDS	NO.	AVG	LG	TD
Harrison, Ind	1524	109	14.0	68	15
Smith, Jax	1373	112	12.3	t35	8
Smith, Den	1343	113	11.9	t65	11
Brown, NE	1199	101	11.9	t60	5
Brown, Oak	1165	91	12.8	t46	9
Rice, Oak	1139	83	13.7	t40	9
Mason, Tenn	1128	73	15.5	t71	9
Conway, SD	1125	71	15.8	t72	6
McCardell, Jax	1110	93	11.9	45	6
Johnson, Cle	1097	84	13.1	t55	9

Rushing

	ATT	YDS	AVG	LG	TD
Holmes, KC	327	1555	4.8	41	8
Martin, NYJ	333	1513	4.5	47	10
Alexander, Sea	309	1318	4.3	t88	14
Dillon, Cin	340	1315	3.9	t96	10
Tomlinson, SD	339	1236	3.6	54	10
Smith, NE	287	1157	4.0	44	12
Rhodes, Ind	233	1104	4.7	t77	9
Bettis, Pitt	225	1072	4.8	48	4
Smith, Mia	313	968	3.1	25	6
George, Tenn	315	939	3.0	27	5

Total Yards from Scrimmage

	TOTAL	RUSH	REC
Holmes, KC	2169	1555	614
Martin, NYJ	1823	1495	328
Alexander, Sea	1661	1318	343
Tomlinson, SD	1603	1236	367
Dillon, Cin	1543	1315	228
Harrison, Ind	1527	3	1524
Garner, Oak	1417	839	578
Smith, Jax	1370	-3	1373
Smith, Den	1370	27	1343
Smith, NE	1349	1157	192

Interceptions

	NO.	YDS	LG	TD
Henry, Cle	10	177	t97	1
O'Neal, Den	9	115	42	0
McNeil, SD	8	55	33	0

Six tied with five.

Sacks

Boulware, Balt	15.0
Miller, Cle	13.0
Abraham, NYJ	13.0
Wiley, SD	13.0
Gildon, Pitt	12.0

Punting

	NO.	YDS	AVG	NET AVG	TB	IN 20	LG	BLK	RET	RET YDS
Lechler, Oak	73	3375	46.2	39.4	12	23	65	1	34	502
Rouen, Den	81	3668	45.3	38.9	8	25	64	1	48	517
Smith, Ind	68	3023	44.5	37.3	12	12	65	0	35	486
Feagles, Sea	85	3730	43.9	38.4	7	26	68	1	43	462
Hanson, Jax	82	3577	43.6	40.0	12	24	59	0	38	295

Punt Returns

	NO.	YDS	AVG	LG	TD
Brown, NE	29	413	14.2	t85	2
O'Neal, Den	31	405	13.1	t86	1
J. Lewis, Bal	39	496	12.7	62	0
Ogden, Mia	32	377	11.8	48	0
Dwight, SD	24	271	11.3	t84	1

Kickoff Returns

	NO.	YDS	AVG	LG	TD
Jenkins, SD	58	1541	26.6	t93	2
J. Lewis, Balt	41	1011	24.7	76	0
Cole, Den	48	1127	23.5	52	0
Kirby, Oak	46	1066	23.2	t90	1
Edwards, Pitt	20	462	23.1	81	0

2001 NFL Individual Leaders (Cont.)

NATIONAL FOOTBALL CONFERENCE

Scoring

TOUCHDOWNS	TD	RUSH	REC	RET	2PT	PTS
Faulk, StL	21	12	9	0	1	128
Owens, SF	16	0	16	0	0	96
Alstott, TB	11	10	1	0	2	70
Green, GB	11	9	2	0	0	66
Moss, Minn	10	0	10	0	0	60
Franks, GB	9	0	9	0	0	54
Schroeder, GB	9	0	9	0	0	54
Horn, NO	9	0	9	0	0	54
Boston, Ariz	8	0	8	0	0	48
Booker, Chi	8	0	8	0	0	48

KICKING	PAT	FG	LG	PTS
Wilkins, StL	58/58	23/29	54	127
Akers, Phil	37/38	26/31	50	115
Feely, Atl	28/28	29/37	55	115
Carney, NO	32/32	27/31	50	113
Edinger, Chi	34/34	26/31	48	112
Longwell, GB	44/45	20/31	54	104
Cortez, SF	47/47	18/25	52	101
Conway, Wash	22/22	26/33	55	100
Andersen, NYG	29/30	23/28	51	98
Gramatica, TB	28/28	23/29	49	97

Rushing

Rushing	ATT	YDS	AVG	LG	TD
Davis, Wash	356	1432	4.0	32	5
Green, GB	304	1387	4.6	t83	9
Faulk, StL	260	1382	5.3	t71	12
Williams, NO	313	1245	4.0	46	6
Hearst, SF	252	1206	4.8	t43	4
Thomas, Chi	278	1183	4.3	46	7
Smith, Dall	261	1021	3.9	44	3
Barber, NYG	166	865	5.2	36	4
Pittman, Ariz	241	846	3.5	42	5
Smith, Atl	237	760	3.2	58	5

Passing

Passing	COMP	ATT	PCT COMP	YDS	AVG GAIN	TD	PCT TD	INT	PCT INT	LG	RATING PTS
Warner, StL	375	546	68.7	4830	8.85	36	6.6	22	4.0	t65	101.4
Garcia, SF	316	504	62.7	3538	7.02	32	6.3	12	2.4	t61	94.8
Favre, GB	314	510	61.6	3921	7.69	32	6.3	15	2.9	t67	94.1
McNabb, Phil	285	493	57.8	3233	6.56	25	5.1	12	2.4	t64	84.3
Chandler, Atl	223	365	61.1	2847	7.80	16	4.4	14	3.8	t94	84.1
Culpepper, Minn	235	366	64.2	2612	7.14	14	3.8	13	3.6	t57	83.3
Plummer, Ariz	304	525	57.9	3653	6.96	18	3.4	14	2.7	t68	79.6
Johnson, TB	340	559	60.8	3406	6.09	13	2.3	11	2.0	47	77.7
Collins, NYG	327	568	57.6	3764	6.63	19	3.3	16	2.8	76	77.1
Batch, Det	198	341	58.1	2392	7.01	12	3.5	12	3.5	76	76.8

Pass Receiving

RECEPTIONS	NO.	YDS	AVG	LG	TD
Johnson, TB	106	1266	11.9	47	1
Booker, Chi	100	1071	10.7	t66	8
Boston, Ariz	98	1598	16.3	t61	8
Owens, SF	93	1412	15.2	t60	16
Horn, NO	83	1265	15.2	56	9
Faulk, StL	83	765	9.2	t65	9
Holt, StL	81	1363	16.8	51	7
Jackson, NO	81	1046	12.9	63	5
Moss, Minn	80	1224	15.3	t73	10
Morton, Det	77	1154	15.0	76	4

Pass Receiving (Cont.)

YARDS	YDS	NO.	AVG	LG	TD
Boston, Ariz	1598	98	16.3	t61	8
Owens, SF	1412	93	15.2	t60	16
Holt, StL	1363	81	16.8	51	7
Johnson, TB	1266	106	11.9	47	1
Horn, NO	1265	83	15.2	56	9
Moss, Minn	1224	80	15.3	t73	10
Morton, Det	1154	77	15.0	76	4
Bruce, StL	1106	64	17.3	t51	6
Booker, Chi	1071	100	10.7	t66	8
Toomer, NYG	1054	72	14.6	t60	5

Total Yards from Scrimmage

Total Yards from Scrimmage	TOTAL	RUSH	REC
Faulk, StL	2147	1382	765
Green, GB	1981	1385	596
Williams, NO	1934	1245	511
Boston, Ariz	1633	35	1598
Davis, Wash	1624	1419	205
Hearst, SF	1553	1206	347
Barber, NYG	1433	856	577
Owens, SF	1433	21	1412
Holt, StL	1363	0	1363
Thomas, Chi	1361	1183	178

Interceptions

Interceptions	NO.	YDS	LG	TD
Barber, TB	10	86	t36	1
Lassiter, Ariz	9	80	25	0
Evans, Car	8	126	49	1
Bronson, SF	7	165	t97	2
Plummer, SF	7	45	24	0

Sacks

Sacks			
Strahan, NYG	22.5	Gbaja-Biamila, GB	13.5
Little, StL	14.5	Kerney, Atl	11.5
Clemons, NO	13.5		

Punting

Punting	NO.	YDS	AVG	NET AVG	TB	IN 20	LG	BLK	RET	RET YDS
Sauerbrun, Car	93	4419	47.5	42.9	17	35	73	1	42	425
Berger, Minn	47	2046	43.5	37.1	10	10	67	0	25	302
Landeta, Phil	97	4221	43.5	38.5	10	26	64	0	56	488
Jett, Det	58	2512	43.3	37.6	6	16	62	0	30	332
Williams, NYG	91	3905	42.9	37.2	8	25	90	0	43	521

Punt Returns

Punt Returns	NO.	YDS	AVG	LG	TD
Gordon, Atl	31	437	14.1	74	0
Swinton, Dall	31	414	13.4	t65	1
Metcalf, Wash	33	412	12.5	t89	1
Mitchell, Phil	39	467	12.0	54	0
Jackson, Ariz	40	461	11.5	55	0

Kickoff Returns

Kickoff Returns	NO.	YDS	AVG	LG	TD
Smith, Car	56	1431	25.6	t99	2
Howard, Det	57	1446	25.4	91	0
Mitchell, Phil	41	1025	25.0	t94	1
Vaughn, Atl	61	1491	24.4	t96	1
McAllister, NO	45	1091	24.2	63	0

2001–2002 NFL Playoffs

AFC First Round
New York 24
Oakland 38

Baltimore 20
Miami 3

AFC Divisional Playoff
Oakland 13
New England 16 (ot)

Baltimore 10
Pittsburgh 27

AFC Championship
New England 24

Pittsburgh 17

Super Bowl XXXVI
February 3, 2002

NEW ENGLAND 20
St. Louis 17

NFC Championship
Philadelphia 24

St. Louis 29

NFC Divisional Playoff
Philadelphia 33
Chicago 19

Green Bay 17
St. Louis 45

NFC First Round
Tampa Bay 9
Philadelphia 31

San Francisco 15
Green Bay 25

Super Bowl XXXVI Box Score

ST. LOUIS 3	0	0	14	—17
NEW ENGLAND 0	14	3	3	—20

FIRST QUARTER
St. Louis: FG Wilkins 50, 11:50. Drive: 48 yards, 10 plays. Key play: Warner 11 pass to Bruce on 3rd-and-4. **St. Louis 3–0.**

SECOND QUARTER
New England: Law 47 interception return

SECOND QUARTER (Cont.)
(Vinatieri kick), 6:11. **New England 7–3.**
New England: Patten 8 pass from Brady (Vinatieri kick), 14:29. Drive: 40 yards, five plays. Key play: Buckley 15 fumble return. **New England 14–3.**

THIRD QUARTER
New England: FG Vinatieri 37, 13:42. Drive: 14 yards, five plays. Key play: Smith 30 interception return. **New England 17–3.**

FOURTH QUARTER
St. Louis: Warner 2 run (Wilkins kick), 5:29. Drive: 77 yards, 12 plays. Key play: Faulk 22 pass from Warner. **New England 17–10.**

FOURTH QUARTER (Cont.)
St. Louis: Proehl 26 pass from Warner (Wilkins kick), 13:30. Drive: 55 yards, three plays. Key play: Hakim 18 pass from Warner. **17–17.**
New England: FG Vinatieri 48, 15:00. Drive: 53 yards, nine plays. Key play: Brown 23 pass from Brady. **New England 20–17.**

Farewells

Willie Stargell

The heart and soul of "The Family"—the 1979 World Series champi-
on Pirates—Stargell (above) played for 21 seasons in Pittsburgh,
amassing 474 homers, 2,232 hits, 1,540 RBIs and a career average
of .282. As captain, he awarded cloth gold stars to his teammates
(who stitched them onto their caps) for individual accomplishments.

SI asked members of the formidable Pirates teams from the 1970s
about their memories of the Hall of Fame slugger:

Phil Garner, second baseman: "He had an unbelievable fire
to play, but his emotions never got out of control. One time we
were in St. Louis, and Darold Knowles came into a tie game
and struck Willie out on a changeup. Willie came back to the
dugout and said, 'I'll hit that changeup later.' Sure enough,
ninth inning, Knowles throws him a change, and Willie hits it
into the upper tier. And he comes back to the dugout very
calmly and puts his bat and helmet away and takes a seat."

Dave Parker, rightfielder: "He was my baseball father.
That's why I called him Pops. In '78 I told the Pirates that the
only way I would re-sign was if they brought Pops back too."

Bill Robinson, leftfielder: "Willie wasn't one to brag, but
every time we'd go to Philadelphia, he'd point to a seat way,
way, way up in the rightfield stands and say, 'I hit Jim
Bunning up there.' Other guys would ask him, 'Should I take
a pitch?' and Willie would say, 'Hit like you live—hard.' "

In Wilmington, N.C., age 61, from a stroke, April 9, 2001.

Earl Anthony

Hall of Fame bowler Anthony was named Bowler of the Year consec-
utively from 1974 to '76 and from 1981 to '83.

SI's Alexander Wolff writes:

"Earl Anthony (above) made pocket money as a kid by setting up pins. His knack for knocking them down as an adult
made him the first bowler to earn $1 million during his
career. ... He dominated bowling when bowling dominated
Saturday-afternoon television. He won a PBA career-record 41
events from 1970 to '83, including 10 titles in the majors. 'Earl
made our broadcasts,' said former ABC host Chris Schenkel.

"His appeal might seem hard to fathom today. With his
nerdy hair and Poindexter glasses, Anthony would go over only
in a hip-to-be-square sense. ... Nonetheless, even as bowling has
all but disappeared from the airwaves, it has come back in vogue
in other ways. A trio of Microsoft millionaires recently bought
the PBA tour and is trying to make the sport cool again. ...

"It's hard to imagine Anthony on this newfangled PBA
tour. Square Earl liked to say, 'You can't ever be too slow to
the line.' ... The poky style that made Anthony an immortal
only underscores how bowling's golden age belonged to
another era entirely—and how daunting a task the PBA
tour's new proprietors face."

In New Berlin, Wis., age 63, of injuries sustained from falling
down a flight of stairs, Aug. 14, 2001.

Eddie Futch

Futch, a Golden Gloves lightweight champ who once sparred with Joe Louis, trained 22 champions during his seven-decade, Hall of Fame career. A legendary cornerman, he trained his last champ in 1997 (light heavyweight Montell Griffin).

SI's Alexander Wolff writes:

"Futch (above) was a gentleman trainer whose good nature didn't seem to interfere with success in the ring. He trained 22 champions, six of them heavyweights, and would have trained who knows how many more if he hadn't been as scrupulous about his fighters' conduct as he was about his own....

"To the younger generation he may be best remembered as the man who somehow whipped the undisciplined Riddick Bowe into a heavyweight champ. Bowe, who found it hard to listen to anyone's instructions, idolized the man he called Papa Smurf but ... ultimately, [didn't listen] enough to keep Futch from dropping him.

"Futch could be impatient that way, ignoring the money when it got in the way of his standards.... Of those Futch did work with, the record is plain: He made them better. Starting with Don Jordan [welterweight champ, 1958], Futch trained such champions as Larry Holmes, Michael Spinks, Alexis Arguello and Mike McCallum.... and he devised upsets of Muhammad Ali by both Joe Frazier and Ken Norton."

In Las Vegas, Nev., age 90, of natural causes, Oct. 10, 2001.

Dale Earnhardt

A NASCAR legend, Earnhardt racked up 76 victories in 676 Winston Cup races, a record 20 Top 10 finishes in Winston Cup points races and a record career prize-money total of $41,639,662.

SI's Mark Bechtel writes:

"In losing Earnhardt, NASCAR didn't just lose the best driver stock car racing had seen. It also lost its heart and soul, the one thing it had that no other sport could claim: a superstar the average blue-jean-wearing fan could identify with.... Front-runners cheered him on as he won seven Winston Cup championships, equaling the record set by Richard Petty. Underdogs appreciated how he had worked his way up from humble beginnings, tinkering with cars in a makeshift garage that his dad built.... Then there were the tough guys, the ones who couldn't get enough of the way he refused to let anyone slow him down on the way to his destination....

"Earnhardt (above) offered this bit of advice last summer to drivers who complained that they were going too fast: 'Get the hell out of the race car if you've got feathers on your legs or butt. Put a kerosene rag around your ankles so the ants won't climb up there and eat that candy ass.'

"The 76th and final win of Earnhardt's career [was the 2000] Winston 500 in Talladega, Ala."

In Daytona Beach, Fla., age 49, of severe neck and skull injuries sustained in a crash during the Daytona 500, Feb. 18, 2001.

Farewells

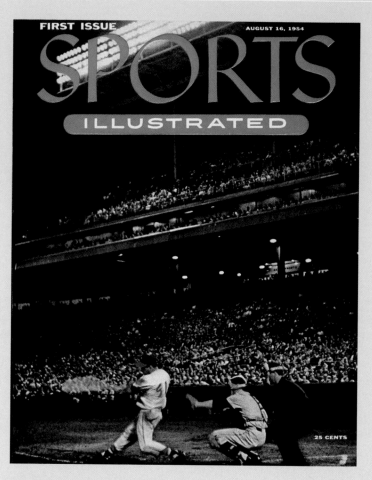

Lou Boudreau

In 1948, Boudreau (above) hit .355, belted 18 home runs and drove in 106 runs for the Indians; the Associated Press named him Male Athlete of the Year. A Hall of Famer, he was also a radio commentator for the Cubs for nearly 30 years.

SI's Mark Bechtel writes:

"The idea seems preposterous now—a 24-year-old shortstop sweet-talking an owner into handing him the manager's job—but it wasn't always so. In November 1941 ... Lou Boudreau convinced Cleveland owner Alva Bradley that he was ready to become the youngest manager in baseball history. No mere stopgap, Boudreau ... managed and played short for the Indians for nine more years and, in 1948, led them to the World Series title, their last to date....

"When Boudreau the manager made a call, he knew he had Boudreau the player to cover his back. After the Indians finished the 1948 regular season tied with the Red Sox, Boudreau chose rookie Gene Bearden over Bob Feller and Bob Lemon to start the one-game playoff.... Bearden beat Boston 8–3; it helped that Boudreau went 4 for 4 with two homers.

"Cleveland went on to defeat the Braves in six games, making Boudreau the only man to manage a World Series winner in the same year he was named MVP. Safe to say, that's a feat that won't be repeated anytime soon."

In Olympia Fields, Ill., age 84, of cardiac arrest, Aug. 10, 2001.

Eddie Mathews

Considered the game's best third baseman in the 1950s and early '60s, Mathews (above, batting) won the NL home run title twice (1953 and '59) and was a nine-time All-Star during a 17-year career. In his last season as a player, his team, Detroit, won the World Series.

SI's Walter Bingham writes:

"As a Hall of Famer and one of only 16 players to hit 500 home runs, Eddie Mathews has a secure place in baseball history. But Mathews also holds a special place in SI's history—as the athlete featured on the cover of our first issue, dated Aug. 16, 1954....

"The selection of Mathews for our inaugural cover was, in retrospect, fortuitous, for he embodied many traits we would come to celebrate: poise, teamwork, durability, all-around excellence. Mathews went on to hit 40 home runs in 1954, and, together with his more celebrated teammate, Hank Aaron, formed the one-two punch that led the Braves to a World Series title in '57 and a National League pennant in '58. Mathews ended his career with 512 homers and was elected to the Hall of Fame in '78. 'It's funny,' he told SI in 1999. 'When that picture was taken, I didn't think of it—or myself—as anything special. SPORTS ILLUSTRATED and me, we were nuthins.' "

In San Diego, age 69, of complications from pneumonia, Aug. 18, 2001.

Other Notable Passings

Al McGuire

The multitalented McGuire played pro basketball with the New York Knicks and Baltimore Bullets, coached three college teams and was a television analyst until 2000. He was named Coach of the Year by four major sportswriting organizations in 1971 and was inducted into the Basketball Hall of Fame in 1992.

SI's Alexander Wolff writes:

"We could recite the details of the life of Al McGuire, but he wouldn't want us to. McGuire didn't believe in details. He blithely forgot names of players in games he telecast and of those on his own team. Jerome Whitehead, a star of McGuire's 1977 NCAA champion Marquette team, was forever Whitehorse. So was Whitehead's father, a minister who must have frowned upon realizing that White Horse is a brand of Scotch.... Forever fuzzy on the particulars, McGuire never erred in the broad strokes. When he said, 'Just show me the numbers,' he didn't mean that literally, only that what interested him was the metaphorical bottom line....

"He'll be remembered for his sensibility, including that picturesque urban argot of which Dick Vitale's is wincingly derivative. He was without peer as a game coach. 'I don't know basketball,' he said. 'I feel basketball. Drop me in the middle of a game, and I could manage it by the ebb and flow.' "

In Milwaukee, age 72, of a blood disorder, Jan. 26, 2001.

Tommie Agee Centerfielder for 1969 Miracle Mets. In New York, age 58, of a heart attack, Jan. 21, 2001.

Chris Antley Jockey. more than 3,000 career wins. In Pasadena, Calif., age 34, of multiple drug intoxication, Dec. 2, 2000.

Eraste Autin College football player. In Gainesville, Fla., age 18, of heatstroke, July 25, 2001.

Sir Donald Bradman Legendary cricketer. In Adelaide, Australia, age 92, of pneumonia, Feb. 25, 2001.

John Cooper Pioneering race car designer (F/1 & Minis). In Worthington, England, age 77, of cancer, Dec. 24, 2000.

Didi Two-time World Cup–winning Brazilian soccer star. In Rio de Janiero, age 71, of liver failure, May 12, 2001.

Stan Fox Race car driver (Indy car and midget-car). In New Zealand, age 48, after a car accident, Dec. 18, 2000.

Werner Fricker Executive and prominent force in U.S. soccer. In Horsham, Pa., age 65, of cancer, May 30, 2001.

Joe Gilliam Jr. Pioneering black NFL quarterback. In Nashville, age 49, of an apparent heart attack, Dec. 25, 2000.

Marty Glickman Track star and broadcaster. In New York, age 83, of heart-surgery complications, Dec. 14, 2000.

Lou Groza Hall of Fame kicker, Cleveland Browns. In Middleburg Heights, Ohio, age 76, of a heart attack, Nov. 29, 2000.

Victor Kiam New England Patriots owner, 1988–92. In Stamford, Conn., age 74, from a heart condition, May 27, 2001.

Stephen Malcom Jamaican soccer player. In Trelawny, Jamaica, age 30, after a car accident, Jan. 28, 2001.

Tyrone McGriff Football player. Three-time Div. 1–AA All-America. In Melbourne, Fla., age 41, of a heart attack, Dec. 9, 2000.

John McKay Football coach for USC and NFL's Tampa Bay Buccaneers. In Tampa, age 77, of diabetes, June 10, 2001.

Murray Murdoch Was oldest living Stanley Cup champ. In Pawley's Island, S.C., age 96, of unknown causes, May 17, 2001.

Bobbi Olson Pillar of Arizona men's basketball program. In Tucson, age 65, of ovarian cancer, Jan. 1, 2001.

Charlie Pell College football player (Alabama) and coach (Florida). In Gadsden, Ala., age 60, of cancer, May 29, 2001.

Lowell Perry Pioneering black football coach and public figure. In Southfield, Mich., age 66, of cancer, Jan. 7, 2001.

Bill Rigney Baseball player, manager and executive. In Walnut Creek, Calif., age 83, of heart disease, Feb. 20, 2001.

Bekzat Sattarkhanov Olympic featherweight champ. In Kazakhstan, age 20, after a car accident, Dec. 31, 2000.

John Steadman Sportswriter; 50-year career with Baltimore newspapers. In Baltimore, age 73, of cancer, Jan. 1, 2001.

Korey Stringer Vikings All-Pro offensive tackle. In Mankata, Minn., age 27, of heatstroke, Aug. 1, 2001.

Mickey Trotman Soccer player (MLS/Trinidad & Tobago). In Trinadad, age 26, after a car accident, Oct. 10, 2001.

Dan Turk NFL center for 15 years with Steelers, Bucs, Raiders and Redskins. In Ashburn, Va., age 38, of cancer, Dec. 23, 2000.

Emil Zatopek Czech runner; won 5,000, 10,000 and marathon at '52 Games. In Prague, age 78, of a stroke, Nov. 21, 2000.

Front Cover
AFP.
Back Cover
Clockwise from left: Garrabrant/NBA Entertainment; David E. Klutho; Glyn Kirk/Action Plus/Icon SMI; Al Tielemans.
Front Matter
1, Brian Bahr/Allsport; 2–3, DPPI/Icon SMI.

6, from left, Al Tielemans; John Biever; Damian Strohmeyer; Walter Iooss Jr.; 7, top left, John W. McDonough; top right, Stewart Shining; center, George Tiedemann; bottom left, Brad Mangin; bottom right, Heinz Kluetmeier; 8, top l–r, Walter Iooss Jr.; David E. Klutho; Bob Rosato; Nitin Vadukul; bottom, l–r, Composite photos, John Biever/John W. McDonough/Manny Millan/Bob Rosato; John W. McDonough; Fred Vuich; Gerard Rancinan; 9, top l–r, John Biever; Walter Iooss Jr.; Jesse D. Garrabrant/NBA Entertainment; Lynn Johnson; bottom l–r, Peter Read Miller; John W. McDonough; Walter Iooss Jr.; David E. Klutho; 10, top, l–r, Walter Iooss Jr.; Gerard Rancinan; Brad Mangin/MLB Photos; Courtesy Jan Kalsu-McLauchlin; bottom, l–r, Robert Beck; Gerard Rancinan; Rich Frishman; Peter Read Miller; 11, top left, Joe Zeff; top right, Michael O'Neill; center, Matt Mahurin; bottom left, Damian Strohmeyer; bottom right, John Biever; 12, top left, Eliot Schechter/Allsport; bottom left, V.J. Lovero; center, John Iacono; top right, John Biever; bottom right, Bob Rosato; 13, top l–r, V.J. Lovero; Al Tielemans; Peter Gregoire; Jeffery A. Salter/SABA; bottom l–r, Al Tielemans; John Biever; Brian Lanker; Walter Iooss Jr.; 14, Robert Beck; 16, Garrabrant/NBA Entertainment; 17, Bob Rosato; 18, Manny Millan; 19, Rocky Widner/NBA Entertainment; 20, Bob Rosato; 21, Manny Millan; 22, Manny Millan; 23, top, Bill Frakes; bottom, John W. McDonough; 24, John W. McDonough; 25, John Biever; 26, Rich Frishman; 28, Gerard Rancinan; 29, Al Tielemans; 30, Peter Gregoire; 34, David E. Klutho; 36, David E. Klutho; 37, David E. Klutho; 38, David E. Klutho; 39, Lou Capozzola; 40, David E. Klutho; 41, Darren Carroll; 42, David E. Klutho; 44, Rafael Fuchs; 45, Manuello Paganelli; 48, John Biever; 50, David E. Klutho; 51, Manny Millan; 53, John Biever; 54, Al Tielemans; 55, Manny Millan; 56, top, John W. McDonough; bottom, David E. Klutho; 57, Bob Rosato; 58, Bob Rosato; 59, Rich Clarkson/NCAA Photos; 60, Manny Millan; 62, Peter Gregoire; 63, David E. Klutho; 66, Simon Bruty; 68, Jamie Squire/Allsport; 69, Tony Gutierrez; 70, Essy Ghavameddini/MLS/Allsport; 71, Damian Strohmeyer; 72, Brian Bahr/Allsport; 73, George Tiedemann/GT Images; 74, Simon Bruty; 76, Damian Strohmeyer; 77, Tony Quinn/MLS/Allsport; 81, Bob Martin; 82, Glyn Kirk/Action Plus/Icon SMI; 83, Glyn Kirk/Action Plus/Icon SMI; 84, Clive Brunskill/Allsport; 85, Heinz Kluetmeier; 86–87, Bob Martin; 88, Clive Brunskill/Allsport; 89, Manny Millan/SI/Icon SMI; 91, Ezra Shaw/Allsport; 95, Bob Martin; 96, Jim Gund; 97, Simon Bruty; 98, Robert Beck; 99, J.D. Cuban; 100–101, Robert Beck; 102, Jim Gund; 104, Martyn Hayhow/AFP; 105, Robert Beck; 108, David E. Klutho; 110, Heinz Kluetmeier; 111, Peter Read Miller; 112, Ezra Shaw/Allsport; 113, Al Tielemans; 114, Chuck Solomon; 115, Chuck Solomon; 116, Heinz Kluetmeier; 117, John W. McDonough; 118–119, John Biever; 120, John W. McDonough; 123, Al Tielemans; 125, V.J. Lovero; 128, Jacob Langston/Orlando Sentinel; 130, George Tiedemann/GT Images; 131, Jockel Finck/AP; 133, George Tiedemann/GT Images; 134, Robert Laberge/Allsport; 135, Bruno Fablet/Presse Sports; 136, Sam Sharpe; 137, Jamie Squire/Allsport; 138, Brian Spurlock; 139, Clive Mason/Allsport; 141, Brian Spurlock; 144, Richard Mackson; 146, Al Tielemans; 147, John Biever; 148, Damian Strohmeyer; 149, John Biever; 150, Al Tielemans; 151, John W. McDonough; 152, Peter Read Miller; 153, Bill Frakes; 154, John Biever; 155, top, John Biever; bottom, Al Tielemans; 157, Jeffery A. Salter/SABA; 158, Heinz Kluetmeier; 160, John Biever; 165, John Biever; 166, Scott Martin/AP; 167, John Biever; 168, Heinz Kluetmeier; 169, Al Tielemans; 170, Damian Strohmeyer; 171, Damian Strohmeyer; 172, Heinz Kluetmeier; 173, Al Tielemans; 174, David E. Klutho; 175, Damian Strohmeyer; 176, Michael O'Neill; 179, Damian Strohmeyer; 180, Otto Gruele; 184, left, Walter Iooss Jr.; right, Lane Stewart; 185, left, Neil Leifer; right, Heinz Kluetmeier; 186, left, Hy Peskin/TimePix; right, *Sports Illustrated*; 187, Heinz Kluetmeier.